"To mobilize action globally in line with the 2030 Agenda for Sustainable Development will require buy-in and commitments not just from governments, but from all segments of society. This book addresses a major component of that challenge – involving stakeholders in every part of the process to deliver on the promise of the SDGs. Many of the contributors have long led efforts to build an inclusive and democratic framework for delivering on sustainable development. Their experience, insights and analysis of what works and what doesn't not only make the case for the benefits of multi-stakeholderism, but allows them to develop crucial practical and detailed guidance on making multi-stakeholder policy dialogues and partnerships legitimate, effective and accountable."

Steven Bernstein, Professor of Political Science and Co-director of the Environmental Governance Lab, Munk School of Global Affairs and Public Policy, University of Toronto, Canada.

"This book is extremely timely. The ability for government institutions to deal with challenges to our society and planet is seemly getting worse day by the day. Government institutions need to be reimagined and this book offers a vision that can help institutions to be more inclusive to society and respectful to nature by their design. The basic idea is to formally involve stakeholders in government decision making and therefore have society at large committed to implementation of policies, delivered through a sense of ownership and partnership. This vision can empower representative democracy in a time of fear of conflict and economic collapse to deal with social inequality and environmentally degradation."

Professor Patrick Paul Walsh, Director of the UCD Centre for Sustainable Development Studies, Senior Advisor UN Sustainable Development Solutions Network

"For those of us wondering 'what exactly does stakeholders mean?' this book provides a comprehensive and useful answer. Beyond that, it outlines the concept of stakeholder democracy both in historical overview and in contemporary political context, as the inevitable next step in democratic progress. *Stakeholder Democracy: Represented Democracy in a Time of Fear* distills decades of knowledge into an engaging, enlightening read, democratically disseminating the wisdom usually only gleaned through a coffee with one of its authors. In UN advocacy, precedent is everything. Outlining the best examples of stakeholder engagement, this book is a guiding light for the next generation of non-government actors seeking to influence global policy."

Kathryn Tobin

"Multi-stakeholder engagement is fundamental for a coherent and integrated implementation of the SDGs. Stakeholders contribute to mobilising resources, informing policy, identifying innovative solutions, supporting transformations and voicing the needs of underrepresented communities. A strong partnership means engaging stakeholders effectively by granting them equal and fair opportunities to be informed and consulted in decision-making. The book *Stakeholder Democracy: Represented Democracy in a Time of Fear* depicts well how partnerships must be aligned with the adoption of the 2030 Agenda for Sustainable Development. With this aspiration, the OECD created the PCSD Partnership that brings together governments, international organisations, civil society, think tanks, the private sector and other stakeholders from all regions of the world, committed and working to enhance policy coherence for sustainable development (SDG 17.14)."

Ebba Dohlman, OECD's head of unit on policy coherence for sustainable development

"It's democracy, period! This book is a must-read for all who want to understand how to work the twenty-first century politics. Having worked long years as eminent advisors, actors, and advocates the authors offer deep insider knowledge. Stakeholder are more than just the opposite to economic shareholder. Stakeholder democracy is part of the mainstream institutional and parliamentary governance. Even more so, engagement of people helps keeping democracies lively, effective and resourceful. This book carefully sketches out how stakeholder democracy came to be the prime important ingredient to our common future. When it comes to ensuring a decent life for all within the planetary boundaries being transparent, reliable, constructively positive are the virtues of cooperation – as opposed to being absorbed in elitist turf battles and selfish positioning in the global awareness economy. For public and stakeholder politics there what can be learned from the rich narrative of this book might simply start a new Stakeholder Social Responsibility."

Günther Bachmann, General Secretary to the German Council for Sustainable Development and activist in a series of stakeholder setups

"There is no doubt about the power of the collective to change the world, even more now, when we are increasingly interconnected. In order for the collective effort to be effective, numbers matter, but strategy is key. This book, which emphasizes multi-stakeholder democracy, makes a truly important contribution to how the whole of society can, and should, come together to solve the world's most pressing problems. This compelling work calls for reflection and action, two sides of the coin of transformative change."

Claudia Mansfield LaRue, Former G77+China negotiator of the United Nations "Towards Global Partnerships Resolution" International Recruitment and Partnerships Specialist, Montclair State University, USA

"Just as the fundamentals of the international architecture are being challenged and on the brink of a period of renewal, there could be no better time to revisit the power and presence of stakeholder democracy as a force for positive change. This book shows how stakeholder democracy can enable us to make the transition to a sustainable future in a way that addresses the political upheaval of our times, and the necessary shift from authoritarian-populism to a people-lead social and political renaissance."

Andrew Higham, Chief Executive of Mission 2020

"There is a vast body of scholarly literature on non-state actors in governance of sustainable development, amongst other in partnerships. There is an even larger body of academic publications on democracy – a crucial principle underpinning meaningful engagement of stakeholders in policy-making and implementation. This book, by a great team of experienced advocates of and specialists in stakeholder engagement, brings these topics together and in a historic context – not from an ivory tower perspective, but from constructive critical 'Vienna Café' perspective. And this makes the book a must-read for all the diplomats, bureaucrats, lobbyist, scientists, and civil society representatives who crowd this coffee corner in the basement of the UN Headquarters."

Ruben Zondervan, Executive Director, Stakeholder Forum

Stakeholder Democracy

In the context of sustainable development, this book describes how we are moving from representative to participatory democracy, and how we are now in a "stakeholder democracy," which is working to strengthen represented democracy in a time of fear.

Since the 1992 Rio Earth Summit the idea of stakeholder democracy has grown, with stakeholders engaged in helping governments and intergovernmental bodies make better decisions, and in helping them to deliver those decisions in partnerships amongst various stakeholders, with and without government. Seen through a multi-stakeholder, sector and level lens, this book describes the history of the development of stakeholder democracy, particularly in the area of sustainable development. The authors draw on more than twenty-five years of experience to review, learn from and make recommendations on how best to engage stakeholders in policy development. The book illustrates successful practical examples of multi-stakeholder partnerships (MSPs) to implement agreements and outline elements of an MSP Charter. This will provide a benchmark for partnerships, enabling those being developed to understand what the necessary quality standards are and to understand what is expected in terms of transparency, accountability, financial reporting, impact and governance.

The book is essential reading for professionals and trainees engaging in multi-stakeholder processes for policy development and to implement agreements. It will also be useful for students of sustainable development, politics and international relations.

Felix Dodds is an Adjunct Professor at the University of North Carolina and an Associate Fellow at the Tellus Institute. He was the co-director of the 2014 and 2018 Nexus Conference on Water, Food, Energy and Climate. In 2019 he was a candidate for the Executive Director of the United Nations Environment Programme (UNEP).

Stakeholder Democracy
Represented Democracy in a Time of Fear

Felix Dodds

with contributions from

Jan-Gustav Strandenaes, Minu Hemmati, Carolina Duque Chopitea, Bernd Lakemeier, Susanne Salz, Jana Borkenhagen and Laura Schmitz

First published 2019
by Routledge
2 Park Square, Milton Park, Abingdon, Oxon OX14 4RN

and by Routledge
52 Vanderbilt Avenue, New York, NY 10017

Routledge is an imprint of the Taylor & Francis Group, an informa business

© 2019 Felix Dodds

The right of Felix Dodds to be identified as author of this work has been asserted by him in accordance with sections 77 and 78 of the Copyright, Designs and Patents Act 1988.

All rights reserved. No part of this book may be reprinted or reproduced or utilised in any form or by any electronic, mechanical, or other means, now known or hereafter invented, including photocopying and recording, or in any information storage or retrieval system, without permission in writing from the publishers.

Trademark notice: Product or corporate names may be trademarks or registered trademarks, and are used only for identification and explanation without intent to infringe.

Chapter 8 © 2019 Minu Hemmati

British Library Cataloguing in Publication Data
A catalogue record for this book is available from the British Library

Library of Congress Cataloging-in-Publication Data
A catalog record has been requested for this book

ISBN: 978-0-8153-8692-6 (hbk)
ISBN: 978-0-8153-8693-3 (pbk)
ISBN: 978-1-351-17442-8 (ebk)

Typeset in Sabon
by Taylor & Francis Books

Printed and bound in Great Britain by
TJ International Ltd, Padstow, Cornwall

Contents

List of illustrations	x
Abbreviations	xii
Author biographies	xv
Foreword by Helen Clark	xx

	Introduction	1
1	Stakeholder democracy – re-engaging the peoples of the world: Definitions, concepts and linkages *by Jan Gustav Strandenaes*	7
2	A short history of democracy	22
3	The emergence of stakeholder democracy	41
4	Civil society discourse	99
5	Literature review *by Carolina Duque Chopitea*	124
6	Examples of successful multi-stakeholder policy development	134
7	Multi-stakeholder partnerships: Making them work for delivering global agreements *by Jan-Gustav Strandenaes*	164
8	Principles for multi-stakeholder processes *by Minu Hemmati*	194
9	Designing successful multi-stakeholder partnerships *by Susanne Salz, Bernd Lakemeier, Laura Schmitz, and Jana Borkenhagen*	212
10	The challenges ahead	226
	Index	229

Illustrations

Figures

2.2 The Constitution of the Roman Republic (authors)	27
6.1 Alignment of the Basque Government Programme with the United Nations 2030 Agenda, Basque Country	159
7.1 The 2030 Agenda for Sustainable Development and multi-stakeholder partnerships at the UN (Beisheim and Nils, 2016)	182
9.1 First steps in an MSP (authors)	213
9.2 Three elements of the institutionalization of MSPs (authors)	216
9.3 Impact of MSPs (authors)	218
9.4 Impact and MSP – three perspectives (authors)	219
9.5 MSP impact chain (authors)	219
9.6 Impact assessment of MSPs (authors)	222
9.7 Impact and impact assessment of MSPs (authors)	225

Tables

2.1 Aristotelian ways to organize societies	24
6.1 Number of interventions by Major Groups per session: Industry (Howell, 2004)	139
6.2 Number of interventions by Major Groups per session: Tourism (Howell, 2004)	143
6.3 Number of interventions by Major Groups per session: Agriculture (Howell, 2004)	144
6.4 Number of interventions by Major Groups per session: Energy/ Transport (Howell, 2004)	146
6.5 Examples of NCSDs supported by NSDSs (Nouhan et al., 2018)	149
6.6 Strengths and weaknesses of the three models of National Councils (Nouhan et al., 2018)	153
7.1 Criteria for reviewing multi-stakeholder partnerships	181
8.1 Levels of engagement (author)	196
8.2 Key principles and strategies of multi-stakeholder processes (Hemmati, 2002)	197

List of illustrations xi

8.3 Seven principles of effective MSPs (Brouwer et al., 2015)   198
8.4 Success factors of partnerships (author)   199
9.1 Overview: Starting a partnership (authors)   215
9.2 Types of MSPs and kinds of impacts (authors)   220
9.3 The M&E process of the MSP for sustainable tuna fisheries in the Philippines MSP case study (WWF, 2019)   224

Boxes

2.1 The Quaker model has been adapted by Earlham College for application to secular settings   35
3.1 The Stakeholder Standard (Stakeholder Forum, 2009) authors   81
4.1 International principles protecting civil society   115
6.1 Summary of the dialogue process (Howell, 2004)   136
6.2 Are regions ready? Implementing the SDGs at the sub-national level, NRG4SD Assessment Questionnaire   158
7.1 Key definitions of terms   165

Abbreviations

ASCEND 21	Agenda of Science for Environment and Development into the Twenty-First Century
BINGO	Business and Industry NGO
CDI	Centre of Development Innovation
CEDAW	Convention on the Elimination of All Forms of Discrimination against Women (UN)
CFCs	Chlorofluorocarbons
CFS	Civil Society Mechanism
CFS	Committee on Food Security
CSD	Commission on Sustainable Development (UN)
CIDA	Canadian International Development Agency
COP	Conference of the Parties
CSO	Civil Society Organization
CSSM	Civil Society Support Mechanism
CUNPA	Campaign for a United Nations Parliamentary Assembly
DAC	Development Assistance Committee
ECOSOC	Economic and Social Council (UN)
ELCI	Environmental Liaison Centre International
ENGO	Environmental NGO
ESG	Environmental, Social and Governance
FANGO	Farmers and Agriculture NGO
FAO	Food and Agricultural Organization (UN)
FE2W	Food, Energy, Environment and Water Network
FSC	Forest Stewardship Council
GATT	Global Agreement on Trade and Tariffs
GAVI	Global Alliance for Vaccines and Immunization
GHG	Green House Gas
GIZ	Gesellschaft für Internationale Zusammenarbeit
GONGO	Government-Organized NGO
GPEI	Global Polio Eradication Initiative
GPF	Global Policy Forum
GPP	Global Public Policy
GRI	Global Reporting Initiative

Abbreviations xiii

HLM	High-Level Meeting (UN)
HLPF	High-Level Political Forum (UN)
ICASO	International Council of AIDS Service Organizations
ICC	International Chamber of Commerce
ICFTU	International Confederation of Free Trade Unions
ICLEI	International Council for Local Environmental Initiatives
ICSC	International Civil Society Centre
ICSU	International Council for Science
ILO	International Labour Organization (UN)
IFAD	International Fund for Agricultural Development
IPCC	Intergovernmental Panel on Climate Change
IPO	Indigenous Peoples Organization
IUCN	International Union for Conservation of Nature
JPol	Johannesburg Plan of Implementation
LA21	Local Agenda 21
LGMA	Local Government and Municipal Authorities
MDB	Multilateral Development Bank
MDGs	Millennium Development Goals
MID	Maurice Ile Durable Commission
MIT	Massachusetts Institute of Technology
MSD	Multi-Stakeholder Democracy
MSI	Multi-Stakeholder Initiative
MSP	Multi-Stakeholder Partnership
MYPOW	Multi-Year Program of Work
NCSD	National Councils for Sustainable Development
NGO	Non-Governmental Organization
NIC	National Intelligence Council (United States)
NRG4SD	Network for Regional Government for Sustainable Development
NSDS	National Sustainable Development Strategy
OECD	Organization for Economic Cooperation and Development
OWG	Open Working Group
PiP	Partnerships in Practice
PPP	Public Private Partnership
PrC	Partnerships Resource Centre
PSM	Private Sector Mechanism
REEEP	Renewable Energy and Energy Efficiency Partnership
RINGO	Research and Independent NGO
SAICM	Strategic Approach to International Chemicals Management
SARD	Sustainable Agriculture and Rural Development
SDG	Sustainable Development Goal
SDG-OWG	Sustainable Development Goals – Open Working Group
SEI	Stockholm Environment Institute
SE4All	Sustainable Energy for All
SF	Stakeholder Forum

xiv *Abbreviations*

SIDS	Small Island Developing States
SIGTARP	Special Inspector General for the Troubled Assets Relief Program
SIWI	Stockholm International Water Institute
TFWW	The Future We Want
TOR	Terms of Reference
TPI	The Partnering Initiative
TTT	Technical Task Team (TTT)
TUNGO	Trade Union NGO
UN	United Nations
UNC	University of North Carolina at Chapel Hill
UN CEB	United Nations Chief Executive Board
UNCCD	United Nations Convention to Combat Desertification
UNCED	United Nations Conference on Environment and Development
UNDESA	United Nations Department of Economic and Social Affairs
UNDP	United Nations Development Programme
UNDSD	United Nations Division on Sustainable Development
UNDPI	United Nations Department of Public Information
UNECE	United Nations Economic Commission for Europe
UNED	United Nations Environment and Development UK Committee
UNEP	United Nations Environment Programme
UNESCO	United Nations Educational, Scientific and Cultural Organization
UNFCCC	United Nations Framework Convention on Climate Change
UNFPA	United Nations Population Fund
UNICEF	United Nations International Children's Emergency Fund
UNGA	United Nations General Assembly
UNGC	United Nations Global Compact
WBA	World Benchmarking Alliance
WBCSD	World Business Council for Sustainable Development
WEDO	Women's Environment and Development Organization
WEF	Water-Energy-Food Security Nexus
WGC	Women and Gender Constituency
WHA	World Health Assembly
WHO	World Health Organization (UN)
WMO	World Meteorological Organization (UN)
WSIS	World Summit on the Information Society
WSSD	World Summit on Sustainable Development
WSF	World Social Forums
WTO	World Trade Organization
WTTC	World Travel and Tourism Council
WWF	World Wide Fund for Nature
YOUNGO	Youth NGO

Author biographies

Jana Borkenhagen

Jana Borkenhagen engages in the Partnerships2030 team, the German national platform for multi-stakeholder partnerships at the Gesellschaft für Internationale Zusammenarbeit (GIZ). Having successfully completed her bachelor's in International Development at the University of Vienna as well as her master's in Governance and Globalization at Ruhr-University Bochum, she now contributes to an inclusive and just global development by supporting the work of  GIZ. Jana gained practical experiences when interacting with stakeholders of German development cooperation, both abroad (in South Africa and Kenya) and in Germany.

Felix Dodds

Felix Dodds is an Adjunct Professor at the University of North Carolina and an Associate Fellow at the Tellus Institute. He was the co-director of the 2014 and 2018 Nexus Conference on Water, Food, Energy and Climate. In 2019 he was a candidate for the Executive Director of the United Nations Environment Programme (UNEP).

In 2016 he was a member of an informal expert group for the President of the UN General Assemblies Brookings Report: "Links in the Chain of Sustainable Finance: Accelerating Private Investments for the SDGs, including Climate Action."

He has written or edited seventeen books including the Vienna Café Trilogy which chronicles sustainable development at the international level: the first, *Only One Earth*, he co-wrote with the father of Sustainable Development Maurice Strong and Michael Strauss; the second, *From Rio +20 to the New Development Agenda*, with Jorge Laguna Celis and Ambassador Liz Thompson; and the last one, *Negotiating the Sustainable Development Goals*, with Ambassador David Donoghue and Jimena Leiva Roesch.

Felix was the Executive Director of Stakeholder Forum for a Sustainable Future from 1992–2012. He played a significant role in promoting multi-stakeholder dialogues at the United Nations and proposed to the UN General Assembly the introduction of stakeholder dialogue sessions at the United Nations Commission on Sustainable Development. In 2011, Felix was listed as one of twenty-five environmentalists ahead of his time.

In 2011 he chaired the United Nations DPI 64th NGO conference – "Sustainable Societies Responsive Citizens." From 1997–2001 he co-chaired the UN Commission on Sustainable Development NGO Steering Committee.

Carolina Duque Chopitea

Carolina Duque Chopitea was born in Panama and raised in the Argentinian Patagonia. She did her undergraduate studies in Canada at the University of Victoria in Political Science and Environmental Studies. Most of her work has been with NGOs and Intergovernmental Organizations. Carolina worked for the Panama Mission to the United Nations in New York where she dedicated most of her time to the First, Third and Fourth Commit-

tees of the General Assembly. Also, she closely worked with stakeholder groups during the 2018 Nexus Conference on Water, Food, Energy and Climate to find ideas and share knowledge on how to implement the Sustainable Development Goals. Currently, she has relocated in San Francisco to peruse a master's in International Business and Business Analytics. Her passion is to find ways in which technology and Big Data can be used to fight climate change, and help businesses and society more broadly transition towards sustainable development.

Bernd Lakemeier

Bernd Lakemeier is Project Leader at the Partnerships2030 team. He studied political science, business studies and (public) international law. After finishing his studies, he joined the Gesellschaft für Internationale Zusammenarbeit (GIZ) and spent three years working in Nepal. Back in Germany, he was part of a small core team working on change management and change processes as an in-house consultant for several years.

Since taking over the project lead for Partnerships2030, he has been sharing and further developing his skills and expertise on multi-stakeholder partnerships. Bernd started heading a second GIZ project "Eradicating Poverty – Reducing Inequality" in June 2018.

Dr. Minu Hemmati

Dr. Minu Hemmati is a clinical psychologist with a doctorate in Organisational and Environmental Psychology, consulting since 1998 with governments; international organisations; women's networks; NGOs; corporations; research institutions. Minu also does non-for-profit work with the MSP Institute – Multi-Stakeholder Processes for Sustainable Development eV, an international charitable association she co-founded in 2016.

Her work includes designing and facilitating change processes that bring together diverse groups of stakeholders in dialogue and collaboration; training; research and advocacy. Minu has wide experience with multi-stakeholder processes at all levels; facilitating small and large groups; international policy making; local and national implementation.

She has published two books and co-authored another, and written over fifty articles, book chapters and reports. Minu is a co-founder of GenderCC – Women for Climate Justice, a Senior Fellow with EcoAgriculture Partners International, and on the Jury of the International Resource Award.

More information at www.minuhemmati.net and www.msp-institute.org.

Susanne Salz

Susanne Salz is an Advisor on multi-stakeholder partnerships for the Sustainable Development Goals (SDGs) in the Partnerships2030 team at the Gesellschaft für Internationale Zusammenarbeit (GIZ). Her professional focus lies on sustainable development and global governance. Previously she worked at the UN SDG Action Campaign as Events Manager, started an initiative on global governance called United Actors, worked as a Project Manager at the "Think and Do Tank" Collaborating Centre on Sustainable Consumption and Production (CSCP) and as Head of the Secretary General's Office at ICLEI – Local Governments for Sustainability. In that role Susanne managed the involvement of local governments in the UN Rio+20 Conference on Sustainable Development. She has also worked at the UN Volunteers and the OECD.

Susanne holds a master's in International Relations from the London School of Economics as well as a bachelor's in International Relations with French from the University of Sussex, including an exchange year at the Institut d'Etudes Politiques (Sciences Po) in Paris. She is a member of the Global Diplomacy Lab, a BMW Foundation Responsible Leader, an alumnus of the Global Governance Futures Fellowship and of the Chinese-German Young Professionals Campus. Susanne loves to row and competes in 100 km rowing races on the Rhine.

Laura Schmitz

Laura Schmitz is a Junior Advisor on multi-stakeholder partnerships for the Sustainable Development Goals (SDGs) in the Partnerships2030 team at the Gesellschaft für Internationale Zusammenarbeit (GIZ). After finishing her studies (BA European Studies, Maastricht University and MSc International Development Studies, Wageningen University and Research Center) she completed her internship with the Partnerships2030 team. Her work as a Junior Advisor focuses on the institutionalization and governance structure of multi-stakeholder partnerships. Previously, she gained practical experience working for the Elsevier Foundation

in Amsterdam, the Netherlands, and during a Global Development Internship in Indore, India. She is passionate in her work on enhancing gender equality, advancing sustainability and fighting for equal opportunities.

Jan-Gustav Strandenaes

Jan-Gustav Strandenaes was educated at the Universities of Oslo, Uppsala, and at St. Olaf College in Minnesota, in modern history, literature, environmental sciences and development issues, and began working with the UN on environment and governance in the 1970s. A first assignment for the UN brought him to Latin America. He taught about the UN for twenty years, worked with the UN Commission for Sustainable Development for ten years, was a liaison officer at the UN HQ for NGOs, worked for the Norwegian Aid Agency in Botswana and Norway's foreign office in Uganda, has extensive NGO/stakeholder experience through forty years in all continents, speaks several languages, is a seasoned lecturer (Oslo University College in Norway), guest lectured all over the world on the UN, governance, sustainable development and stakeholder engagement, evaluated projects and organizations in Africa, Asia and Latin America, advised governments, chaired UN meetings, facilitated UN processes, translated and authored books and numerous articles on environment and sustainable development, assessed sustainability consequences for a Norwegian Olympic Games project, and officially assessed the German National Sustainability Strategy for the government in 2018.

He now works for Stakeholder Forum, UK, and Pure Consulting, Norway, advising private sector, NGOs and municipalities on implementing the SDGs. Jan-Gustav is also an independent researcher on environment, governance and sustainability issues. A global traveller – he crossed the Kalahari Desert in a Land Rover – but when he is not travelling the world, he works out of his home outside Oslo, Norway.

Foreword

Seventy-four years ago, the United Nations Charter was agreed with its opening words being "We the peoples...."

Yet, for the best part of its first half century, the voices of the peoples found relatively few entry points in the United Nations system. It was very much the preserve of the Member States where non-state entities were accorded little effective status.

The Earth Summit in Rio de Janeiro in 1992 broke new ground in the formal recognition it gave to nine sectors of society which became known as the Major Groups in the UN context. From that, a system of engagement with non-state actors has developed which is a logical evolution from those ringing words of the 1945 Charter.

The importance of this new publication is that it makes this history of engagement between stakeholders and the UN system accessible. It draws not only on formal documentation, but also on first hand recollections of how stakeholders came to be included in UN processes, and how effective they were able to be.

Inclusion of the major groups in Agenda 21 agreed at Rio was significant not only because of the importance of representation of key sectors of society in UN processes. It also was an acknowledgement that achieving sustainable development could not be achieved by central governments acting alone, but rather required society-wide buy-in.

Twenty-three years on from Rio, the Sustainable Development Goals were gaveled through the UN General Assembly meeting in New York. They were the product not only of intense and intensive Member State negotiations, but also of the many contributions of stakeholders made in New York, at the national level, and in thematic consultations around the world.

That matters, and it was a different process from that which produced the Millennium Development Goals. Worthy as they were, the lack of broad engagement in their development bears some considerable responsibility for their slow start. The SDGs, on the other hand, were launched with broad stakeholder support because of the opportunity to contribute. That, in turn, has built expectations of ongoing involvement, including at the national level of input into implementation and monitoring and evaluation of progress.

Foreword xxi

In recognising the role of Major Groups, the UN has been well ahead of many Member States which have yet to come to terms with the potential of civil society to contribute to their countries' development. Yet the most sustainable development results will come from strategies into which stakeholders have had input and for which there is broad support. Inclusive governance enhances sustainability. It also enhances accountability for implementation and progress.

As this book documents, not all stakeholder engagement in multilateral processes has been impactful. It shares valuable lessons about what has worked and what hasn't. The Multi Stakeholder Partnership Charter project has developed useful principles on what the future of partnerships could be- not only at the multilateral level, but at all levels where decisions are made.

I commend the authors for producing an authoritative account of how multi stakeholder processes have developed at the global level and how they could be enhanced to be more meaningful and impactful in future.

Rt Hon Helen Clark
Former Prime Minister of New Zealand 1999–2008 and Former UNDP
Administrator 2009–2017.

Introduction

A changing world

> A revolution is coming – a revolution which will be peaceful if we are wise enough; compassionate if we care enough; successful if we are fortunate enough – But a revolution which is coming whether we will it or not. We can affect its character; we cannot alter its inevitability (Kennedy, 1966).

The revolution that Bobby Kennedy was talking about isn't the one we are talking about in this book, but the sentiments are the same. Kennedy was also known for quoting a Chinese proverb which says, "May we live in interesting times." We definitely are living in interesting times.

This is a book about democracy in the context of sustainability. The theory of change we are using is that involving stakeholders in the decision-making process will result in better-informed decisions by governments at all levels. It further argues that involving stakeholders in the decision-making process makes them more likely to partner with each other and with governments at all levels to help deliver on the commitments associated with those agreements.

Today this argument might be viewed as mainstream, or as a kind of geopolitical comfort food akin to that icon status of apple pie in the United States, but twenty-five years ago, at the United Nations Rio Earth Summit (1992), it seemed radical.

The outcome document from that summit – Agenda 21 – was the first intergovernmental text that recognized the rights and responsibilities of a set of stakeholders (nine) that were not governments.

I have been an observer, participant and advocate for stakeholder engagement at the local, sub-national, national and global levels since that first summit in 1992. Stakeholder Forum, for which I was Executive Director (1992–2012), was one of the first multi-stakeholder bodies set up in response to the summit. I worked with local authorities in the United Kingdom on the development of some of the first local Agenda 21s and local sustainable development indicators projects. I witnessed and participated in the birth of the UN Commission on Sustainable Development and the setting up of the Network for Regional Government for Sustainable Development.

2 *Felix Dodds*

But all of this wouldn't have been possible without the role that two particular people played in this emerging theory. Those two were Maurice Strong (Secretary-General of the Earth Summit) and Chip Lindner (Executive Director of the Center for Our Common Future). It is doubtful if we would be where we are now if they hadn't advocated for stakeholders in 1991 and 1992, as chapters in this book will show.

Democracy has been an evolving system of who should have a voice in how we are governed.

The emergence of "stakeholder democracy" should be seen in that historical context. It is an expansion and strengthening of Madisonian democracy (representative) and the next step towards Jeffersonian democracy (participatory).

The objective of this book is to try and learn from the experience of the last twenty-five years and to give the readers some understanding about what has been achieved, especially (where policy development is concerned) at the intergovernmental level. Among other things, the book looks at successful models of multi-stakeholder partnership for helping to deliver global agreements.

The stakeholder concept in the Earth Summit process for the first time enabled nine unique stakeholder voices to be heard. It enabled women to articulate the "gender perspective" of different policies, and youth to be heard before policy decisions would impact on their lives. It recognized that Non-Government Organizations play a critical role in advocating for policy development and monitoring the implementation of agreements, but also in implementing change either by themselves or in partnership with others.

The inclusion of local and sub-national governments at the table ensured a local knowledge and delivery mechanism for global policy decisions. The inclusion of science and academics guaranteed that the best science was in front of the policy makers, and engaging the trade unions meant that any transition would have to be a just transition. Farmers were included because it was seen as critical to address the challenge of feeding the growing population. The eighth stakeholder group is Indigenous Peoples – this represented the start of a long overdue recognition for Indigenous Peoples which in 2000 saw the setting up at the UN of the Permanent Forum on Indigenous Peoples, and in 2001 the establishment of the UN Special Rapporteur on the Rights of Indigenous Peoples.

The most controversial stakeholder to be included was business and industry, but it's vital to have them at the table because they produce the goods and services we all use. Bringing business and industry to the table safeguards their place in the discourse and also ensures that they can be held more accountable.

Here I have focused mostly on the nine stakeholders recognized in 1992, but as time passed, it became clear that there were others that needed to be included depending on the issue being addressed.

The 2030 Agenda for Sustainable Development (2015) added a number of other stakeholders, including disabled people, older people, volunteers (of any age or condition) and the education community. The reality is that any engagement with stakeholders for policy or for developing a partnership should always start by mapping out the relevant stakeholders. The book takes the point of view that a relevant stakeholder is any stakeholder that is impacted by a decision or can impact on a decision.

The development of multi-stakeholder partnerships for the World Summit on Sustainable Development (WSSD) in 2002 was a reaction to a number of realities, as Paul Hohnen, the former Strategic Director of Greenpeace, said:

> Business as usual, government as usual, and perhaps even protest as usual are not giving us the progress we need to achieve sustainable development. Let's see if we can't work together to find better paths forward (Hohnen, 2001).

The concept of stakeholder democracy can build strong coalitions that can shape international, national and local policies and practices. Diverse categories of stakeholders can come together and work to develop a direction that can motivate governments to act, that can bring high-quality policy and practical advice to international forums, and that can prod governments to take domestic action to implement international agreements when they are hesitant or timid. In all these situations, stakeholder democracy has empowered new constituencies to work together to alter multilateral and government directions and to deliver global agreements through multi-stakeholder partnerships.

Has multi-stakeholderism (if there is such a word) developed robust new forms of governance? Are these new processes transparent? Are they accountable to anyone other than the stakeholders engaged in a partnership? What reporting do they do? Are they taking up roles that government should do, and, if so, is that a good idea? These are questions we hope to address in the book while giving the reader some ideas on what can be done so that the answer to the questions is "yes" or at least can be "yes" in the future. There definitely needs to be more transparency and accountability within the stakeholder world. Whether it's a multi-stakeholder policy dialogue or a multi-stakeholder partnership among groups, representation should be empirically verifiable.

I would like to thank my co-authors, Jan-Gustav Strandenaes, Carolina Duque Chopitea, Minu Hemmati, Susanne Salz, Bernd Lakemeier, Laura Schmitz and Jana Borkenhagen, for their chapters. I would also like to underscore that the co-authors do not necessarily agree with the chapters written by other people.

The book has ten chapters that tell the story. These are as follows:

Chapter 1: Stakeholder democracy – re-engaging the peoples of the world: Definitions, concepts and linkages by Jan-Gustav Strandenaes

To enable the reader to understand the terms that the book will use, this chapter sets the scene as far as the world we are engaging in and then defines key terms such as stakeholders, engagement, dialogue, partnerships, multi-stakeholder partnerships, civil society, public private partnerships, etc.

4   *Felix Dodds*

It also identifies and defines key issues such as legitimacy, transparency and power, discussing the linkages between multilevel, multisector and multi-stakeholder processes and approaches.

Chapter 2: A short history of democracy by Felix Dodds

Democracy has developed over the course of human history, from its origins in fifth century Athens to present-day Madisonian (representative) democracy. Over time, the definition of democracy has expanded whose views should be considered. This chapter reviews that development and starts to place stakeholder democracy within present democracy.

Chapter 3: The emergence of stakeholder democracy by Felix Dodds

Following the short history of democracy in the previous chapter, this one goes into more depth on how the ideas behind stakeholder democracy developed and how they fit current thinking. It explains stakeholder democracy as a strengthening of present-day Madisonian (representative) democracy and a step towards Jeffersonian (participatory) democracy. It explains how the theory change we are using is that involving stakeholders in the decision-making process will result in better-informed decisions by governments at all levels. It further argues that involving stakeholders in the decision-making process makes them more likely to partner with each other and with governments at all levels to help deliver on the commitments associated with those agreements.

Chapter 4: Civil society discourse by Felix Dodds

There have been two different discourses that have developed over the past twenty-five years, these being civil society in the area of development and stakeholder engagement in the area of sustainable development. This chapter reviews the three major versions of the civil society discourse (associational life, the good society and public sphere). It finds that they limit engagement by excluding key stakeholders. It also groups together key stakeholders into one space therefore reducing the voices of those individual stakeholders. It suggests that civil society works best to mitigate totalitarianism on both the left and right; however, as an organizing principle within democracy, it is found wanting.

Chapter 5: Literature review by Carolina Duque Chopitea

This chapter synthesizes research and current thinking on stakeholder democracy, shedding light on the academic discourse and the political debate. The literature review undertaken in this section relies on normative and empirical studies that highlight the strengths and weaknesses, the opportunities and risks of the role of stakeholders and multi-stakeholder partnerships (MSPs) in decision-making, decision-finding and implementation.

Chapter 6: Examples of successful multi-stakeholder policy development by Felix Dodds

This chapter builds on some of the examples discussed in Chapter 3. The chapter explores part of the theory of change that engaging stakeholders helps governments make better-informed policy decisions.

It explores in more depth the impact that stakeholder engagement has had on sustainable development policy-making, focusing on an example from each of the global, national, sub-national and local levels. It offers suggestions on how to improve policy development between levels of government and between governments and other stakeholders.

Chapter 7: Multi-stakeholder partnerships: Making them work for delivering global agreements by Jan-Gustav Strandenaes

This chapter reviews examples from different levels and all regions of the world using a common framework of presentation for issues, goals, stakeholders, governance, financing and measures of success. It also traces some of the history behind the development of multi-stakeholder partnerships.

Chapter 8: Principles for multi-stakeholder processes by Minu Hemmati

This chapter provides a summary of existing guidance for MSPs with a focus on principles; some of the key literature is being presented along with the MSP Charter developed 2017–2019. The MSP Charter includes references to practical aspects of putting its principles into practice. In addition, the chapter offers implementation guidance by providing summaries of key handbooks and tool guides as well as links to relevant organizations, institutes and networks.

Chapter 9: Designing successful multi-stakeholder partnerships by Susanne Salz, Bernd Lakemeier, Laura Schmitz and Jana Borkenhagen

A multi-stakeholder partnership (MSP) brings together various stakeholders willing to contribute to sustainable development. In themselves, MSPs are complex; there is no one-size-fits-all approach concerning its design and operation. This chapter gives practical tips along the process of (i) initiating, (ii) institutionalizing and (iii) assessing the impact of MSPs. The tips on the first steps in MSPs elaborate how to find potential partners, initiate a partnership and tackle challenges along the way (i). Once an MSP is operating, its institutionalization helps to define a governance structure, general rules and to approach the question of funding (ii). Lastly, the chapter identifies the potential impact of MSPs and ways of impact assessment, illustrated using a case study on sustainable tuna fisheries in the Philippines (iii).

6 *Felix Dodds*

Chapter 10: The challenges ahead by Felix Dodds

This chapter summarizes what the book has addressed and explores what real world challenges we might face over the coming decade and why stakeholder democracy is a way by which represented democracy might be supported in a time of fear.

Thanks

I would like to thank the following people, in particular Patrick O'Hannigan, and Tanner Glenn, who helped Felix's English sound more intelligent. This is always challenging because I am dyslexic. Michael Strauss for his amazing support, patience and creative energy even at 4 in the morning ... mostly 4 or 4:15 in the morning ...

I would very much like to thank Tim Hardwick at Routledge, who has overseen nearly all of my books going back to before Earthscan became part of the Taylor and Francis Group. This is my first book – of many I hope – with my new editor, Amy Johnston.

I would also like to thank those that reviewed some of the text and helped address some of my own preconceptions. They include: Guenther Bachmann, Jamie Bartram, Andrew Binns, Chandana Das, Michael Dorsey, Eela Dubey, Thomas Forster, Herman Greene, Jeffery Huffines, Alexander Juras, Frans de Man, Paul Raskin, Michael Strauss, Stacey Wilenkin and Ruben Zondervan.

Finally, thank you, esteemed reader, for buying this book. We all hope you enjoy the story here. We believe that it's an important story, and one that hopefully you will take part in over the coming years.

Perhaps American pastor Harry Emerson Fosdick best expressed the hope of democracy when he said, "democracy is based upon the conviction that there are extraordinary possibilities in ordinary people" (Fosdick, 1935).

References

Fosdick, E. H. (1935) Harry Emerson Fosdick. Available online at: https://en.wikiquote.org/wiki/Harry_Emerson_Fosdick

Hohnen, P. (2001) Multi-Stakeholder Processes: Why, and Where Next? Paper presented to the Stakeholder Forum Workshop: Examples, Principles, Strategies. New York: Stakeholder Forum. Available online at: https://earthsummit2002.org/msp/workshop/Paul%20Hohnen%2028%2004%2001.pot

Kennedy, R. (1966, May 9) Speech in the United States Senate. Washington, DC: United States Senate.

1 Stakeholder democracy – re-engaging the peoples of the world
Definitions, concepts and linkages

Jan Gustav Strandenaes

Introduction to multi-stakeholder democracy (MSD) – a multi-lateral background

As explained in the introduction of this book, we are examining the development of stakeholder democracy in the context of sustainability specifically, but advocating the engagement of stakeholders at all levels as a way of strengthening representative democracy as a whole.

Our definition of stakeholders is those who have an interest in a particular decision, either as individuals or representatives of a group. This includes people who influence a decision, or can influence it, as well as those affected by it.

As far as sustainability is concerned, our guide is the "Transforming Our World: The 2030 Agenda for Sustainable Development" agreed by heads of state in 2015. Within that document, it committed the world community to "leaving no one behind."

The almost slogan-like statement is understood to embody everything we fight for today – justice for all, equality for all, sustainability for all, well-being for all. Any person in the world today, with a basic understanding of the planet's situation and with some interest in his or her own well-being, including the well-being of the closest family or group of friends, will most probably be anxiously concerned with what possibilities there are to sustain, let alone develop, that level of well-being. The perilous state of the world outlining our options for future well-being is most eloquently and dramatically expressed as follows:

> Today we are also taking a decision of great historic significance. We resolve to build a better future for all people, including the millions who have been denied the chance to lead decent, dignified and rewarding lives and to achieve their full human potential. We can be the first generation to succeed in ending poverty; just as we may be the last to have a chance of saving the planet. The world will be a better place in 2030 if we succeed in our objectives (UN, 2015).

There are two axioms in this quote, one positive and one, well, rather pessimistic, though as with most pessimistic statements, it is also imbued with a

8 *Jan-Gustav Strandenaes*

challenge. The first axiom emphasizes the possibilities humanity has, after all these centuries, to finally end poverty, and hence build a platform for well-being for all. The second comes with a warning: we may presently be the last generation to have the chance to rectify what is wrong with our world. The choice is obviously ours.

The 2030 Agenda for Sustainable Development centred around seventeen goals, known as the Sustainable Development Goals (SDGs), to which were added 169 targets. This ambitious plan contained language criticized as lofty by some; it was not bereft of concrete proposals on how to implement it, and, in particular, it contains a commitment to partnerships.

> The scale and ambition of the new Agenda requires a revitalized Global Partnership to ensure its implementation. We fully commit to this. This Partnership will work in a spirit of global solidarity, in particular solidarity with the poorest and with people in vulnerable situations. It will facilitate an intensive global engagement in support of implementation of all the Goals and targets, bringing together Governments, the private sector, civil society, the United Nations system and other actors and mobilizing all available resources (UN, 2015).

In the coming chapters, we will cover two key elements of stakeholder democracy: that of the engagement of stakeholders in policy development and that of engaging them in delivering global agreements in partnerships.

Stakeholder democracy is already part of our political discourse, and it functions as such parallel to the "mainstream political landscape." What is surprising to us is that no one has actually attempted to describe it as such, something we will attempt to change with this book.

The mainstream political landscape today is not perceived as a positive one. In the second decade of the twenty-first century, a new and dramatic political situation has descended on this world. Politicians with subversive ideas have reared their ugly heads and formulated ideas we all thought were long gone and buried once and for all in the post–WWII settlements. Aggressive and often antidemocratic political sub-currents have not only seen the light of day in this decade, but have come to dominate much of the political discourse. In a world subjected to numerous problems that are global in consequence, and clearly demand globally coordinated and cooperated solutions, isolationism, sectarianism and sometimes extreme individualism projecting short-term and narrow-minded actions have become the order of the day.

We entered this century on a positive note

Long-term planning and multi-lateral cooperation through multi-lateral institutions, meticulously developed over the past seventy years, have provided us with a world that by and large has enjoyed political predictability during these years.

A global consensus to follow global agreements has contributed to reasonable global stability.

The multi-lateral system, largely through the UN system, was hugely important in developing this consensus. The political scientist Samuel Huntington wrote about what he described as the "third wave of democratization," stating that liberal democracies had by the turn of the last century become the default form of government. In his magnum opus, *The Origins of Political Order*, the political scientist Frances Fukuyama writes that by the late 1990s more than 60 percent of the world's independent states had become electoral democracies (Fukuyama, 2011).

We might therefore assert that the political roots to the present century are good in the sense that more and more people have been able to participate in the development of their own well-being. We entered the twenty-first century with a sense of optimism.

Of course, there have been many setbacks and problems have been piling up around us, such as climate change, war, refugees or the global economy crash of 2008.

Yet, despite all these challenges, and despite the recent political reaction and narrow-minded short-termism, more initiatives and different efforts were taken to counter the all-out negative tendencies. And one of these initiatives was the idea of engaging stakeholders more in the decision-making process and in partnerships between governments and stakeholders on sustainable development.

To foster more understanding of stakeholder democracy, this chapter will also outline some of the key terms that we think are all part of such a landscape. You, the reader, may find there are no new concepts in our list of terms. What is new, we think, is their application and the context in which they will be applied. The list of terms is also important as these are key terms to be used and contextualized to frame what we mean when defining and explaining stakeholder democracy.

Multi-level and multi-sector approaches stimulate interlinkages

But before going into the terms, allow us to give you a simple overview of multi-level, multi-sector and multi-stakeholder approaches.

One more caveat; this book has a focus on global level approaches to multi-stakeholder processes; global level approaches entail agreements between nations in multi-lateral and intergovernmental systems. These systems are represented by the UN family of organizations and units, but also of other multi-lateral organizations, such as the OECD, DAC, etc. as well as regional constructs, such as found in Europe, Africa, Asia, the Pacific or the Americas. Within this framework of multi-lateralism, and their focus on identifying, developing and implementing global agreements, the various chapters of the book will also attempt to address the global level approaches and multi-stakeholder processes from a variety of aspects: community to local, sub-national to national, regional to global.

10   *Jan-Gustav Strandenaes*

A multi-stakeholder approach to policy development, where all stakeholders are respected and taken seriously and where their views and inputs are reflected in the final outcome, as we have said has its roots in the 1992 UN Earth Summit, but is still a novelty.

Our planet, though finite, is complex, almost dauntingly so. Our continuous and expanding knowledge of our world only seems to exacerbate this complexity. Finding solutions to the many-faceted problems that we identify in this complexity cannot be done through a singular lens.

This approach – a singular-focused approach – has, however, dominated policy-making up until now: we have either discussed how to solve environmental problems, and established environmental institutions to deal with that; or we have delved into social issues and tried to find solutions through establishing institutions with expert knowledge on social issues; or we have identified economic issues that needed to be dealt with, and have established a multitude of institutions with expert knowledge on finance and economy. This has resulted in establishing a number of single issue-silos imbued with expert knowledge on issues pertaining to that specific silo. Integrating different issues, which at first glance may seem unrelated to each other, has never properly been done.

The report "Our Common Future," delivered to the UN in 1987 by Ms. Gro Harlem Brundtland, the then Prime Minister of Norway, introduced sustainable development as a concept, and firmly placed the issue on the global agenda. It centred on the need to balance economic, social and environmental concerns.

With the emergence of the concept of sustainable development, the theory of integrating its three dimensions was launched.

Interlinkages between sectors or issues is not a new idea. But there was a lack of understanding, even accepting how to apply a multi-sector approach that would illustrate how interlinked the issues were. Because of this, few had seen and realized, let alone assessed, the value and benefits of trade-offs between sectors.

This apparent ignorance had also inadvertently blocked the development of policies that would benefit from these trade-offs. There is accordingly an urgent need to realize this. A recurring problem with multi-sector approaches is that people too often see the multi-sector approach as a replacement for a sector approach. This is a huge mistake as "siloed expertise" and strong thematic and organizational sectors are also needed. But to address the complex world of 2030, mechanisms to address and operationalize interlinkages between themes and sectors are needed.

An integrated element of such mechanisms must have innovative, accountable, strong and resilient governance structures. One significant purpose of such governance structures must be to allow for multi-stakeholder input.

The relevance and content of the 2030 Agenda with the SDGs mentioned earlier in the chapter is largely a result of the integrative openness of the Open Working Group (OWG), which steered the negotiations and allowed for relevant and active participation of all stakeholders as well as heeding their input (Dodds et al., 2016). It is also one of the few global agreements that tries to address the issue of interlinkages between policy areas.

A new era – Same concepts in a new context

There has been in the past a belief that governments should be the delivery mechanism for everything. If only governments would take responsibility, then everything would be great. Such a view has often been reflected in various academic writings as well as expressed by non-state actors. There is, however, strong evidence that this approach does not always work, the latest "proof" being the Inter-governmental Panel on Climate Change (IPCC) Report of 2018:

> "One of the key messages that comes out very strongly from this report is that we are already seeing the consequences of 1°C of global warming through more extreme weather, rising sea levels and diminishing Arctic sea ice, among other changes," said Panmao Zhai, Co-Chair of IPCC Working Group I (IPCC, 2018).

Despite government commitment to the 2015 Paris Agreement on Climate to reduce drastically greenhouse gas emissions, these emissions are still on the increase.

The 1992 Rio Earth Summit played, as I mentioned above, a critical role in readjusting the global policy-negotiating narrative to welcome the involvement of stakeholders in policy development as well as in implementation. The Summit outcome document known as Agenda 21 contains nine chapters on non-state stakeholders, called Major Groups (see p. 15 for the list).

The chapters hold both rights and responsibilities. This has led to considerable engagement by these nine stakeholders in policy development on sustainable development and in working together to help deliver those policies in practical projects on the ground.

In the complex world of the twenty-first century, policy and practice need to be multi-level, multi-sector and multi-stakeholder to ensure that global agreements are delivered.

This book will attempt to describe some of the key elements of stakeholder democracy – where it has come from what role it might play in policy and practice. There is still much of this to be developed as far as governance issues within stakeholder democracy are concerned.

This book will rely on newly researched and available material as well as on our own experience having been an integrated part of the last twenty-five years of multi-stakeholder approaches.

The Yale historian Timothy Snyder observed:

> History does not repeat, but it does instruct (Snyder, 2017).

With recorded history and experience, we may find ways of engaging stakeholders. Twenty-five years of trial and error and of experimentation offer a formidable amount of experience and knowledge that can contribute to making a stakeholder democracy a robust and accountable system ready and eager to deliver.

12 Jan-Gustav Strandenaes

To enable such development, there will clearly need to be better knowledge management and capacity building for and among all stakeholders. The UN multi-lateral system has played a strategic role in helping to create the space for learning approaches that will delineate the topography of the new landscape. Engaging stakeholders will strengthen our democracy at all levels against the enormous challenges we will face in the coming decades. It will help us understand, protect and respect democracy and good governance.

Some terms that are helpful in understanding the narrative

Accountability: In ethics and governance accountability is answerability, blameworthiness, liability and the expectation of account-giving. As an aspect of governance, it has been central to discussions related to problems in the public sector, nonprofit and private and individual contexts. In leadership roles, accountability is the acknowledgment and assumption of responsibility for actions, products, decisions and policies including the administration, governance and implementation within the scope of the role or employment position and encompassing the obligation to report, explain and be answerable for resulting consequences.

In governance, accountability has expanded beyond the basic definition of "being called to account for one's actions." It is frequently described as an account-giving relationship between individuals, e.g., "A is accountable to B when A is obliged to inform B about A's (past or future) actions and decisions, to justify them, and to suffer punishment in the case of eventual misconduct." Accountability cannot exist without proper accounting practices; in other words, an absence of accounting means an absence of accountability (Wikipedia, 2019).

Accreditation: Most multi-lateral intergovernmental organizations, such as the UN family of organizations, have rules and procedure to allow the different actors to participate in their meetings or conferences. As the name implies, the intergovernmental organizations belong to member states and their governments, and thus their official delegations are almost automatically admitted. However, even government representatives must carry a visible sign – a passport to be recognized as a participant to the international conference, and this sign ensures you that they are accredited to participate. Non-state stakeholders are subjected to different procedures, specifically designed to cater to the non-state stakeholder community. In the case of the UN, the overarching rules of admittance or accreditation is found in a resolution from 1996 taken in the Economic and Social Council (ECOSOC 1996/31). As long as the organization is accredited to the UN, or accepted by the UN for participation, a passport can be issued to a person belonging to that organization. The UN has different levels of accreditation, some organizations have been given ECOSOC status, after application and rigid vetting, and some organizations may only participate at special conferences, provided they apply for registration.

Civil society: has its historical origin in Greek antiquity and is today recognized as the "third sector" of society. Institutions like OECD, the World Bank, and several donor organizations explain society as consisting of three sectors: (1) government representatives, national and local, including elected parliamentarians; (2) the market, comprising the private sector and business enterprises; and (3) civil society. Civil society comprises civil society organizations, community-based organizations and **non-governmental organizations** (NGOs) depending on their constituency. United Cities and Local Governments (UCLG) and Local Governments for Sustainability (ICLEI) are both organized as NGOs, but they represent local authorities and hence are not of civil society; the International Chamber of Commerce (ICC) and the World Business Council on Sustainable Development (WBCSD) are both organised as NGOs, but represent the business sector. Accordingly, they are not of civil society. Hence all civil society organizations are NGOs – but not all NGOs are of civil society (see also **non-state actors** and **stakeholders**). For a thorough discussion on these concepts and the UN, see Strandenaes, 2014. (Cf. also the World Bank and OECD on stakeholders.)

Collaborative democracy: is a political framework where electors and the elected actively collaborate to attain the best possible solution to any situation using collaborative enabling technologies to facilitate wide scale citizen participation in government.

Communication: exchange of opinions, news and information by writing, speech or gestures including body language and facial reactions.

Conflict: perceived incompatibility of goals between two or more parties.

Consensus: general agreement; accepted unanimity; the judgement arrived at by most of those concerned; group solidarity in sentiment and belief. The UN system is often adverse to voting procedures, and makes adamant efforts to reach consensus agreements. The jargon is: nothing is agreed until everything is agreed, nothing is decided until everything is decided.

Constituencies: a group or body that patronizes, supports, or offers representation.

Consult: to have regard to; consider; to ask the advice or opinion of <consult a doctor>; to refer to <consult a dictionary>; to consult an individual; to deliberate together; confer; to serve as a consultant. Synonyms: confer, advise, confab, confabulate, huddle, parley, powwow, treat. Related words: cogitate, counsel, deliberate; consider, examine, review.

Debate: The term refers to stakeholders stating their views, both arguing "their case." Debates imply a party-political approach and are usually "won," meaning that they don't lead to an integration of views.

Decision-making: the act or process of deciding something especially with a group of people.

Decision-shaping: a term used in certain UN organizations as synonymous with **decision-making**. The difference is, however, that certain member states of the UN feel that non-state actors should not be part of the decision-making processes of the UN as they are not of member states and have no voting rights in the organization. They are, however, allowed to lobby for their views, and hence help shape the final decided outcome (see UNEP, 2018).

14 Jan-Gustav Strandenaes

Democratic deficit: an insufficient level of democracy in political institutions and procedures in comparison with a theoretical ideal of a democratic government. The expression "democratic deficit" may be used to denote the absence or underdevelopment of key democratic institutions, but it may also be used to describe the various ways in which these institutions may fail to function properly (e.g., lack of transparency and accountability, technocratic decision-making, inadequate participation of citizens in policy-making). Evaluations of the level of democratic deficit focus on the procedural aspects of democracy, reflected in the mechanisms of representation and decision-making. Therefore, the notion of democratic deficit encompasses distortions in the flow of influence from citizens to government. As such, it is closely associated with the issue of democratic legitimacy.

Dialogue: a conversation between two or more persons; an exchange of ideas and opinions; a discussion between representatives of parties to a conflict that is aimed at resolution.

Direct democracy: also called pure democracy, forms of direct participation of citizens in democratic decision-making, in contrast to indirect or **representative democracy**, based on the sovereignty of the people. This can happen in the form of an assembly democracy or by initiative and referendum with ballot voting, with direct voting on issues instead of for candidates or parties. Sometimes the term is also used for electing representatives in a direct vote as opposed to indirect elections (by voting for an electing body, electoral college, etc.) as well as for recalling elected officeholders. Direct democracy may be understood as a full-scale system of political institutions, but, in modern times, it means most often specific decision-making institutions in the broader system environment of representative democracy.

Discussion: consideration of a question in open and usually informal debate; a formal treatment of a topic in speech or writing. More than **dialogue**, the term "discussion" recognizes the differences between views and people and is less focused on mutual understanding in order to open possibilities to con-sensus-building.

Forum: the marketplace or public place of an ancient Roman city forming the centre of judicial and public business; a public meeting place for open discussion; a medium (as a newspaper) of open discussion or expression of ideas; a judicial body or assembly; court; a public meeting or lecture involving audience discussion; a programme (as on radio or television) involving discussion of a problem usually by several authorities.

Franchise: a special privilege granted to an individual or group, the right or license granted to an individual or group to market a company's goods or services in a particular territory and a team and its operating organization having such membership.

Freedom: the power or right to act, speak, or think as one wants; the power of self-determination attributed to the will; the quality of being independent of fate or necessity.

Stakeholder democracy 15

Globalization: is also a social, cultural, political and legal phenomenon. In social terms, globalization represents greater interconnectedness among global populations. Culturally, globalization represents the exchange of ideas and values among cultures, and even a trend towards the development of a single world culture. Politically, globalization has shifted countries' political activities to the global level through intergovernmental organizations like the United Nations and the World Trade Organization. With regard to law, globalization has altered how international law is created and enforced.

Global public policy (GPP) networks: a term used by Reinicke et al. (2000) in their work with the World Bank Global Public Policy Program. GPP networks are described as multi-sectoral collaborative alliances, often involving governments, international organizations, companies and NGOs. They "take advantage of technological innovation and political liberalization"; "pull diverse groups and resources together"; "address issues that no single group can resolve by itself"; and, by doing so, rely on "the strength of weak ties" (ibid).

Governance: refers to a process whereby elements in society wield power, authority and influence and enact policies and decisions concerning public life and social upliftment.

Hearing: opportunity to be heard; to present one's side of a case; or to be generally known or appreciated. The term refers to processes where governments or intergovernmental bodies invite stakeholders to state their views on a particular issue.

Ideology: a manner or the content of thinking characteristic of an individual, group or culture; the integrated assertions, theories and aims that constitute a socio-political programme; a systematic body of concepts especially about human life or culture.

Implementation of decisions: includes conveying the decision to those affected and getting their commitment to it. Groups or committees can help a manager achieve commitment. The people who must carry out a decision are most likely to enthusiastically endorse the outcome if they participate in the decision-making process.

Liberty: the positive enjoyment of various social, political or economic rights and privileges.

Liquid democracy: is a new form for collective decision-making that gives voters full decisional control. Voters can either vote directly on issues, or they can delegate their voting power to delegates (i.e., representatives) who vote on their behalf. Delegation can be domain specific, which means that voters can delegate their voting power to different experts in different domains.

Major Groups: Since the first United Nations Conference on Environment and Development in 1992 – known as the Earth Summit – it was recognized that achieving sustainable development would require the active participation of all sectors of society and all types of people. Agenda 21, adopted at the Earth Summit, drew upon this sentiment and formalized nine sectors of society as the main channels through which broad participation would be facilitated in UN activities related to sustainable development. These are officially called "Major

16 Jan-Gustav Strandenaes

Groups" and include the following sectors: Women, Children and Youth, Indigenous Peoples, Non-Governmental Organizations, Local Authorities, Workers and Trade Unions, Business and Industry, the Scientific and Technological Community and Farmers.

Meta-communication: [from Greek "meta" = higher] communication about communication; exchanging information, views, opinions about the way we communicate in a given situation and structure. An important tool in communication processes, particularly in groups of high diversity of language, culture and background.

Multi-Stakeholder Partnerships (MSPs) for sustainable development: specific commitments and contributions, undertaken together by various partners, intended to support the implementation of transformation towards sustainable development and help achieve the Sustainable Development Goals (SDGs) and other relevant sustainable development agreements.

Multi-Stakeholder Partnerships for sustainable development are by definition using a multi-stakeholder approach: they are inclusive in nature, involving all relevant actors in their area of work. MSPs can be arranged among any combination of partners, including governments, regional groups, local authorities, non-governmental actors, international institutions, private sector partners and other relevant stakeholders. All partners should be involved in the development of the MSP from an early stage, so that it is genuinely participatory in approach. Yet as partnerships evolve, there should also be opportunities for additional partners to join on an equal basis.

New social partnerships: people and organizations from some combination of public, business and civil constituencies who engage in voluntary, mutually beneficial, innovative relationships to address common societal aims through combining their resources and competencies.

Non-Governmental Organization (NGO): An NGO is as the designation implies different from government organizations. It is more often than not an organization with a civil society constituency, but not necessarily so (see **civil society**). Within the UN system, an NGO has a proper definition including minimum requirements to be recognized as a valid NGO (see ECOSOC resolution 1996/31). The legal position for an NGO within the UN system is found in Article 71 of the UN Charter. The Specialized Agencies of the UN (such as UNESCO, WHO, ILO, FAO, etc.) are, however, mandated through their mandating charters to establish other rules of procedure and accept other non-state constellations. Some have also done that – see FAO and World Food Programme.

Non-state actor: As there has been a proliferation of stakeholders working on the global multi-lateral scene, the concept "non-state" actor has been frequently used to refer to stakeholders other than governments. The concept is slightly controversial, as many NGOs do not accept the term. There is, however, a tendency in academia to use the term synonymously with NGOs, which only adds to the growing confusion. The term "non-state actor" is also context dependent, has no legal status within the UN system and can be used to refer to any organizational construct – except governments, including regional and local.

On behalf of: When a person speaks in a meeting, he or she does so in different contexts. The person speaking "on behalf of" has been mandated to do so. That means that the person has been given a job, an assignment or a mandate by a constituency in an organization or a political party to speak on their behalf. But a person may feel the need to speak up in a meeting because the person feels that he or she knows the issue being discussed as well as how the larger group of stakeholders may think about this particular issue. In such a case, the person may not claim to be speaking on behalf of, but can safely say that the views of the stakeholder community are being represented and thus the person may be "speaking for that particular stakeholder group." Such a statement must also reflect and respect the issue of **representativity**.

Other stakeholders: Two decades after the Earth Summit, the importance of effectively engaging the nine Major Groups of society was reaffirmed by the United Nations Conference on Sustainable Development (Rio+20), in 2012. Its outcome document, "The Future We Want," highlights the role that Major Groups can play in pursuing sustainable societies for future generations. In addition, governments invited other stakeholders, including local communities, volunteer groups and foundations, migrants and families, as well as older persons and persons with disabilities, to participate in UN processes related to sustainable development, which can be done through close collaboration with the Major Groups. These are delineated in paragraph 43 of the Rio+20 outcome document; there are further additions to "other stakeholders" in the UNGA resolution A/Res/67/290 (§§ 14 and 16) which mandates the High Level Political Forum (HLPF) to function as a coordination mechanism for the 2030 Agenda and the SDGs.

Participation: Meaningful participation requires that individuals are entitled to participate in the decisions that directly affect them, including in the design, implementation and monitoring of health interventions. In practice, meaningful participation may take on a number of different forms, including informing people with balanced, objective information, consulting the community to gain feedback from the affected population, involving or working directly with communities, collaborating by partnering with affected communities in each aspect of decision-making including the development of alternatives and identification of solutions, and empowering communities to retain ultimate control over the key decisions that affect their well-being.

Participatory democracy: individual participation by citizens in political decisions and policies that affect their lives, especially directly rather than through elected representatives.

Power: a relationship among social actors in which one social actor, A, can get another social actor, B, to do something that B would not have otherwise done. The bases for power can be "coercive-force/threat," "utilitarian-material/ incentives" and/or "normative-symbolic influences."

Process: progress, advance; something going on; proceeding; a natural phenomenon marked by gradual changes that lead towards a particular result; a

18 *Jan-Gustav Strandenaes*

natural continuing activity or function; a series of actions or operations conducing to an end; the series of actions, operations or motions involved in the accomplishment of an end.

Public private partnerships: are principally contractual arrangements between single or several public agencies (federal, state or local) and single or several private sector entities. Through such arrangements, the skills and assets of each sector (public and private) are shared, in delivering a service or facility for the use of the general public. Other stakeholders might be sub-contractors in a PPP.

Representative democracy: is a form of democracy founded on the principle of elected individuals representing the people. Here, people allow representatives who form an independent ruling body to represent them in the various forms of democratic process and are not directly involved in any of the processes of legislation or law-making.

Representativity: Much of the intergovernmental system rests on a foundation of so-called **representative democracy**, but representativity can also mean other things: you can represent an issue over time, and thus build a credible and respected position with colleagues, an issue which is hugely important in networks; you can represent an issue with in-depth and expert knowledge, and you can also represent views of many different stakeholders, (see also **on behalf of**).

Stakeholder forum: forum as an inclusive process wherein stakeholders of all types feel welcome to participate and express their views, which will be respected and taken into account as authorities move forward ... is not a one-off event, but a living, evolving process (OGP, 2011).

Stakeholders: The term can often be misleading as it is context dependent. A stakeholder can refer to a government, a business person or a person from civil society. At the UN and in certain other multi-lateral organizations the term stakeholder is often used in reference to civil society. That may often be the case, but again – it would be the context of the document that gives the reader the proper understanding of what the term refers to. The term NGO is also often used as being synonymous with civil society, which it may not be (see discussion under **civil society** and **NGO**). An NGO is definitely a stakeholder, but unlike the term NGO, a "stakeholder" has no legal definition or standing within the UN system (see **NGO**). The term stakeholder is mostly used synonymously with NGOs in the Rio+20 outcome document, which has delineated in paragraph 43 a number of interest groups to be included as participants in the SDG process (see **other stakeholders**).

Statement: Synonyms: expression, utterance, vent, voice. Related words: outgiving; articulation, presentation, presentment, verbalization, vocalization.

Transparency: is a belief that there is a general right of the public to know, and pro-active transparency is a mechanism for exercising this right.

Understand: to grasp the meaning of; comprehend; to have a sympathetic attitude. Understanding: knowledge and ability to apply judgment; ability to comprehend and judge.

Values: the principles that help you to decide what is right and wrong, and how to act in various situations.

Vanguard: people who are making changes or new developments in something.

Voluntary initiatives: are activities or contributions made by single governments or organizations, or groups of them, towards a certain goal, and above and beyond legally binding or UN-agreed commitments.

References

Civil Society (2018) Civil Society Definition from the United Nations, New York, UN. Available online at: http://www.un.org/en/sections/resources-different-audiences/civil-society/

Collaborative Democracy (2007) Collaborative Democracy Definition, New York. Available online at: www.collaborative-democracy.com/cdDefinition.html

Communication (2018) Communication Definition, Your Dictionary. Available online at: www.yourdictionary.com/communication

Conflict (1995) Glossary in *Social Psychology*, third edition, by Smith and Mackie, London, Psychology Press.

Consensus (2018) Consensus Definition, Merriam-Webster. Available online at: www.merriam-webster.com/dictionary/consensus

Constituency (2018) Constituency Definition, a group or body that patronizes, supports, or offers representation, Merriam-Webster. Available online at: www.merriam-web ster.com/dictionary/constituency

Debate (2002) Definition in *Multi-Stakeholder Processes for Governance and Sustainability*, by Hemmati, Dodds, Enayati and McHarry, London, Earthscan.

Decision-Making (2018) Decision-Making Definition, Merriam-Webster. Available online at: www.merriam-webster.com/dictionary/decision-making

Democratic Deficit (2018) Definition of Democratic Deficit, Encyclopaedia Britannica. Available online at: www.britannica.com/topic/democratic-deficit

Dialogue (2018) Dialogue Definition, Merriam-Webster. Available online at: www.mer riam-webster.com/dictionary/dialogue

Direct Democracy (2018) Direct Democracy Definition, Encyclopaedia Britannica. Available online at: www.britannica.com/topic/direct-democracy

Discussion (2018) Discussion Definition, Merriam-Webster. Available online at: www.merriam-webster.com/dictionary/discussion

Dodds, F., Donoghue, D. and Leiva-Roesch, J. (2016) *Negotiating the Sustainable Development Goals*, London, Routledge.

Forum (2018) Forum Definition, Merriam-Webster. Available online at: www.merriam -webster.com/dictionary/forum

Franchise (2018) Definition of Franchise, Merriam-Webster. Available online at: www.merriam-webster.com/dictionary/franchise

Freedom (2018) Freedom Definition, Oxford Living Dictionary. Available online at: http s://en.oxforddictionaries.com/definition/freedom

Fukuyama, F. (2011) *The Origins of Political Order*, Profile Books.

Globalization (2018) Globalization Definition, Investopedia. Available online at: www.investopedia.com/terms/g/globalization.asp

Governance (2018) Understanding the Concept of Governance, GRDC. Available online at: www.gdrc.org/u-gov/governance-understand.html

Hearing (2018) Hearing Definition, Merriam-Webster. Available online at: www.merriam-webster.com/dictionary/hearing

Ideology (2018) Ideology Definition, Merriam-Webster. Available online at: www.merriam-webster.com/dictionary/ideology

Implementation of Decisions (2010) What is Decision Making?Citeman. Available online at: www.citeman.com/8288-what-is-decision-implementation.html

IPCC (2018) Press Release IPCC: Summary for Policymakers of IPCC Special Report on Global Warming of 1.5°C Approved by Governments, Geneva, IPCC. Available online at: https://ipcc.ch/pdf/session48/pr_181008_P48_spm_en.pdf

Liberty (2018) Liberty Definition, Merriam-Webster. Available online at: www.merriam-webster.com/dictionary/liberty

Liquid Democracy (2015) Liquid Democracy: True Democracy for the 21st Century, by Dominik Schiener, Medium Organizer Sandbox. Available online at: https://medium.com/organizer-sandbox/liquid-democracy-true-democracy-for-the-21st-century-7c66f5e53b6f

Major Groups (2018) Major Groups Definition, United Nations. Available online at: https://sustainabledevelopment.un.org/majorgroups/about

New Social Partnerships (2001) *Partnership Alchemy: New Social Partnerships in Europe,* by J. Nelson and S. Zadek, Copenhagen, Denmark, The Copenhagen Centre.

Open Government Partnership (OGP) (2011) *Designing and Managing an OGP Multistakeholder Forum: A Practical Handbook with Guidance and Ideas,* Washington DC, OGP. Available online at: http://www.opengovpartnership.org/sites/default/files/Multistakeholder%20Forum%20Handbook.pdf

Other Stakeholders (2018) Other Stakeholders Definition, United Nations. Available online at: https://sustainabledevelopment.un.org/majorgroups/about

Participation (2018) Participation Definition, World Health Organization. Available online at: www.who.int/gender-equity-rights/understanding/participation-definition/en/

Participatory Democracy (2018) Participatory Democracy Definition, Dictionary.com. Available online at: www.dictionary.com/browse/participatory-democracy

Power (1981) Definition in *Power in Organizations,* by J. Pfeffer, Marshfield, MA: Pitman.

Process (2018) Process Definition, Merriam-Webster. Available online at: www.merriam-webster.com/dictionary/process

Public Private Partnerships (2017) Definition in Principles and Practices of Multi-Stakeholder Partnerships for Sustainable Development – Guidance and Oversight from UN Decisions, by M. Hemmati and F. Dodds, in *Governance for Sustainable Development: Implementing the 2030 Agenda,* Apex New World Frontiers.

Reinicke, W., Witte, J. M. and Benner, T. (2000) *Critical Choices: The United Nations, Networks, and the Future of Global Governance,* New York, The United Nations Vision Project on Global Public Policy (GPP) Networks.

Representative Democracy (2018) Representative Democracy Definition, US Legal.com. Available online at: https://definitions.uslegal.com/r/representative-democracy/

Snyder, T. (2017) *On Tyranny – Twenty Lessons from the Twentieth Century,* Tim Duggan Books.

Stakeholder (2002) Stakeholder Definition in *Multi-Stakeholder Processes for Governance and Sustainability,* by Hemmati, Dodds, Enayati and McHarry, London, Earthscan.

Statement (2018) Statement Definition, Merriam-Webster. Available online at: www.merriam-webster.com/dictionary/statement

Strandenaes, J. G. (2014) Participatory Democracy – HLPF Laying the Basis for Sustainable Development Governance in the 21st Century: Modalities for Major Groups, Non-Governmental Organisations and Other Stakeholders' Engagement with the High Level Political Forum on Sustainable Development, UNDESA. Available online at: https://sustainabledevelopment.un.org/content/documents/3682The%20High%20Level%20Political%20Forum,%20major%20groups%20and%20modalities.pdf

Transparency (2018) Transparency Definition, Good Governance, Belgrade Open School. Available online at: www.bos.rs/du-eng/transparency/931/2017/06/29/transparency-as-a-principle-of-good-governance.html

Understand (2018) Understand Definition, Merriam-Webster. Available online at www.merriam-webster.com/dictionary/understand

United Nations (UN) (2015) Transforming Our World: The 2030 Agenda for Sustainable Development, A/Res/70.1. Available online at: http://www.un.org/en/development/desa/population/migration/generalassembly/docs/globalcompact/A_RES_70_1_E.pdf

UNEP (2018) Discussion Papers, Major Groups and Stakeholders, UNEP Knowledge Repository.

Values (2018) Values Definition, Cambridge Dictionary. Available online at: https://dictionary.cambridge.org/us/dictionary/english/values

Vanguard (2018) Vanguard Definition, Cambridge Dictionary. Available online at: https://dictionary.cambridge.org/us/dictionary/english/vanguard

Voluntary Initiatives (2017) Voluntary Initiatives Definition in Principles and Practices of Multi-Stakeholder Partnerships for Sustainable Development – Guidance and Oversight from UN Decisions, by M. Hammati and F. Dodds, New York, Friends of Governance for Sustainable Development. Available online at: http://friendsofgovernance.org/index.php/section-2/

Wikipedia (2019) Accountability. Available online at: https://en.wikipedia.org/wiki/Accountability

2 A short history of democracy

Introduction

This book is being written in 2018, a time when we are celebrating the eightieth anniversary of the release of the first issue of *Superman*. Superman's catchphrase illustrated the values he believed in: "Truth, Justice and the American Way." These values are now clearly under attack. The "American Dream" is also, in essence, a global dream as it exemplifies hope for the opportunity to achieve prosperity and success. It is based on a belief that this can be achieved through hard work and that the opportunity exists for each individual to achieve upward mobility through that hard work. Brian Michael Bendis, who has taken up the writing of *Superman*, said the following at the Emerald City Comic Convention:

> Truth is under siege in our society today... Justice — we see it every day on video, justice is not being handed out to everybody. The American dream, that is also under siege. These things, that seemed cliché just five years ago, are now damn well worth fighting for (Bendis, 2018).

It isn't as if we had absolute justice in the past. One only needs to look at the twentieth century to see widespread instances of persecution based on race or religion. With the beginning of a new century, the fact that issues like marriage equality had become increasingly mainstream created a feeling among many that the world was moving towards a more just society.

The idea of trying to create a short history of democracy is probably a very bad one, but discussing stakeholder democracy it is important in understanding how democracy more broadly has developed over time. The contention here is that we are in a process of democracy of moving from what is called in the United States "Madisonian democracy" (representative) to "Jeffersonian democracy" (participatory).

This book examines the growth of stakeholder democracy and how it can be seen as a way to strengthen representative democracy. Representative democracy isn't perfect, but engaging with it so that it listens to voices in a more inclusive, transparent and accountable way can only be beneficial and can address some of the risks we are now observing.

A *short history of democracy* 23

So, to start with let's try and understand how democracy has evolved.

Democracy begins?

"Democracy is a government in which the supreme power is vested in the people and exercised by them directly or indirectly through a system of representation, usually involving periodically held free elections" (Merriam-Webster, 2018a).

The definition above is the traditional view of democracy. Over time our understanding and application of democracy has changed. Most obviously, it has moved from voters being only landowners, to all men above a particular age, to all people regardless of race or sex. These advancements were not without conflict, and history has shown that the renewal of democracy is something that each generation needs to engage in.

At this point in history, democracy is being challenged on many fronts with a growth of right-wing populism, the lack of acceptance of science as a basis for decision-making, the corporatization of our democracy and the creation of fake news or even alternate realities. It would be fair to say that none of this is new, but the extent to which these forces now exist is very concerning. Democracy is only really possible when a society has a shared social contract on issues such as truth, justice and free speech. If this is undermined, then justice will suffer as well as democracy.

These are but a few of the challenges that this and future generations are facing. Unlike previous times, we are also living through, and dealing with, a period when governments have enormous information on all of us across our activities on the Internet. How this could play out in countries which develop into repressive regimes has yet to be seen fully. But we are starting to see worrying signs emerging of how this data can be mined and used. Cambridge Analytica famously marketed themselves for the Brexit vote in the UK and the US Presidential Election in 2016 as offering: "big data and advanced psychographics to grow audiences, identify key influencers, and move people to action" (Murphy, 2018).

The development of a strong transparent stakeholder engagement with governments at ALL levels can strengthen democracy and can address some, though not all, of these problems.

Before examining stakeholder democracy, it's important to look more fundamentally at the roots of democracy.

Different types of democracy

Today we have, in most countries, a form of representative democracy, which is defined as: "based on or constituting a government in which the many are represented by persons chosen from among them usually by election" (Merriam-Webster, 2018b).

At of the end of 2016, the Pew Research Center announced that: "97 out of 167 countries (58%) with populations over 500,000 were democracies and only 21 (13%) were autocracies." Freedom House, which conducts research into democracy, political freedom and human rights, says in its 2018 report that

24 Felix Dodds

democracy is in crisis: "Seventy-one countries suffered net declines in political rights and civil liberties, with only 35 registering gains. This marked the 12th consecutive year of decline in global freedom" (Freedom House, 2018).

To be clear, representative democracy is not just about elections. It is also about building a society based on the rule of law, which has free speech and ensures human rights and civil liberties.

Greek democracy

One of the earliest forms of democracy was practiced in the Greek city of Athens in the fifth century BC. This was one of the forms closest to participatory democracy that we have seen.

Athenian democracy was an early attempt at a form of direct democracy that enabled citizens to vote directly on legislation. However, it was not open to everybody: you had to be a man over 20 and a citizen of the city. Out of a population that was thought to be between 250,000 and 300,000, only 30,000–50,000 were eligible to participate.

The Athenian Assembly was open to anyone among those eligible. It had four roles, which were to legislate, to make executive pronouncements such as going to war, to elect people to take particular roles, and to try any political crimes. Figure 2.1 tries to capture who was included and who was excluded in this democracy.

Greece was also a hotbed of political philosophers such as Aristotle and Socrates as well as Sophist philosophers such as Protagoras, who would teach the active Athenians the art of rhetoric. Aristotle defined three different types of systems that were in place in the different Greek cities (Table 2.1). The first were those that were ruled by the many (democracy/polity), the second by the few (oligarchy/aristocracy) and the third by a single person (tyranny, or today: autocracy/monarchy).

In his book *Politics*, Aristotle expressed his view on democracy:

> Now a fundamental principle of the democratic form of constitution is liberty—that is what is usually asserted, implying that only under this constitution do men participate in liberty, for they assert this as the aim of every democracy. But one factor of liberty is to govern and be governed in turn; for the popular principle of justice is to have equality according to number, not worth, and if this is the principle of justice

Table 2.1 Aristotelian ways to organize societies

	The One	The Few	The Many
For the Common interest	Monarchy	Aristocracy	Polity
For the interest of the Ruler(s)	Tyranny	Oligarchy	Democracy

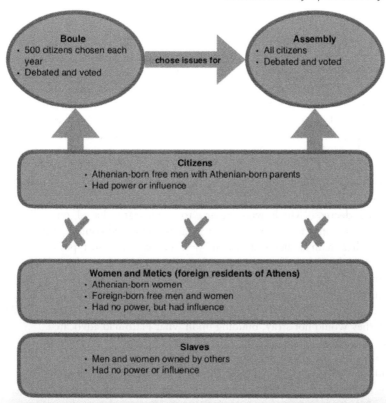

Figure 2.1 Diagram representing Athenian democracy in the fourth century BC (authors)

prevailing, the multitude must of necessity be sovereign and the decision of the majority must be final and must constitute justice, for they say that each of the citizens ought to have an equal share; so that it results that in democracies the poor are more powerful than the rich, because there are more of them and whatever is decided by the majority is sovereign. This then is one mark of liberty which all democrats set down as a principle of the constitution. And one is for a man to live as he likes; for they say that this is the function of liberty, inasmuch as to live not as one likes is the life of a man that is a slave. This is the second principle of democracy, and from it has come the claim not to be governed, preferably not by anybody, or failing that, to govern and be governed in turns; and this is the way in which the second principle contributes to equalitarian liberty (Aristotle, 1944).

In summary the Greeks tended to look at justice as "mind your own business" and with its democratic institutions they reflected participation based on position. This enlightened approach (at the time) of the Greeks would last only a couple of centuries.

26 Felix Dodds

The Roman Republic

One of the first nations to have a representative government was the Roman Republic. Grown again out of a city state – Rome – this period of experimentation took elements from different cities in Greece. The Republic came about when the aristocrats rebelled in 510 BC against the King and established a new constitution. What followed was a conflict between the ruling families and the rest of the population, otherwise known as the plebs (free Roman citizens). The plebs wanted to see a constitution that had clear secular laws. To address the problems, the Romans sent a commission to review what had happened and was happening in Greece.

The result of this was a kind of hybrid constitution: a Senate (300–500 Senators) initially made up of the aristocracy who served for life. The Senate produced decrees, which were advice to magistrates based on a law. This included directing the government on what it could and couldn't fund.

The other main bodies were assemblies. There were two types of assemblies, one of which was made up of Roman citizens who decided on laws, elected magistrates and tried judicial cases. The other was a council made up of a group of citizens brought together to address issues relating to a particular sector of society. This framework was based on people having a place they knew in society and from which they would not stray, building upon what Plato had advocated.

To engage the large population, a convention was used as an unofficial mechanism to debate future laws and bills. When they were ready to vote, they would then come together in small units called committees or councils.

For this book, the most interesting aspect is the Tribal Assembly or Assembly of the People. In this structure, citizens were organized into thirty-five tribes – four for the city of Rome and the others for the areas that had been conquered. Each tribe would meet separately to decide on an issue by majority, and then the President of each tribe would convey the result. When a majority was secured among the Tribal Assemblies, the issue would be settled. These tribes were defined on geographical constituencies and, to some extent, they reflect what has become the system of most parliamentary democracies if they had not been mostly based on powerful families and those who owed their livelihood to them – what could be called client communities. It is important to note these tribes were not equal in population, area or wealth and for that matter influence (see Figure 2.2).

For the Romans, justice was about being free from constraints and it saw politics as a way to regulate the all against all fight of self-interest by uniting people through a social contract, a key idea of western democracy.

Guilds

Another interesting development under the Romans were the first guilds. These were merchants who organized themselves around particular crafts. Guilds included ship owners, masons, carpenters, glass works and similar other traders. Guilds

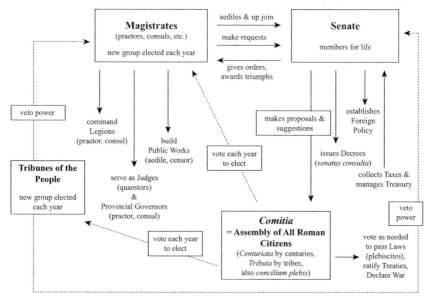

Figure 2.2 The Constitution of the Roman Republic (authors)

grew in the Middle Ages into two main areas of merchant guilds and craft guilds. These were perhaps an early example of stakeholders in society coming together around their profession and then negotiating with the governments.

A short English interlude for representative democracy

England and ultimately the United Kingdom more broadly has been a monarchy or a constitutional monarchy except for twice in its history. The first challenge to the "divine right of kings" was the rebellion of Simon de Montfort, 6th Earl of Leicester, against King Henry III, which established on January 20, 1265, a parliament that was not only made up of barons, senior churchmen, four knights from each county but also two burgesses from each of the major towns. This was the first time that this had happened. Even after Montfort had been defeated and killed and the King reinstated, the parliamentary approach continued. By the early fourteenth century, the meetings would be known as the Commons of England and ultimately the House of Commons.

During the first of the English Civil Wars (1642–1651), there was an interesting development called the Putney Debates. These took place beginning on October 28 and finished on November 9, 1647. The participants were the soldiers and officers of Oliver Cromwell's New Model Army which also included civilian representation. The debates held:

> discussions on the constitution and the future of England. Should they continue to negotiate a settlement with the defeated King Charles I?

28 *Felix Dodds*

- Should there even be a King or Lords?
- Should suffrage (a civil right to vote, known as the franchise) be limited to property-holders? Would democratic changes lead to anarchy? (Putney Debates, 2018)

The leaders in this opening up were the Levellers, who were made up of the radical elements within the military and the civilian population. They advocated for:

a constitution based upon manhood suffrage ("one man, one vote") and a fairer reorganisation of parliamentary constituencies. Further, they also wanted authority to be vested in the House of Commons rather than the King and Lords (with elections every two years) and "native rights" to be declared sacrosanct for all Englishmen:
freedom of conscience, freedom from impressment into the armed forces, everyone equal under the law and no penalties should be made for not going to church, or attending other acts of worship (Putney Debates, 2018).

Ultimately, they were defeated by Cromwell and the leaders put to death.

The second civil war in 1688, known as the Glorious Revolution, overthrew King James II of England and introduced a Bill of Rights (1689) which was then accepted by William III and Mary II who had replaced King James. The Bill of Rights stopped any return to an absolute monarchy in the country. Now parliament had the power to oversee the monarch who could no longer suspend laws, levy taxes, make royal appointments or maintain a standing army during peacetime without parliament's permission. Although presented as a revolution, it was more a coup with William being hired for his army to defeat the Catholics.

The Age of Enlightenment

The emergence of the scientific and industrial revolutions, starting mid-way through the seventeenth century, had a major impact on the thinking in the eighteenth century. Philosophers who contributed to this "Age of Enlightenment" addressed issues such as religion, reason, nature and humanity. Their impact was felt in society, particularly in the realms of art, philosophy and politics. The key thinkers of that time included Bacon, Descartes, Locke, Hume, Kant, Rousseau, Adam Smith and Voltaire. They developed theories of government that, at their core, asserted the necessity for a social contract between people in society and institutions (Rousseau) and the guarantee of individual liberty (Thomas Hobbes). Rousseau, in his opening to his work *The Social Contract*, expressed his belief that man (people) was basically good and it was society and institutions that corrupted him/her; he said: "everywhere man is free and everywhere in chains. One man thinks himself the master of others, but remains more of a slave than they are" (Rousseau, 1762).

A short history of democracy 29

In other words, we are bound by our obligations to one another. According to Rousseau, the modern state repressed the physical freedom that we have when we are born and, too often in history, has done nothing to secure our civil liberties.

These ideas would ultimately differentiate the state from civil society – the balance of freedom, liberty and equality. Different views on the balance between these three ideals ultimately began to be reflected in political parties.

There was change in the air, and one of critical questions was whether it would be revolutionary change or transformational change. In his book *On Liberty*, John Stuart Mill discussed the need for institutions to support the rights of individuals: "There is confessedly a strong tendency in the modern world towards a democratic constitution of society, accompanied or not by popular political institutions" (Mill, 1859).

He went on to say:

> Representative government, in particular, is a form which best encourages individuality. It leads people to take a more active and intelligent participation in society. It provides moral training and encourages the development of natural human sympathies. The result is the habit of looking at social questions from an impersonal perspective rather than that of self-interest (Mill, 1859).

In 1871 there was a short-lived attempt at participatory democracy for two months with the Paris Commune (March 18 to May 28). In the aftermath of the French defeat by Prussia, the Paris National Guard rebelled and held free elections for the citizens of Paris electing a Commune council of ninety-two members. There was instant recourse and recall of representatives from the different communes to the Council should they not follow that commune's wishes. They worked to implement a number of reforms, including the conversion of some workplaces into cooperatives.

Only a few of their decrees were actually implemented. These included:

- separation of church and state.
- remission of rents owed for the entire period of the siege (during which payment had been suspended).
- abolition of night work in bakeries.
- granting of pensions to the unmarried companions and children of national guardsmen killed in active service.
- free return by pawnshops, of all workmen's tools and household items, valued up to 20 francs, pledged during the siege.
- postponement of commercial debt obligations, and the abolition of interest on the debts.
- right of employees to take over and run an enterprise if it were deserted by its owner; the Commune, nonetheless, recognized the previous owner's right to compensation.
- prohibition of fines imposed by employers on their workmen (Wikipedia, 2018a).

30   *Felix Dodds*

The national government put down the Paris Commune by force on June 10.

In the United States, advocates such as Thomas Paine, James Madison and Thomas Jefferson contributed to creating a new social contract with the constitution of a brand new country: the United States.

Later the French Revolution would change France forever. Thomas Jefferson proclaimed that France had "been awakened by our [American] Revolution" (Dunn, 1999).

Madison and Jeffersonian democracy and the French

> Democracies have ever been spectacles of turbulence and contention; have ever been found incompatible with personal security, or the rights of property; and have in general been as short in their loves as they have been violent in their deaths (Madison, 1787).

At the beginning of the creation of the United States, there were unsurprisingly differing views on how the new country should be governed. Madison promoted a more restrictive form of indirect democracy for the President, writing in the Federalist Papers that the United States constitution should both promote state-based and population-based government through the use of an Electoral College model for choosing the President. Both Madison and Alexander Hamilton argued for a strong federal government.

The United States is nearly unique in that the electorate does not elect the President, but rather by an Electoral College which would be selected based on population in each State. The College ultimately selects the President. There have been four elections where the President won the Electoral College but did not win the popular vote (1876, 1888, 2000 and 2016).

Jefferson argued for more decentralized governments with power at the state or local level – more in the hands of the people. He was the principal author of the Declaration of Independence, its preamble proclaiming the phrase that "all men are created equal." It would not be until 1920 when the Nineteenth Amendment to the US Constitution was ratified, stating, "The right of citizens of the United States to vote shall not be denied or abridged by the United States or by any State on account of sex" (United States, 1920).

The creation of separation of powers between the executive, legislative and judicial branches was critical to balancing the interests of the different branches at any one time. They each have defined roles and powers that are unique. The new United States also learned from the European experience the importance of the separation of church and state, as many of the colonists had themselves been fleeing from religious persecution in Europe.

France was going through its own revolution against its monarchy. Louis XVI had become King in 1774 and found the state nearing bankruptcy. This was in no small part because of the Seven Years War and later the role that France played in the American Revolutionary War. By late 1788, it was clear that there needed to be a new tax, this time on the nobility and clergy; most of the taxes in the past had been levied on the lower classes. Unable to get an Assembly of Notables to agree, the King announced the calling of the Estates-General for May 1789; the last time the body had been summoned was 1614.

The Estates-General had three constituencies: the clergy (303 members), the nobility (291 members) and the rest of France (610 members). By June 17, they had declared themselves a National Assembly. By August 11, they had abolished privileges and feudalism in the August Decrees which swept away personal serfdom, seigneurial rights (land tenure – payment of money to lords by peasants for living on the land) and the 10 percent tax for the Church.

The French Declaration of the Rights of Man and of the Citizen (August 26, 1789), which had been written by General Lafayette with the help of Thomas Jefferson and Honore Mirabeau, was a statement of principles rather than a constitution. The new constitution ratified in 1791 created only one assembly – it did not include a Senate. Also, the King would only have a "suspensive veto." In other words, he could only stall and not block a decision. In August 1792, the first elections were held under universal suffrage for the National Convention. The first government of the French Revolution on September 21 abolished the monarchy.

A new Constitution was agreed upon in August 1793, which was put to a popular vote (1,801,918 for and some 17,610 against) and marked the first time a constitution had been ratified by popular vote.

An odd one – Switzerland

Since the ratification of its 1848 constitution, Switzerland has allowed for referenda. Its first use of referendum occurred in the canton of Graubünden in the sixteenth century – this was an early form of direct democracy. Any changes to the constitution require not only winning a majority in the country, but also a majority of the cantons – there are 26 cantons in total. Any citizen may challenge a law if they can gather 50,000 signatures or propose an amendment to the constitution if they can gather 100,000 signatures. The Federal Council of Seven that governs the country is elected individually by both of the Swiss chambers of the Federal Assembly. These elections, in theory, are open to any Swiss citizen who wishes to become a candidate. The Council is made up of representatives of many political parties. With the presidency of the country rotating every year, it represents one of the few successes from the revolutions that swept across Europe in 1848 – this wave of revolutions also included Denmark, France, Germany, Hungary, Ireland, Italy, Poland, Romania and Sweden. Though it would be fair to say some of these countries were not countries as we understand them now. The German revolution (1848–1849), which established democratic rights, was around a German Confederation which ultimately became a nation-state in 1871.

The twentieth century

Much of the twentieth century became a conflict between democracy and different types of dictatorships, whether they were from the right (fascism) or the

32   Felix Dodds

left (communism). But it was also a time of expanding the franchise to vote to women, young adults and to all people regardless of the color of their skin.

In some of the writings of Marx and Engels, there was the support for a form of direct democracy through worker councils and communes. This was attempted at the beginning of the Soviet Union, perhaps for the first year, but didn't last for long. Marx argued: "The first step on the revolution by the working class is to raise the proletariat to the position of the working class, to win the battle of democracy" (Marx and Engels, 1848).

The commune, according to Neil Harding in his excellent book *Democracy: The Unfinished Journey*, was to be:

> at once a legislative, executive, judicial, and defensive body. It was to make reality of democracy by involving all the citizens in all aspects of the governmental process and it was to retain control over all its functionaries by electing them all, paying them workers' wages, and keeping them subject to immediate recall by their constituents (Harding, 1992).

Whether the turn to an authoritarian approach was due to the lack of full implementation of the Marxist theory is up for debate. Marx argued that you first had to develop an industrial society (the Soviet Union was basically still an agrarian society). Furthermore, the reality of civil war, attacks from hostile countries, and the enormous administrative needs to reorganize a very large country may have ultimately given rise to an authoritarian leadership and an anti-democratic approach.

This had a big impact on intellectual arguments, particularly because many on the left did not initially believe what was reportedly happening within the Soviet Union. It made it very difficult in the United States, in particular, as the Soviet Union moved from being an ally in the Second World War to being its primary adversary from the beginning of the 1950s. This was best reflected through the work of the House Committee on Un-American Activities (1938–1975). This work was supplemented in the Senate by Joseph McCarthy, chairman of the Government Operations Committee and its Permanent Subcommittee on Investigations of the United States.

By the late 1950s, some of the European countries had socialist or social democratic governments and there were growing social movements around civil rights and reducing tensions between the West and the Soviet Union. Even the Catholic Church seemed to be undergoing reform, particularly with Pope John XXIII and his reforms at the Second Vatican Council. This laid the foundation for a more reflective time as economies emerged out of the post-war restrictions – food rationing in the UK ended in 1954.

The Soviet Union and its satellite states never recovered a democratic approach. There were attempts, but these were put down by military force in Hungary (1956) and in Czechoslovakia during the Prague Spring (1968). It wasn't until Mikhail Gorbachev became General Secretary of the Communist Party of the Soviet Union that reforms started to be introduced. Gorbachev introduced the policies of perestroika (restructuring) in 1986 and glasnost (openness) in 1988, changing the Soviet Union forever and resulting in the first

A short history of democracy 33

democratic elections in over seventy years in March 1989. Gorbachev acknowledged that these reforms owed much of the policies of Alexander Dubcek's Prague Spring in 1968.

"Many legitimate forms of ownership, mainly cooperative and communal, had not been used to any effective extent mainly because of the imposition of Stalinist restrictions" (Dubcek, 1968).

Students for a democratic society

In January 1961, President Kennedy echoed the new feeling of hope in his inaugural speech:

> We stand today on the edge of a new frontier – the frontier of the 1960s – a frontier of unknown opportunities and perils – a frontier of unfulfilled hopes and threats.
>
> … the New Frontier of which I speak is not a set of promises – it is a set of challenges. It sums up not what I intend to offer the American people, but what I intend to ask of them. It appeals to their pride, not to their pocketbook – it holds out the promise of more sacrifice instead of more security.
>
> … the New Frontier is here, whether we seek it or not. Beyond that frontier are the uncharted areas of science and space, unsolved problems of peace and war, unconquered pockets of ignorance and prejudice, unanswered questions of poverty and surplus. It would be easier to shrink back from that frontier, to look to the safe mediocrity of the past, to be lulled by good intentions and high rhetoric – and those who prefer that course should not cast their votes for me, regardless of party.
>
> But I believe the times demand new invention, innovation, imagination, decision. I am asking each of you to be pioneers on that New Frontier (Kennedy, 1961).

The Students for a Democratic Society (SDS) was formed in the United States in 1960 and served as the youth wing of the League for Industrial Democracy, a socialist education organization, taking over that role from the Student League for Industrial Democracy. SDS was to become a place for intellectual discourse on the left in what became known as the New Left.

SDS met in Port Huron in June 1962 and produced a political manifesto: "The Port Huron Statement." In the introduction, it set out its analysis:

> The decline of utopia and hope is in fact one of the defining features of social life today. The reasons are various: the dreams of the older left were perverted by Stalinism and never recreated … the horrors of the twentieth century, symbolized in the gas-ovens and concentration camps and atom bombs, have blasted hopefulness. To be idealistic is to be considered apocalyptic, deluded (SDS, 1962).

34   *Felix Dodds*

The draft of the Statement, which became known as the "Agenda for a Generation," was first written by one person, Tom Hayden, and was amended over five days by fifty-eight students who had attended as members of SDS branches from across the country. The outcome document was called a "statement" as opposed to a "manifesto" because the authors saw it as a living document addressing the key issues of the day such as disarmament, civil rights, reform of the Democratic Party and university reform. It reflected the tension between communitarianism and individualism, but more than anything it issued a non-ideological call for "participatory democracy."

There have been different views on what was meant by the term. Those that led the discussion in 1962 seem to see it in retrospect as supporting and strengthening representative democracy, while others who came afterwards interpreted it more as a replacement for representative democracy. The Port Huron Statement said: "We seek the establishment of a democracy of individual participation."

It went on to say:

> In a participatory democracy, the political life would be based in several root principles:
>
> - That decision-making of basic social consequence be carried on by public groupings;
> - That politics be seen positively, as the art of collectively creating an acceptable pattern of social relations;
> - That politics has the function of bringing people out of isolation and into community, thus being a necessary, though not sufficient, means of finding meaning in personal life;
> - That the political order should serve to clarify problems in a way instrumental to their solution; it should provide outlets for the expression of personal grievance and aspiration; opposing views should be organized so as to illuminate choices and facilitate the attainment of goals; channels should be commonly available to relate men to knowledge and to power so that private problems—from bad recreation facilities to personal alienation—are formulated as general issues (SDS, 1962).

Hayden took a position that it was a supplement to representative democracy. Richard Flacks, the founder of SDS, perhaps put it best:

> Participatory democracy did not mean abandoning organizational structures of the usual sort, like elected officials and parliamentary procedures. We were thinking of participatory democracy at that time as a concept of social change, not as a set of principles for guiding the internal organizational life of SDS (Flacks, 1987).

Participatory democracy by the mid-1960s had evolved into more a viewpoint that decisions had to be taken by consensus, picking up the Quaker-

A short history of democracy 35

based model (see Box 2.1). It is often thought that Quakers "invented" consensus decision-making as they have been using it for more than 300 years. But a version of consensus decision-making had been used since 1142 by the Haudenosaunee Confederacy Grand Council – known by most of us as the Iroquois nation. Each of the five Iroquois nations had their own council and then representatives from each nation that would govern the Confederacy as a whole. At the Confederacy level, the representatives would meet at the Grand Council meetings to decide by consensus how to address the issue.

Box 2.1 The Quaker model has been adapted by Earlham College for application to secular settings

- Multiple concerns and information are shared until the sense of the group is clear.
- Discussion involves active listening and sharing information.
- Norms limit number of times one asks to speak to ensure that each speaker is fully heard.
- Ideas and solutions belong to the group; no names are recorded.
- Ideally, differences are resolved by discussion. The facilitator ("clerk" or "convenor" in the Quaker model) identifies areas of agreement and names disagreements to push discussion deeper.
- The facilitator articulates the sense of the discussion, asks if there are other concerns, and proposes a "minute" of the decision.
- The group as a whole is responsible for the decision and the decision belongs to the group.
- The facilitator can discern if one who is not uniting with the decision is acting without concern for the group or in selfish interest.
- Ideally, all dissenters' perspectives are synthesized into the final outcome for a whole that is greater than the sum of its parts.
- Should some dissenter's perspective not harmonize with the others, that dissenter may "stand aside" to allow the group to proceed, or may opt to "block". "Standing aside" implies a certain form of silent consent. Some groups allow "blocking" by even a single individual to halt or postpone the entire process (Wikipedia, 2018b).

Other faiths such as the Bahá'í have a model of "consultation." Individual development involves investigating the "truth" for oneself.

> Continual reflection, based on experience in applying this truth, is critical to the process of individual (spiritual) development. For collective investigation of the truth and group decision-making, consultation, which draws on the strength of the group and fosters unity of purpose and action, is indispensable. Consultation plays a major role in Bahá'í communities because it is seen as the only way to get all relevant expertise to the table,

36 Felix Dodds

to come to consensus about future action and to create the commitment to implement solutions. The basic assumption is that no member of a community has some kind of exclusive access to the "truth", and that everybody's subjective views and knowledge have to be integrated in order to achieve the best results. Bahá'í communities and elected assemblies conduct consultations on the basis of detailed rules – for example the rule of honesty; openness and not holding back any views; group ownership of any ideas; striving for consensus if possible and voting if there is no consensus (Hemmati et al., 2001).

There were lots of experiments with participatory democracy, often using the Quaker Decision-Making model, in different urban centers with varying levels of success. Hayden practiced closer to his vision when he stood for the California State Senate, reaching out to local environmentalists, small and medium-sized businesses, labor, tenant associations, peace activists and feminists.

Hayden's candidacy is representative of the early way of developing a political agenda that resonates within a community or among whom we today refer to as stakeholders. There are clear paths from what SDS articulated in 1962 and our present-day conception of stakeholder democracy. Getting from there to here has itself been a journey that wasn't easy.

Types of democratic governments

"You can't start with a democracy. You have to work up through stuff like tyranny and monarchy first. That way people are so relieved when they get to democracy that they hang on to it" (Pratchett, 2015).

I hope that Terry Pratchett's quote isn't true, but at times in the last century it has seemed like it has exhibited some truth. In the twenty-first century, our democratic governments have evolved in different ways. We would be amiss if we didn't briefly mention them. They fall into basically eight different versions of how "the people" should be represented. These are:

1   Presidential republics: This includes countries such as the United States and much of South Africa and African states such as Nigeria and Kenya as well as Asian states such as Indonesia and the Philippines. These countries operate with an executive presidency separate from the legislature.
2   Semi-presidential republics: These include countries such as Egypt, Russia, France and some of their former colonies such as Algeria, Democratic Republic of the Congo, Mali, Mozambique, Niger and Tunisia. Here countries have both an executive presidency and a separate head of government that leads the legislature. They are appointed by the president.
3   Parliamentary republics: These include countries like Czech Republic, Fiji, Greece, Hungary, Italy and Singapore. These countries have an executive presidency dependent on the legislature.
4   Parliamentary republics with a ceremonial/non-executive president: This includes countries such as Germany and Ireland. In these countries a

A *short history of democracy* 37

separate head of government leads the executive. There are some which are mixed such as South Africa and Botswana.

5 Constitutional monarchies: These include Belgium, Cambodia, Denmark, Netherlands, Norway, Spain, Sweden and the UK and many of their former colonies – such as Barbados, Canada, Jamaica, Malaysia and New Zealand. These countries have a ceremonial/non-executive monarch, while a separate head of government leads the executive branch of the government.

6 Constitutional monarchies: Countries with this model have a ceremonial monarch, but the monarchy still holds a significant executive and/or legislative power. This includes countries such as Jordan, Monaco, Morocco and Thailand.

7 Absolute monarchies: There are still seven countries with this system; they are Brunei, Eswatini, Oman, Qatar, Saudi Arabia, United Arab Emirates and the Vatican City. In each of these countries, the monarch leads the executive.

8 One-party states: These include China, Cuba, North Korea, Laos and Vietnam. In these countries, the dominant role of a political party is codified in the constitution.

These is no one definition of how democracy should be practiced. It often is based on the history and culture of a country and, in many developing countries, the impact of colonialism. This book isn't designed to go into depth on the examples above, but to say that in all of them you will have seen an increased role for stakeholders over the last twenty years.

Deliberative democracy, citizens panels and advocates for a global parliament

We have also seen a number of new terms and experiments as far as democracy is concerned, which are worth a mention here. These include (but are not limited to):

- Advocacy democracy: This is where every elected official would have a citizens' advisory council.
- Anticipatory democracy: This is built on the use of "experts'" predictions on what will happen to inform voters in advance.
- Cellular democracy: Not what you think – not based on cell phones! This model advocates breaking down larger areas into smaller neighborhood councils of 500 people – very Jeffersonian.
- Deliberative democracy: Too often legislators pass bills without debate – this is returning to a more classical Athenian approach where there is real "deliberation" on an issue before agreement.
- Guided democracy: This is close to Plato's view that an ideal ruler would guide the state. Decisions would be left to only the well informed.
- Interactive democracy: This embraces new Internet options with "e-democracy" including "e-petitions" for government proposals. It is a top-

38   *Felix Dodds*

down approach. A bottom-up approach would be "i-democracy" where proposals would bubble up from the grassroots. Interactive democracy still keeps legislators as part of the system, but they would now act more as recipients from the people.

- Liquid democracy: This is where educated citizens of a particular issue might serve when that issue is being discussed.
- Network democracy: It is sometimes called "digital democracy" – again a new concept around the use of the Internet where networks, which could be stakeholders that can mobilize, put pressure on legislators.
- Radical democracy: This is perhaps the closest to the civil society approach. It is where dissident groups and mass movements emerge to challenge a system.

With the invention of the Internet, there have been many experiments in how this technology might help engage people in a way that informs decision-making. With the 2016 US Presidential Election and Brexit as the most reported examples, there have already been problems with this. In the coming chapters, we will return to this issue. On the positive side, it is clear that there now is a much easier way for representatives to hear from the people they are representing.

The use of citizens panels as a mechanism in a geographical area is an additional way to help local or sub-national government to assess public preferences and opinions. The participants here are selected similar to how jurors are currently selected, whereby participants are randomly chosen through an electoral roll or postcode; this enables some balance, but often needs to be supplemented with other means to ensure that the socially excluded are reached.

All of these different types of democracy are in many ways attempts to enrich the debate and conversation around how to better govern ourselves.

As this is a book primarily focused at the global level, it would be erroneous not to mention advocates for a global or world parliament. The advocates for this argue that to achieve a more sustainable world that we need to elect a world (UN) parliament to be able to address global issues that national states cannot do due to their interests.

> A world parliament in the context of global challenges such as climate change and planetary boundaries, the management of public goods, the stability of the financial system, combating tax evasion, terrorism and organized crime, disarmament, and protecting human rights. The construction of global democracy also plays a decisive role in combating hunger, poverty and inequality and in global water policy. Rapid developments in the fields of bio- and nanotechnology, robotics and artificial intelligence are giving rise to fundamental questions that humanity is not institutionally prepared for (Leinen and Bummel, 2018).

The Campaign for a United Nations Parliamentary Assembly (CUNPA) is a global network of over 300 non-governmental organizations and 1,500 current or former parliamentarians from over 150 countries. Its secretariat is provided by Democracy Without Boarders and in 2016 secured the support from the Pan-African Parliament. The Commission on Global Security, Justice and Governance, chaired by former US Secretary of State Madeleine Albright and former Nigerian Foreign Minister Ibrahim Gambari, has also called for the creation of a United Nations Parliamentary Network.

To achieve this there are basically three options:

1 Amend the Charter of the UN.
2 Create it as a subsidiary body of the UN General Assembly.
3 Create it as stand-alone treaty body.

With the present challenge to multi-lateralism, this campaign will find it very difficult to find traction. There are different viewpoints on how it would be constructed, but if it was by population then clearly the largest amount of members would be from Asia – population figures in 2019 are as follows: Asia (4,584,807,000), Africa (1,320,038,000), Europe (743,102,600), Latin America and the Caribbean (658,305,557), Northern America (366,486,000) and Oceania (41,826,000). If the principle of one person, one vote was the basis and those that are advocating for the UN as a "We the People" from the UN Charter should be doing this, then the parliament members would have a majority from Asia. The other idea is through appointment by national parliaments which then retains the link to the country and probably to a party in power having the most appointed seats. In China, that would mean all seats would go to the Communist Party.

The conversation about democracy is an ongoing one and perhaps well said by another Terry Pratchett quote: "You can't go around building a better world for people. Only people can build a better world. Otherwise it's just a cage" (Pratchett, 1988).

References

Aristotle (1944) *Aristotle in 23 Volumes*, Vol. 21. Translated by H. Rackham. Cambridge, MA: Harvard University Press. Available online at: https://en.wikipedia.org/wiki/History_of_democracy#cite_note-AristotlePol1317b-59

Bendis, M. B. (2018) Reported from a panel discussion at the Emerald City Comic Con, CBR. Available online at: https://www.cbr.com/bendis-superman-truth-justice-american-way/

Dubcek, A. (1968) Speech. Available online at: https://www.brainyquote.com/quotes/alexander_dubcek_303642

Dunn, S. (1999) *Sister Revolutions*. New York: Faber and Faber.

Flacks, R. (1987) Interviewed by James Miller for the book *Democracy is in the Streets*. New York: Simon and Schuster Inc.

Freedom House (2018) Freedom in the World. Washington: Freedom House. Available online at: https://freedomhouse.org/report/freedom-world/freedom-world-2018

Harding, N. (1992) *Democracy: The Unfinished Journey, 508 BC to AD 1993*. Edited by John Dunn. Oxford: Oxford University Press.

40 *Felix Dodds*

Hemmati, M., Dodds, F., Enayati, J. and McHarry, J. (2001) *Multi-Stakeholder Processes for Governance and Sustainability: Beyond Deadlock and Conflict*. London: Earthscan.

Kennedy, J. (1961) Inaugural Speech for President of the United States, Washington DC. JFK Library. Available online at: https://www.jfklibrary.org/About-Us/News-and-Press/Press-Releases/50-Years-Ago–Senator-John-F-Kennedy-of-Massachusetts-Wins-Presidential-Nomination-at-Democratic-Nat.aspx

Leinen, J. and Bummel, A. (2018) *A World Parliament: Governance and Democracy in the 21st Century*. Berlin: Democracy Without Borders.

Madison, J. (1787, November 22) Federalist No. 10, "The Utility of the Union as a Safeguard Against Domestic Faction and Insurrection (continued)," *Daily Advertiser*. Available online at: https://thefederalistpapers.org/federalist-papers/federalist-10-democracies-have-ever-been-spectacles-of-turbulence-and-contention

Marx, K. and Engels (1848) *Selected Works*. Available online at: https://www.marxists.org/archive/marx/works/1848/communist-manifesto/

Merriam-Webster (2018a) Definition of Democracy. Available online at: https://www.merriam-webster.com/dictionary/democracy

Merriam-Webster (2018b) Definition of Representative. Available online at: https://www.merriam-webster.com/dictionary/representative

Mill, J. S. (1859) Chapter IV, Of the Limits to the Authority of Society over the Individual. In *On Liberty*. The Harvard Classics 1909–1914. Available online at: http://www.bartleby.com/25/2/4.html

Murphy, M. (2018) 'Mind-Reading' Software Cambridge Analytica Boss Denies Brexit Influence, *The Telegraph*. Available online at: https://www.telegraph.co.uk/technology/2018/02/27/mind-reading-software-cambridge-analytica-boss-denies-brexit/

Pratchett, T. (1988) *Wyrd Sisters*. London: Gollancz.

Pratchett, T. (2015) *A Blink of the Screen*. London: Penguin Random House.

Putney Debates (2018) The Putney Debates of 1647 - The Conception of British Democracy. Available online at: http://www.putneydebates.com/

Rousseau, J. (1762) *The Social Contract*. CreateSpace Independent Publishing Platform.

Students for a Democratic Society (SDS) (1962) Port Huron Statement. Available online at: www2.iath.virginia.edu/sixties/HTML_docs/Resources/Primary/Manifestos/SDS_Port_Huron.html

United States (1920) Nineteenth Amendment to the Constitution. Washington DC US Government. Available online at: https://constitutioncenter.org/interactive-constitution/amendments/amendment-xix

Wikipedia (2018a) Paris Commune. Available online at: https://en.wikipedia.org/wiki/Paris_Commune

Wikipedia (2018b) Consensus Decision-Making. Available online at: https://en.wikipedia.org/wiki/Consensus_decision-making

3 The emergence of stakeholder democracy

Introduction

The previous chapter, the history of democracy, attempted to set the scene. This chapter focuses principally on the global level and on how stakeholder engagement has developed there in particular in the area of sustainable development.

Too often, books can look at ideas outside of the political reality that they developed in or find themselves in. This book attempts to address both today's reality and the landscape of global politics at the time when stakeholder democracy started to develop. One major influence on both the historical and contemporary landscapes has been the growth and development of globalization.

Emerging globalization

Lexicologists at the Merriam-Webster dictionary define "globalization" as "the act or process of globalizing: the state of being globalized; especially: the development of an increasingly integrated global economy marked especially by free trade, free flow of capital, and the tapping of cheaper foreign labor markets" (Merriam-Webster, 2018).

Globalization has been an emerging issue, some scholars suggest, since the fifteenth-century Age of Exploration, a time when Europeans started exploring and trading beyond their continent. This led to the emergence of global trade between Old World European countries, and countries in Asia and Africa, as well as Australia and the newly discovered Americas.

To facilitate trading, European colonial powers created the Columbian Exchange (named after Christopher Columbus by American historian Alfred Crosby, several centuries after the global diffusion of plants, seeds and crops from the New World back into the Old World). Trade in commodities such as plants, animals and food (including potatoes, maize and tomatoes), not to mention enslaved human populations, accelerated with the industrial revolution of the nineteenth century, which was the next large-scale globalization occurring as the world's economies and cultures became much more connected.

42 *Felix Dodds*

The emergence of global rules

The twentieth century saw the development of new rules, first through the League of Nations and then, with the end of the Second World War, through the United Nations, the Bretton Woods Agreement of 1944, and the Global Agreement on Trade and Tariffs (GATT) of 1947.

The trading system was originally envisioned by its "three architects," US Treasury Secretary Henry Morganthau, his chief economic advisor Harry Dexter White, and British economist John Maynard Keynes as a postwar economic and trading system which would be built on consensus.

In addressing the Bretton Woods Conference (so named because it took place in Bretton Woods, New Hampshire) in July 1944, Henry Morganthau suggested that "bewilderment and bitterness" as a result of the Great Depression became "the breeders of fascism, and finally, of war." The Bretton Woods monetary system and the multi-lateral institutions finding their footing at about the same time were set up to try and ensure that there would never be another world war. The thinking was that if the economies were interlinked so much, then linkage would be a deterrent and would help to maintain international peace and security. The institutions would, in Morganthau's words, facilitate "[the] creation of a dynamic world community in which the peoples of every nation will be able to realise their potentialities in peace" (Morganthau, 1944).

The present version of globalization coincided with the elections of Mrs. Margaret Thatcher as Prime Minister of the United Kingdom (1979) and Ronald Reagan as President of the United States (1980). Both leaders embraced neo-liberal policies in the economies of their respective countries, and this resurgence of nineteenth-century ideas associated with laissez-faire economic liberalism was a major factor in expanding globalization. Thatcher and Reagan turned their backs on the economics developed by British economist and Liberal John Maynard Keynes in the 1930s. Where Keynes had advocated increased government spending and laid the foundation for the welfare state, the new economic order of neo-liberalism championed the rollback of trade barriers and regulations.

A number of factors contributed to the rise of this ideology, including substantially lower costs for travel, and the migration of people from developing countries to developed countries in search of work. Norman Tebbit's speech to the 1981 Conservative Conference immortalized this development in the United Kingdom. Tebbit said: "I grew up in the '30s with an unemployed father. He didn't riot; he got on his bike and looked for work and he kept looking 'til he found it'" (Tebbit, 1981).

In tandem with neo-liberal economic policies, cultural globalization, helped ultimately by the Internet, saw dominant cultures (in particular that of the United States) expand the reach of popular brands like McDonalds, Kentucky Fried Chicken and Starbucks. This contributed to an increasing homogenization of culture, as indicated by the dominance of western TV programmes, music and films across world markets.

Environment and globalization

Several generations after the end of the Second World War, threats to the environment started to be recognized as a by-product of globalization through transboundary pollution (meaning pollution between adjoining countries or across a contiguous cluster of countries).

To help address this, the first United Nations Conference on the Human Environment was held in Stockholm in June 1972. One of its outcomes was the establishment of the United Nations Environment Programme (UNEP) to begin addressing transboundary environmental issues. UNEP is perhaps most significantly remembered for its approach to the destruction of the ozone layer by the release of chlorofluorocarbons (CFCs) formerly found in aerosol sprays.

Joe Farman of the British Antarctic Survey (d. 2013) was the researcher who found a hole (or, more accurately, a softening) in the ozone layer of Earth's atmosphere in 1983 and again in 1984. He was initially disbelieved by NASA scientists. In May 1985, he published his findings in *Nature*. They showed a startling 40 percent drop in the density of the ozone layer relative to previous measurements.

This explosive finding was catalyst enough to get UNEP to facilitate the negotiation of the Vienna Convention for the Protection of the Ozone Layer in 1985 and the subsequent Montreal Protocol of 1987. This short interval between when the ozone problem was recognized and when policy was codified to address that problem remains the best example of the international community addressing a global environmental threat quickly. The UN's World Metrological Organization (WMO) now estimates that the ozone layer "will recover to 1980 levels near the middle of the 21st century."

This concerted push to eradicate the use of CFCs for the sake of protecting Earth's ozone layer is a good example of a global public good. Global public goods are "goods with benefits that extend to all countries, people, and generations" (Kaul and Menoza, 2003).

By the time of the UN Conference on Environment and Development (UNCED), more commonly known as the "Earth Summit," in 1992, UNEP had facilitated many Multilateral Environmental Agreements (MEAs) on issues such as hazardous waste, wildlife trade in endangered species and the protection of regional seas and the Antarctic.

The Earth Summit ultimately created a large number of MEAs, all of which were developed with major stakeholder engagement. These agreements were as follows:

- The United Nations Framework Convention on Climate Change (UNFCCC) [1992].
- The United Nations Convention on Biological Diversity (CBD) [1992].
- The United Nations Convention to Combat Desertification (UNCCD) [1994].

44   *Felix Dodds*

- Conservation and Management of Straddling Fish Stocks and Highly Migratory Fish Stocks [1995].
- Rotterdam Convention on the Prior Informed Consent Procedure for Certain Hazardous Chemicals and Pesticides in International Trade [1998].
- Aarhus Convention on Access to Information, Public Participation in Decision-making, and Access to Justice in Environmental Matters [1998].
- Stockholm Convention on Persistent Organic Pollutants [2001].

As the world becomes more interdependent, the need for global rules has become increasingly clear. These environmental agreements dealt with the transboundary consequences of disregarding the environment in the production and consumption of goods.

The General Agreement on Trade and Tariffs (GATT), signed by twenty-three countries in 1947, was for several generations the primary avenue that countries used to reduce or eliminate trade barriers. But it became clearer in the 1980s that the GATT was not robust enough to address globalization, and so a new permanent body, the World Trade Organization (WTO), was established in 1995. As countries moved to global intergovernmental agreements, their national stakeholders also had to globalize.

NGO/stakeholder engagement up to UN Earth Summit (1992)

"Governance is the sum of the many ways individuals and institutions, public and private, manage their common affairs" (Commission on Global Governance, 1995).

In writing this book, it is difficult to imagine there was ever a time when stakeholders were not a formal part of the global process in the sustainable development and environment arena. But until 1992, they were all bunched together under the term Non-Governmental Organizations (NGOs).

To provide a bit of historical perspective, there were only four "Non-Governmental Organizations" that were accredited to the United Nations when it was created in 1946. This is hardly surprising, as the United Nations was set up recognizing the supremacy of the nation-state. Nevertheless, Article 71 of the Charter of the United Nations states that its Economic and Social Council "may make suitable arrangements for consultation with non-governmental organizations which are concerned with matters within its competence" (UN, 1946).

By the mid-1960s, those NGOs in consultative status with the UN wanted more access. Led by the International Union for Conservation of Nature (IUCN), NGOs campaigned for a new status within the United Nations and, on May 23, 1968, the Economic and Social Council agreed on Resolution 1296, which established consultative relations with non-governmental organizations it distinguished between those that were global, and covered a large number of countries (category I), and those that had special competence in particular areas or support the aims of the UN (category II) and a final category of roster was

The emergence of stakeholder democracy   45

given to organizations that can make occasional and useful contributions to the work of the Council or its subsidiary bodies (UN, 1968).

IUCN is an unusual organization in that it brings government agencies, international organizations and non-governmental organizations together in a kind of early multi-stakeholder organization.

By 1968, the number of accredited non-governmental organizations was 377. It's difficult to appreciate now the impact that the landing on the moon by Apollo 11 on July 20, 1969, would have on changing the consciousness of many people worldwide.

Neil Armstrong, the Commander of Apollo 11, and first human to walk on the Moon, expressed it well:

> It suddenly struck me that that tiny pea, pretty and blue, was the Earth. I put up my thumb and shut one eye, and my thumb blotted out the planet Earth. I didn't feel like a giant. I felt very, very small (Armstrong, 1969).

One result of the shift in perspective sparked by the lunar landing was that, in 1970, we saw the first Earth Day. The emergence of serious stakeholder involvement in global processes started in essence around that first United Nations Conference on the Human Environment in 1972. Maurice Strong, the father of sustainable development and the secretary-general of the conference, opened with this warning:

> The world desperately needs hope; and we must build on this hope. If we fail, we will add to the growing divisions of this planet. Is it realistic to think that we can continue to reap the benefits of exploiting our precious planetary heritage while continuing to permit its accelerating desecration?
>
> The fate of Planet Earth lies largely in our own hands and in the knowledge and intelligence we bring to bear in the decision-making process. In the final analysis, however, man is unlikely to succeed in managing his relationship with nature unless in the course of it he learns to manage better the relations between man and man (Strong, 1972).

Many people do not realize that the Founex Report on Development and Environment, the critical input document for the Stockholm Conference, was produced by NGOs and academics. It played a vital role in framing many of the issues that would be reflected in the outcome document.

It is interesting, though probably not surprising, to note that with increased awareness of the environment, some key environmental organizations were set up in the period leading up to this conference and in its immediate aftermath. Greenpeace, one of the most powerful environmental advocacy organizations today, was established in 1971. Friends of the Earth, which became an international network in 1971, was first established in the United States in 1969.

For the Stockholm Conference, Maurice Strong employed an NGO advisor in the secretariat. He was Henrik Beer, the Secretary-General of the International

46 *Felix Dodds*

Federation of Red Cross Societies. Strong also engaged Baron Axel von dem Bussche, who was a member of the presidency of the Evangelical Church in Germany and had before that as an army officer been involved in the attempt to assassinate Hitler.

Attending the conference were 114 countries, 400 representatives of NGOs and over 1,500 members of the press. The NGOs convened at a separate venue for their Environment Forum. Maurice Strong informally tried to advance the ideas that emerged from the Forum, but there was no formal interaction between the two events.

One of the outcomes from the 1972 conference was the creation of the United Nations Environmental Programme (UNEP). UNEP's mission is "To provide leadership and encourage partnership in caring for the environment by inspiring, informing, and enabling nations and peoples to improve their quality of life without compromising that of future generations" (UNEP, 1972).

Emerging stakeholders

Beginning in 1975, IUCN with its multi-stakeholder membership started working on the idea of a World Conservation Strategy. It was launched in thirty-five countries on March 5, 1980, and was the first document that mentioned sustainable development. Out of this strategy, the World Charter for Nature was adopted by the United Nations General Assembly in 1982 after preparation by IUCN. The UNEP Governing Council in 1982 also discussed the idea of the United Nations creating a world commission to address environment and development issues.

This was followed up in 1983 with the General Assembly Resolution 38/161, "Process of Preparation of the Environmental Perspective to the Year 2000 and Beyond," which established the Commission.

Gro Harlem Brundtland, the former Prime Minister of Norway, was appointed to chair the Commission by the UN Secretary-General Javier Pérez de Cuéllar. The Commission took a new approach to the production of their report, deciding to consult with stakeholders and hold hearings on the drafts of the report.

In total, the Commission held fifteen public hearings around the world. These hearings were organized by Chip Lindner, the secretary to the Commission and formerly Deputy Director of WWF International. They represented the first serious and sustained attempt to engage stakeholders in the work of a UN Commission.

After the Commission's report was published, Gro Harlem Brundtland – again Prime Minister of Norway, which she was for a total of three terms – helped establish the Centre for Our Common Future as a way to promote the outcomes from the Commission. To run the Centre, Chip Lindner was asked to take the same approach of building up support among stakeholders for the Commission's recommendations.

The report, titled "Our Common Future," called for a new form of development and addressed the political changes necessary for that to be achieved. Its definition of "sustainable development" became one of the most widely used over the coming years.

In December 1989, the General Assembly formally agreed to convene another global conference, the United Nations Conference on Environment and Development (UNCED). This conference, better and more informally known as the Earth Summit, would ask Maurice Strong to again be its secretary-general. The Summit's preparatory process would become the birthplace for new stakeholder engagement.

Key people and institutions that created the stakeholder approach

It's useful to understand where this stakeholder engagement around the 1992 Earth Summit came from, so as to grasp the involved context and a sense of the people who played critical roles in building where we are now.

The Centre for Our Common Future played a critical role in reaching out to stakeholders through their newsletter, *Network 92*. This was published at the birth of the Internet. It was August 6, 1991, when the World Wide Web went live to the world. The newsletter was posted out to more than 125,000 people in five languages. Chip Lindner, the Executive Director of the Centre, described how this network began:

> The Centre for Our Common Future also established a network of working partners around the world. Originally, we targeted 100 key global networking groups such as the International Chamber of Commerce, the Global Tomorrow Coalition, etc. We got them to associate with the Centre for Our Common Future publicly as working partners by way of making a public commitment to further the concept of sustainable development (Lindner, 1992a).

Preparing to step back into his role as Secretary-General for the Earth Summit, Maurice Strong convened a meeting in March 1990 in Vancouver, BC. Originally this had been intended to be only a meeting of NGOs and nonprofits. However, organizers at the Centre for Our Common Future and Maurice Strong together decided to widen the constituencies beyond the traditional nonprofits. Chip Lindner remembers:

> I went to [Strong] and said we would be happy to provide our assistance and support to mobilize in the broader constituencies, but we could not work solely from an NGO point-of-view. The Centre brought together 152 of its working partners from 60 countries, representing the broader constituencies they had endeavoured to involve in dialogue on the Brundtland Report. These included industry, trade unions, women,

48 *Felix Dodds*

youth, media, and NGOs. Half of those present were from developing countries, half from developed (Lindner, 1992a).

At this point, stakeholders were being called constituencies. The Vancouver meeting played a critical role in expanding the understanding of the non-governmental designation. It questioned the use of the term NGOs as a catchall term because meeting attendees did not believe it reflected the different inputs and roles that they could play in negotiating outcomes from the Earth Summit.

Building on the outreach done by the Brundtland Commission, these new constituencies endorsed a call for broad participation by all sectors of society in the UNCED process. They also gave the Centre a mandate to extend its work in this area. This had an important impact on how Maurice Strong then prepared for the Summit as far as engaging other constituencies through the UNCED Secretariat. Steve Lerner described this preparation in his book *Beyond the Earth Summit: Conversations with Advocates of Sustainable Development*:

> At the time, the whole question of who could participate in the UNCED process had not been [resolved]. First, out of the meeting came a very strong call for broad participation. There was also a recognition that we had to find new mechanisms for resolving problems. Second, participants in the Vancouver conference called for at least 50 percent participation from developing countries and women in all strategizing and planning for the UNCED conference at all levels – national, regional, and international. Third, it was recognized that the development side of the environment/ development nexus was extremely weak in the proposed agenda for 1992; and that the inter-sectorial or cross-cutting issues, as they are now called, were elementary issues that had to be seriously addressed. And fourth, it was decided that the Centre for Our Common Future should call a meeting of heads of institutions to get a mandate to play some kind of focal point role in 1992 (Lerner, 1992).

The second meeting of this group happened a few months later in Nyon, Switzerland. Over 100 representatives from the different constituencies (stakeholders) and geographical regions attended this June 1990 meeting. To help with outreach for Earth Summit preparations, the different stakeholders established an International Facilitation Committee (IFC), which had two different responsibilities.

The first was to organize the Global Forum – an independent space similar to the Environment Forum that had been organized around the Stockholm 1972 Conference.

The second was to help support and increase access to the negotiations and preparatory meetings for the Earth Summit whenever possible.

There were four such meetings in preparation for the Summit to ensure that there were facilities for these constituencies or stakeholders (as we will refer to them from now on). Different stakeholder groups organized their own input independently. For example:

> The major international NGO Roots of the Future conference was held in Paris in December 1991 – through the support of the government of France and organized by the Environmental Liaison Centre International (ELCI) – in preparation for the Earth Summit. [It] saw the development of global stakeholder networks in areas that had none before committed to sustainable development and the strengthening of others. Over 800 non-governmental organizations and citizens' organizations attended the conference, with nearly three-quarters coming from developing countries. The main outcome document was Agenda ya Wananchi [ELCI, 1991] which in Swahili means "Sons and Daughters of the Earth." The document called for governments to support participatory democracy and a powerful and effective UN. It also called for governments to reduce their military spending [by at least half] and [requested that] developed countries reform the world's trading system and increase financial flows to the developing countries and the newly independent countries of the former Soviet Union (Dodds et. al., 2012).

The meeting in Paris called for building global NGO coalitions to work together in the "struggle for global justice and sustainability" and for a commitment to "campaign against all those national and international organizations and interests [that] disregard the imperatives of justice and sustainability." Moreover, the meeting also called for "the development of equitable and sustainable natural resource management systems and technologies ... [and] empowerment of socially and ecologically marginalized people," as well as a commitment to "a struggle for women's empowerment and equal status in society" (ELCI, 1991).

In addition to the aforementioned conference, a parallel but broader process was also occurring within the secretariat and beyond for the Earth Summit.

To understand this, we need to understand Maurice Strong a little more. He had an unusual background prior to his role as secretary-general of the conference. He started as an entrepreneur in Alberta, BC, working in the oil and natural gas industries. After travelling around Africa for two years, he became involved with YMCA and served as its national President and Chairman. He was then brought into the Canadian government to set up the Canadian International Development Agency (CIDA) in 1968, and he subsequently joined the UN as Secretary-General of the Stockholm Environment Conference. In many ways, Strong had experience through a number of stakeholders, so perhaps it wasn't surprising that he recognized that each had a unique role to contribute to the development and implementation of the agenda.

Industry was one of the areas – to some a controversial one – that Strong felt needed to be engaged. He was aware that the International Chamber of Commerce (ICC) was a conservative force which would seek to block some of the policy ideas. He was also aware that there were progressive industry leaders

50 Felix Dodds

who understood the need to address environmental issues sooner rather than later.

The problem of the hole in the ozone layer had shown that companies could address pollution issues quickly if required and if there they were under political pressure. Strong approached Swiss businessman Stephan Schmidheiny to serve as his principal business advisor. He tasked Schmidheiny with the job of mobilizing the participation and support of the progressive business community. Schmidheiny, who sat on numerous boards of directors such as those for ABB, Asea, Brown Boveri, Nestlé, Swatch, and UBS AG, was ideally placed to bring these business leaders together into a new organization, the Business Council for Sustainable Development (BCSD).

This approach forced the ICC to engage more positively, such as by producing the "Business Charter for Sustainable Development" for the Earth Summit. The Charter was endorsed by members at their pre-Rio Conference. Some of the green NGOs saw this as a greenwash because it did not obligate any company that signed the Charter to follow through. The ICC also did not set up any mechanism to audit companies that signed up, so there was validity to the criticism.

Most of the forty chapters in the initial drafts for Agenda 21 (the blueprint for sustainable development) were produced by UN Agencies and Programmes reaching out to the academic and research community.

Agenda 21 was the first real attempt to integrate a gender perspective into a UN document on environment. This was another example where a small number of key individuals helped create an effective voice for a stakeholder group. Former US Congresswoman Bella Abzug teamed up with feminist activist and journalist Mim Kelber to create the Women's Environment and Development Organization (WEDO) in 1991 to bring a (progressive) female perspective into the negotiations. Abzug explained her motivation by declaring that "As women, we know that we must always find ways to change the process because the present institutions want to hold on to power and keep the status quo."

In a way similar to what BCSD did for industry stakeholders, WEDO facilitated a large conference called the World Women's Congress for a Healthy Planet. It brought together more than 1,500 women from 83 countries; together they worked on a strategy for the Earth Summit.

Strong was a huge supporter of integrating scientific input into the Agenda 21 chapters. He wanted to ensure that the text being prepared by the UN Secretariat and UN Programmes and Agencies was in line with the best science. The International Council for Scientific Union (ICSU) played a critical role in this effort. Like other stakeholders, ICSU also held its own conference, gathering in November 1991 for the Vienna International Conference centered around an Agenda of Science for Environment and Development into the Twenty-first Century (ASCEND 21).

The trade unions, which had often been in conflict with the environmentalists, were similarly active because some of them also recognized the

The emergence of stakeholder democracy   51

need for change. Trade unions met in March 1992 in Caracas, Venezuela, for the World Congress of the International Confederation of Free Trade Unions (ICFTU) to finalize their input to Rio. Two of the key trade union leaders, Lucien Royer and Winston Gereluk, would continue to build a strong constituency in the trade union movement for sustainable development over the coming decade.

One of the most interesting stakeholders that emerged from preparation for the Earth Summit was local government. As a form of government designed for geographically modest impact, it hadn't been engaged in the workings of the UN much up to this point. But Strong brought together progressive local authorities that were addressing environmental issues. Leading this effort was Jeb Brugmann, who created the International Council for Local Environmental Initiatives (ICLEI) in 1990. It held its inaugural conference – the World Congress of Local Governments for a Sustainable Future – in New York in September 1990 to prepare input for the Earth Summit. It also met just prior to Rio in Curitiba, Brazil, to host a World Urban Forum.

These organizations and conferences became the roots of the stakeholder movement for sustainable development.

UN preparatory process and stakeholders

The preparatory process for the Earth Summit involved four global meetings and also regional meetings convened by the five UN Regional Commissions.

The first global preparatory meeting is always an organizational meeting, and this was held in Nairobi in August 1990. What was significant about this meeting as far as stakeholders were concerned is that some government delegations included stakeholders for the first time. These initial countries were Canada, Norway and the United Kingdom. This would grow over the coming years as governments began to see the value of having access to stakeholder knowledge and advice on their delegations.

After the first global preparatory meeting, the regional UN Commissions held meetings that gave countries and stakeholders a chance to discuss priorities for the Earth Summit.

From a stakeholder point of view, the most significant of these meetings was the UN Economic Commission for Europe (UNECE) regional meeting held in Bergan, Norway. It engaged stakeholders in the discussion, and this influenced the outcome document discussed at ministerial level. The conference came up with the term "independent sector," which continued in use until "Major Groups" was chosen for the nine stakeholder chapters of Agenda 21.

The quarterly *Brundtland Bulletin*, produced by the Centre for Our Common Future, stated that:

> For most observers, what really mattered about Bergen was that it saw the emergence at an international level of a new and unique participatory process in which bodies representing the "independent sector" (i.e. industry,

52 Felix Dodds

trade unions, the scientific community, youth, and non-governmental organizations concerned with environmental issues) not only conducted their own parallel conferences but participated with the ministerial delegations in the quest for the broadest possible consensus. The "Bergen Process" of consensus-seeking between independent and official channels had been evolving over the two years in which Bergen was in preparation and seems set to become the model for "the 1992 process", as we now move towards the all-important UN Conference on Environment and Development in Brazil (Centre for Our Common Future, 1990).

Bergen would have two vital impacts on the approach by stakeholders to the intergovernmental meetings in the area of sustainable development: The first was that stakeholders were meeting in their own groups to prepare their input. The second was that governments now recognized that for their decisions to be accepted domestically, they needed to engage and involve stakeholders while developing their positions.

Maurice Strong attended the Bergen meeting and met with representatives from the independent sector, stressing his support for the principle of broad representation and participation. After this, the UN Secretariat prepared guidelines for NGOs/stakeholders to participate in the Summit preparatory process. Chip Lindner expressed the new vision when he commented:

> We have to find a way to move from confrontation through dialogue to cooperation; and we have to get all the players at the table. It is no longer good enough to be critical. Each of us has to accept a share of the responsibility to do something. And we all have to have the humility to recognize that our solutions are not necessarily the only ones or ultimately the right ones. The world works inter-relatedly and we have to work inter-relatedly (Lindner, 1992b).

Agenda 21 and other Rio agreements in relation to stakeholders

In the previous section, we mentioned the enormous impact that the Earth Summit (1992) had in the development of Multilateral Environmental Agreements (MEAs). Summit attendees included 178 governments, of which 108 sent their heads of state or government, 2,400 registered stakeholder representatives, over 10,000 journalists and between 40,000 and 50,000 others attending the parallel Global Forum – a place of workshops, mini-conferences, stalls and cultural events.

There were a number of outcomes from the Earth Summit, three of which are relevant to our discussion here. The major outcome text was *Agenda 21: The Blueprint for Sustainable Development*, a forty-chapter document that was the first UN text to have specific chapters for different stakeholder groups, giving them rights and responsibilities. Agenda 21 as a whole was broken down into four sections:

The emergence of stakeholder democracy   53

- Section 1: Social and Economic Dimensions
- Section 2: Conservation and Management of Resources for Development
- Section 3: Strengthening the Role of Major Groups
- Section 4: Means of Implementation

Looking in more depth at Section 3 of the Agenda 21 blueprint, it identified nine major groups (stakeholders) as well as their rights and responsibilities relative to their anticipated roles in advancing Agenda 21. These stakeholders were Women; Children and Youth; Indigenous Peoples; Non-Governmental Organizations; Local Authorities; Workers and Trade Unions; Business and Industry; Scientific and Technological Community; and Farmers.

Why these stakeholders specifically? Despite overlapping memberships among some of them (as, for example, might be the case with an indigenous woman farmer who is a local authority by virtue of serving on the town council of the municipality closest to her farm), these groups organized substantive input for Agenda 21 and ran an effective lobbying strategy to be recognized. Other stakeholders, such as professional educators, focused on chapter 36 of Agenda 21 – "Promoting Education, Public Awareness and Training." They believed that this gave them the recognition they expected in the follow-up process, and did not therefore lobby to be recognized as a Major Group.

This turned out to be incorrect.

The major group stakeholders were seen by governments as players whom they should engage with to implement Agenda 21, and when they were establishing Sustainable Development Councils or Commissions (see Chapter 6). One of the primary reasons for this is that governments were tasked to report on what they had done to engage these nine stakeholders, so it was logical to involve them. Stakeholder groups outside of these nine were at a huge disadvantage. However, this would ultimately be resolved twenty years later at the Rio+20 Conference and the subsequent 2030 Agenda for Sustainable Development negotiated in 2015.

The second critical outcome from Agenda 21, which had an impact on the ability of stakeholders to engage in the follow-up process, was the establishment of a new Commission of the Economic and Social Council. The Commission on Sustainable Development (CSD) text in Agenda 21 makes clear that governments were expected to achieve a different level of engagement with stakeholders than had been experienced in the UN before "Chapter 38: International Institutional Arrangements" integrated stakeholders into the new body:

> 38.11 ... The Commission should provide for the active involvement of organs, programmes and organizations of the United Nations system, international financial institutions and other relevant intergovernmental organizations, and encourage the participation of non-governmental organizations, including industry and the business and scientific communities. The first meeting of the Commission should be convened no later than 1993.

54 Felix Dodds

It went on to stipulate in section 38.13 that the Commission on Sustainable Development should have the following functions:

d   To receive and analyse relevant input from competent non-governmental organizations, including the scientific and private sectors, in the context of the overall implementation of Agenda 21.
e   To enhance the dialogue, within the framework of the United Nations, with nongovernmental organizations and the independent sector, as well as other entities outside the United Nations system.

Section 38.14 explained:

> Within the intergovernmental framework, consideration should be given to allowing nongovernmental organizations, including those related to Major Groups, particularly women's groups, committed to the implementation of Agenda 21 to have relevant information available to them, including information, reports and other data produced within the United Nations system (UN, 1992).

The third outcome was a large number of stakeholders now wanted to engage with and ultimately receive accreditation from the UN. Getting accredited to a UN conference only means that you are accredited to that conference specifically – indeed, getting accredited to the UN could take up to three years at that time. Stakeholders seeking accreditation were required to go through the Committee on Non-Governmental Organizations, which is a standing committee of the Economic and Social Council (ECOSOC). The countries on this committee were not particularly receptive to stakeholders. Many countries still saw the UN as only a member state forum.

Strong took it on himself to lobby for the acceptance of the Rio stakeholders onto the roster of the UN as a group. A process was agreed that ultimately let in just over 500 stakeholders out of the 2,400 originally accredited. It was the single largest entry of stakeholders to the roster of the UN in its history. By the end of 1992, accredited stakeholders had grown to 928. By 1996, the number of accredited stakeholders reached 1,226, and by 1998, it was 1,519.

Follow-up on the Earth Summit by stakeholders

After the Earth Summit, many stakeholders believed the process had finished – governments would just implement what had been agreed. In June 1992, however, the UN established the new Commission on Sustainable Development under the aegis of the Economic and Social Council. How would governments interpret the paragraphs in Agenda 21 which attempted to integrate stakeholders into the workings of this new Commission? The General Assembly Resolution 47/191 establishing the Commission on Sustainable Development charged it with doing the following:

The emergence of stakeholder democracy   55

f To receive and analyse relevant input from competent non-governmental organizations, including the scientific and the private sector, in the context of the overall implementation of Agenda 21.

g To enhance the dialogue, within the framework of the United Nations, with non-governmental organizations and the independent sector, as well as other entities outside the United Nations system (UN, 1993a).

The UN General Assembly had instructed the new Commission in its establishment to maintain the spirit of the Earth Summit and Agenda 21 by identifying the role of stakeholders through two of its ten modalities. The first would enable the UN to include stakeholder input in producing any Secretary-General Report on the implementation of Agenda 21. The second was promoting the idea of a "dialogue" between member states and stakeholders. This would develop much further in the period 1998–2001.

The Commission on Sustainable Development mandate included:

- Monitor progress on the implementation of Agenda 21 and activities related to the integration of environmental and developmental goals by governments, NGOs and other UN bodies.
- Receive and analyze relevant information from competent NGOs in the context of Agenda 21 implementation.
- Enhance dialogue with NGOs, the independent sector and other entities outside the UN system, within the UN framework (UN, 1993b).

At the 1993 CSD, stakeholders were admitted for the first time to informal and "informal-informal" meetings, and then invited to speak at the discretion of the chair. This practice became popular with stakeholders interested in holding their governments accountable for implementing the action items that emerged from the Earth Summit.

Also in 1993, a working group was set up under ECOSOC to review and evaluate the relationship of NGOs with the UN. In 1996, member states adopted ECOSOC Resolution 1996/31 to replace Resolution 1296 from 1968 in an effort to expand the participation of NGOs into all areas of the work of the UN.

In the Stakeholder Forum's Stakeholder Empowerment Project report (2009), Emily Benson, the author of the report, interviewed Tony Hill, who was then the UN Non-Governmental Liaison Service. Benson summarized their conversation as follows:

According to Hill, this second generation of NGOs can be characterised in a number of ways. Firstly, they were far more numerous and more diverse in terms of their structures, practices and ideologies. Their activities spanned from research and policy analysis to providing services and to lobbying and advocacy activities. They ranged from small grassroots organisations working with local communities to international networks and coalitions

56   *Felix Dodds*

of like-minded NGOs collaborating on specific issues. Of particular significance was the emerging role of business and industry groups.

Second, relative to their predecessors, many of these NGOs were far more politically active and engaged in the negotiations and the outcomes of the meetings. No longer were NGOs content to observe the process [but] they also wanted to inform, contribute [to] and challenge intergovernmental decision-making.

A third development has been the levels of operational cooperation between the Secretariats of UN organisations and non-governmental actors. UN agencies such as the United Nations Population Fund (UNFPA), United Nations International Children's Emergency Fund (UNICEF), United Nations Development Programme (UNDP), and others such as International Fund for Agricultural Development (IFAD), Food and Agriculture Organization (FAO) and the International Labour Organization (ILO) support and fund a range of NGOs in the south, whereas in the past UN funding had been channeled to governments. For example, over issues such as humanitarian crises and refugee-related work, between 33 percent and 50 percent of UNHCR's operational budget is distributed through NGOs. The Organisation for Economic Cooperation and Development (OECD) reported that Civil Society Organizations (CSOs) were channeling some US $11–12 billion development aid annually to developing countries by the late 1990 (Stakeholder Forum, 2009).

At the 1994 CSD, stakeholders were for the first time able to ask their governments questions in front of their peers (other governments) in response to presenting their national reports. This CSD also saw the establishment of the CSD NGO Steering Committee, which had two important functions: (1) to facilitate NGO involvement in the CSD and (2) to enable all Major Groups to deal with any administrative problems between stakeholders and the UN. The Committee was interesting in other ways; 70 percent of its membership was from developing countries, and it had gender balance built into its charter. It was the first Committee at the UN to be established with a Major Group focus.

> To enhance the flow of information about the CSD process to regional, focal points and networks for NGOs, Indigenous Peoples and Major Groups and their constituents.
> Steering Committee members will serve as focal points to ensure participation of issue and regional networks within the NGO community through their ability to disseminate information using communication tools such as mail. telephone, fax and e-mail (CSD NGO Steering Committee, 1994).

Further development of the terms of reference happened in 1998 after a review of the work of the Steering Committee for the Rio+5 Conference.

UK stakeholder follow-up to 1992 Earth Summit – A case study

In the follow-up to the 1992 Earth Summit, national governments established multi-stakeholder councils and commissions (which we will deal with in Chapter 6). Some of these were led by governments and others by the UN or stakeholders. In October 1993, in the United Kingdom, the National Committee for UNEP (UNEP-UK) became the first national committee for both UNEP and UNDP and the first multi-stakeholder platform at the national level. The committee became known as the United Nations Environment and Development UK Committee, or UNED-UK, which in turn would go on (in 2000) to become an international multi-stakeholder platform known as the Stakeholder Forum for a Sustainable Future. One of its original objectives was "helping to mobilize the UK political process, particularly through national and local government, the voluntary sector and the commercial and industrial sector, in order to promote sustainable development in the work of the UN institutions both nationally and internationally" (UNED-UK, 1993).

Its first Chairperson was Jonathon Porritt, the leading UK Green and former Executive Director of Friends of the Earth. In explaining the purpose of UNED-UK, Porritt said:

> UNED-UK will provide a unique forum on which all the Major Groups can be formerly represented. There's a lot of work to be done together, [exchanging] information, developing joint projects, promoting lively debate, forming new partnerships. We all have a part to play in achieving sustainable development (UNED-UK, 1993).

This action in the UK started a process of establishing similar platforms in other developed countries. At their heart, these platforms were national committees for UNEP and UNDP. These committees had originally been set up to advocate for UNEP/UNDP and to channel input from NGOs to UNEP/UNDP discussions on policies, but they expanded to include the other stakeholders identified in Agenda 21, thus becoming (for all intents and purposes) multi-stakeholder platforms that were monitoring, advocating for and helping to implement Agenda 21.

UNED-UK was one of the first groups to organize national roundtables to review the implementation of the different chapters of Agenda 21, which would be reviewed in following years by the Commission on Sustainable Development. The approach that UNED-UK took included three roundtables per issue, with the final roundtable organized as part of a combined mini-conference. These mini-conferences typically featured a Deputy Minister from the UK government and the relevant UN staff person working together to write the Secretary-General's Report and to speak and comment on the reviews of the different chapters of Agenda 21.

The first Secretary-General's Report was written by Socrates Litsios, Secretary of the WHO Task Force on Health, Environment and Sustainable

58   Felix Dodds

Development. He attended the Health and the Environment UNED-UK Roundtable in July 1994 and in his comments said:

> The various activities of UNED-UK have been particularly useful for those of us "in" the system as they adhere to the official work as defined by Agenda 21 while at the same time mobilizing "grass root" interest and activities of direct relevance to that agenda of work (Litsios, 1994).

By 1995, the approach was gaining international recognition as expressed by then-US Vice President Al Gore, who predicted that the UNED work "will serve as a model for others throughout the world" (Gore, 1995).

Praise for UNED-UK was also offered by the European Commission:

> The European Commission team preparing for Rio+5 regards UNED-UK's contribution to the CSD process and particularly their role in coordinating the input of northern NGOs, as important, positive and useful. UNED-UK have played a key role in ensuring that NGIs are able to reach agreement on a united position and make their input early enough to have a real influence. As a result, the preparations for Rio+5 [are] a real example of multi-stakeholder participation in action. The continued involvement UNED-UK seems to us essential if we are to reach a successful conclusion to what is becoming an ever more difficult process (MacKenzie, 1997).

Debuting "Days of Major Groups" in 1995

This new Commission needed to develop new ways to engage with stakeholders to enable them to share their experience with member states.

The 1995 CSD introduced the "Day on a Major Group" focus, with the first such called a "Day of Local Authorities." Chapter 28 of Agenda 21, which focused on local authorities, had as one of its objectives that by "By 1996, most local authorities in each country should have undertaken a consultative process with their populations and achieved a consensus on 'a Local Agenda 21' for the community" (UN, 1992).

This was the first time this level of government engaged in the follow-up to a United Nations Conference. This was a huge step for communities around the world, with local authorities engaging in creating their own local Agenda 21s by working with local stakeholder groups. ICLEI played a critical role in engaging their members. As a result of this effort, other local authorities and even some national authorities, were inspired to get involved.

In 1996, the CSD's second "Day on a Major Group" was titled the "Day of the Workplace." It focused on the work of industry and the trade unions.

Habitat II (1996)

The preparatory process for Habitat II, the second United Nations Conference on Human Settlements, was fascinating. At the second preparatory meeting,

The emergence of stakeholder democracy   59

stakeholders established the International Facilitation Committee, and its membership consisted entirely of stakeholders. Even more interesting was the informal process that member states set up between the second preparatory committee meeting in Nairobi and the third preparatory meeting in New York. At an informal meeting in Paris, stakeholders could propose text and, if endorsed by a government, the text became part of the negotiations. There were times when governments, UN Agencies and Programmes and stakeholders would work together on certain text, even facilitating breakout groups. This continued at the conference itself. Habitat II also saw, for the first time, the UN publish a set of amendments the NGOs wanted to see added to the text reflected in an official UN information document.

Habitat II itself was made up of two committees. Committee 1 was reserved for negotiations, while Committee 2 featured half a day of presentations from each stakeholder group on what challenges they envisioned in implementing the Habitat II Agenda and how they might be able contribute. The recognized stakeholders – referred to as Partners – were:

- Local Authorities
- Business and Industry
- Parliamentarians
- Professionals and Researchers
- Foundations
- Trade Unions
- NGOs and Community-Based Organizations (CBOs)
- Wisdom Seekers (experienced old persons)
- The UN System

Although the stakeholder group representing women was not given a unique space to contribute in Committee 2, they were very active again under the inspirational leadership of WEDO and Bella Abzug and the organizational leadership of Anita Nayar. Their morning briefing sessions were attended by many others as well for they delivered best and up-to-date information about the negotiations, and the (progressive) women's caucus lobbying was well reflected in the final outcome document.

The era of multi-stakeholder dialogues

The approach of Habitat II's Committee 2 was then promoted in the UN General Assembly in October, through the UN General Assembly's Second Committee. The Second Committee would be discussing and agreeing to the modalities for the five-year Review of Agenda 21, scheduled for 1997. A proposal to have hearings/dialogues with the Major Groups, as had occurred during the Habitat II process, was put forward by the Stakeholder Forum. Given that stakeholders had no right to speak in the UN General Assembly (UNGA) processes, Arjan Hamburg of the Netherlands, Chair of the UNGA

60   *Felix Dodds*

Second Committee, went into an informal session to enable the proposal to be put forward. It already had European Union support and also support among key G77 countries. The session then introduced the proposal and it was accepted. This entitled each of the Major Groups to half a day to present on what they had done to implement Agenda 21. Unfortunately, those presentations were scheduled in times parallel to ongoing negotiations.

Ten Major Group representatives presented at the Heads of State session in 1997. During the whole of the preparatory process and at what in reality was the 19th UN General Assembly Special Session – this time focusing on reviewing Earth Summit 1992 outcomes and their implementation – negotiating committees operated in a way consistent with the norms from the UN Commission on Sustainable Development. These norms included allowing stakeholders to attend the sessions and, where there was agreement from the chair of the session, to have the opportunity to speak – a first in the UN. This was helped enormously by the fact that the President of the UN General Assembly was Ambassador Ismail Razali of Malaysia, who had been the Chair of the first session of the CSD.

Oran Young, one of the leading academic scholars in environmental governance, clearly saw why stakeholders were engaging at the global level when he said: "[i]t is increasingly difficult for states and various non-state actors to isolate themselves from events taking place in other parts of the world, however much they may wish to do so" (Young, 1997).

The review of the Major Groups implementation of Agenda 21 chapters produced a number of interesting conclusions:

> 100. Together with the Agenda 21 emphasis on partnership, the concept of Major Groups provides sustainable development with a fundamentally different background from the global action plans adopted previously. Actions that are based on partnership and the involvement of Major Groups open up a wider political space for a broad list of social and economic actors, which puts the sustainable development challenge in the hands of not only Governments and United Nations bodies but also and equally of local communities, individuals, professional societies, businesses of all sizes and the various organizations of civil society at all levels. Hence, the emphasis on major group participation and partnership constitutes one of the most forward-looking elements of Agenda 21.
>
> 101. The five-year review shows that major group actors are actively involved in Agenda 21 implementation and monitoring. Activities are carried out at all levels, from the local to the international. The degree of success of those activities is not always clear, given that some are conducted by newly created mechanisms or institutions, many are carried out with meager financial and technical resources, and most are not well linked with international processes for regularly sharing and exchanging information on their experiences.

The emergence of stakeholder democracy 61

102. The involvement of Major Groups as members, experts and advisers in the national coordination mechanisms is a positive factor, with potential long-term benefits at both the national and the international levels. However, those mechanisms are not in place in all countries, and those that are in place do not always involve the full spectrum of major group sectors or benefit from their full contributions as independent organizations. Furthermore, information at the national level on partnerships with or support for Major Groups, particularly from Governments, is scant (UN, 1997).

In October 1997, the Director of the UN Division on Sustainable Development (UNDSD), Joke Waller Hunter, brought together industry and trade union representatives with the CSD NGO Steering Committee co-chairs to review how to improve the dialogues for the next CSD.

They together developed a new approach which integrated the dialogue session into the agenda for the 1998 and subsequent CSDs through to 2002. This involved reserving the first two days of the CSD for dialogue between member states and stakeholders. Some member states were not happy at losing twelve hours of negotiations. The idea behind this was that governments would debate with stakeholders on four topic areas that the governments would subsequently negotiate. Advocates of the new approach hoped the result would be better-informed decisions by member states.

These multi-stakeholder dialogues (MSDs) will be considered in more depth in Chapter 6. For now, it is important to appreciate the impact that the MSDs had in developing stakeholder engagement in policy-making.

The MSDs at the CSD in 1998 were on industry and water, the one for the 1999 CSD on tourism, the 2000 CSD on agriculture, and the MSD for the 2001 CSD on energy. None of these tried to have every stakeholder group debate, because there was a selection process within the stakeholder organizations to choose the three or four most relevant to each of the three-hour sessions. Other stakeholders that were less relevant were asked to work with those stakeholders that were selected to ensure that their viewpoints were not lost.

As a method for informing governments before they formulated policy, this was and still is a very interesting and impactful approach.

Unlike subsequent attempts at MSDs these had a long preparation process that started with choosing themes for each of the three-hour sessions in October for a dialogue that would happen the following June. Selected stakeholders would then be asked to consult within their group and write a paper about their views of six or fewer pages within a common structure. The UN then produced a comparative analysis of these views for the chair of the session, who was also the chair of the CSD. The chair would then use this to focus the dialogue about issues that were common to each of the papers, consulting with the stakeholders before the dialogue to ensure that everyone was on the same page.

One of the interesting aspects of this period was that the committee Chairperson and governments could challenge what stakeholders were saying. This parliamentary mechanism encouraged solid research, ensuring through peer

62   Felix Dodds

pressure over time that content put forward was of a much higher quality than it might otherwise have been.

The most impactful MSD session was the one on tourism, and the reason for this was because the chair of the session, New Zealand Minister Simon Upton, introduced the elements of the MSD chairs outcome text as amendments to the tourism text. This meant that instead of governments having to introduce elements of what they heard in the MSD, they now had to delete sections they didn't like.

Another interesting by-product of the MSD process is it opened up a much clearer understanding among stakeholders about what each stakeholder group saw as important and cleared up some linguistic differences which had not been helpful.

An example of dialogues outside the UN

In November 2001, the German government hosted the International Bonn Water Conference to feed into the World Summit on Sustainable Development (WSSD). They reserved the first day for multi-stakeholder dialogues and contracted the Stakeholder Forum to run the process. Stakeholder Forum had (through Executive Director, Felix Dodds, in his role as Co-Chair of the NGO Steering Committee for the CSD) been engaged in all of the previous CSD MSDs.

Stakeholder Forum brought in David Hales, former Deputy Assistant Administrator of USAID, to facilitate the process, building on lessons of the previous three years. One of the ways he improved the dialogue was by taking a more informal but directed approach. He did this by facilitating dialogue from the floor, and walking up to delegates to push them for more details – or to suggest their time was up. This approach was more like a TV talk show format. It enabled him to get the most interactive dialogue session seen so far. Franklin Moore, then Acting Deputy Assistant Administrator and Director for the Agency's Global Center for the Environment for USAID, said of the Bonn Dialogues:

> Multi-stakeholder dialogue stood out because of how it was put together, the way it was facilitated and because other instructions given to the participants actually turned it into a dialogue. Having done multi-stakeholder dialogue at the Commission on Sustainable Development meetings quite often you either end up with the stakeholders talking to each other or the stakeholder and governments in a room but you don't get a proper dialogue (Moore, 2001).

World Summit on Sustainable Development Dialogues

The UN was impressed with Hales' approach. Nitin Desai, the UN Secretary-General for WSSD, requested the videos of the MSDs to review. He then initiated a process which he hoped would emulate it in the dialogue sessions during the preparatory sessions for WSSD. Desai had been Maurice Strong's deputy for

The emergence of stakeholder democracy 63

the Earth Summit in 1992 and the chief economist for the Brundtland Report and of course oversaw the creation of the CSD. It is therefore not surprising that he was so interested in developing the stakeholder engagement to the next level.

The first preparatory meeting for WSSD opened with statements by the nine Major Groups. This enabled stakeholders to set the stage with their views on what WSSD should achieve. In recent years this has been abandoned, and stakeholders have spoken at the end of sessions.

The second preparatory meeting for WSSD had an element referred to as dialogues, which in practice was more a set of statements by stakeholders. There was no attempt to focus those statements on the issues in the Secretary-General's Report, which would form the basis of the negotiations taking place immediately afterwards. The second preparatory meeting was also significant because a new NGO Network had been set up to replace the CSD NGO Steering Committee, which had folded the previous year.

The Sustainable Development Information Network (SDIN) was coordinated initially through three networks: ANPED, Environment Liaison Center International, and Third World Network. It was meant to be a temporary arrangement until after the Summit when a new, more representative network would be set up. These networks would continue to facilitate the NGO input to Rio +20 in 2012. They took a much more hands-off approach to coordinating the NGOs, and did not include the other Major Groups.

The final preparatory meeting for WSSD in May 2002 also included an MSD session.

The four sessions of the MSD, starting with a plenary discussion on sustainable development governance, continued with two parallel discussion groups (one on capacity-building for sustainable development and the other on a Major Group framework for partnership initiatives) and concluded with a final plenary session aiming to identify Major Groups' priorities for the future. The stakeholders made many good points, but input on the political outcome was put forward too late for governments to consider. At the time, stakeholders expressed their displeasure and many felt there were some key people in the UN Secretariat who had lobbied for this to ensure that the impact of their voices would be muted. Very few of the issues brought forward saw progress in the coming decade.

Megan Howell has a PhD thesis that includes a useful summary of the lessons from the dialogues. She says they yielded the following:

1   Focus on the values that are being expressed in the Dialogues, in the proceedings and in the surrounding context, at both institutional and individual levels.
2   Detailed examination of the structural, conceptual and historical context the Dialogues are operating in, including the question of how the Dialogues came to be, with the hope of informing where they might go.

64 Felix Dodds

To this must also be added an examination of the theoretical constructs.

3 Emphasis on understanding how power operates in the Dialogues.
4 [Willingness to unfold] the narrative of the Dialogues, and [seek] lessons in the small, revealing moments as well as drawing conclusions from the bigger picture.
5 An inherently grounded, dialogical approach, going beyond the official texts to engage with participants to discover their attitudes towards the Dialogues and the broader subject matter.
6 An orientation to action, contributing the findings of the research to the ongoing debate at the specific level of how the Dialogues and other similar processes might go forward, and the more general level of the possibilities of a communicative approach to sustainable development (Howell, 2004).

In the past, comments were informally offered to governments in the corridors, but comments had now been made in a more "interactive" forum where governments could learn about the reasoning behind different arguments. They also had gone through an internal stakeholder peer group review before they emerged into the dialogue.

Local Agenda 21

One of the outcomes from the 1992 Earth Summit which no one predicted was how successful Chapter 28 of Agenda 21 – "Local Authorities' Initiatives in Support of Agenda 21" – would be. Local government hadn't been very engaged with the UN system previously and in part that was because central government functionaries in many cases were nervous about having their sub-national governments at the UN. This in part was because some of them would have opposition parties in power. The relevant text in Agenda 21 said: "By 1996, most local authorities in each country should have undertaken a consultative process with their populations and achieved a consensus on 'a local Agenda 21' for the community" (UN, 1992).

It further said:

Each local authority should enter into a dialogue with its citizens, local organizations and private enterprises and adopt "a local Agenda 21 (LA21)." Through consultation and consensus-building, local authorities would learn from citizens and from local, civic, community, business and industrial organizations and acquire the information needed for formulating the best strategies. The process of consultation would increase household awareness of sustainable development issues. Local authority programmes, policies, laws and regulations to achieve Agenda 21 objectives would be assessed and modified, based on local programmes adopted. Strategies could also be used in supporting proposals for local, national, regional and international funding (UN, 1992).

The emergence of stakeholder democracy   65

To some extent, this gave UN decisions for the first time a real link from global to local. LA21 offered a framework for local stakeholders to work with their local governments to address the critical environmental issues of their community.

One of the best thinkers on the issue of local sustainable development, former Chief Planner for Seattle, Washington (USA), Gary Lawrence, contributed one of the Millennium Papers for WSSD for the Stakeholder Forum. In it, he said:

> On closer examination, however, LA21 can look unfamiliar and create discomfort, as it calls for a significant reorientation of the planners' role. It asks for a change of orientation from technocratic to political (not partisan). This fundamental difference has not been well recognized by the planning profession, or those who employ planners. Not too surprisingly, NGOs and individuals have expectations for changed institutional behaviors consistent with the principles of LA21. However, even among those progressive local authorities committed to making LA21 work, the public's expectation for different corporate and professional behaviors is seldom being met.
>
> In its construction LA21 makes clear through its call for involvement, empowerment and devolution of power that planning is primarily a political activity that relies upon science and planning techniques. Most rational planning models assume the opposite, that planning is primarily technical with political consequences. With this shift in emphasis, the customary relationship between planners and the planning profession, the public and politician's changes significantly. Planning done under LA21 should:
>
> - Change community decisions about what can or will be discussed and who has a right to be at the table. LA21 threatens the role and power of traditionally empowered groups. Therefore, it increases political risk for elected officials and senior civil servants through empowerment of new constituencies with different and/or heightened expectations. The expectations of these new groups will often differ from significantly from the expectations of more established constituencies. Revamping the local balance of power.
> - Greatly increase professional risk for the planner if he or she appears to be eroding the political influence of traditional community powers by increasing the voice of those historically disempowered. As the shift from "top down" – the "top" being institutions of government or community elite – to "bottom up" planning and decision-making occurs, institutional risk can also increase (Lawrence, 1998).

For the 2002 World Summit on Sustainable Development, ICLEI produced the Second Local Agenda 21 Survey for the UN Department of Economic and Social Affairs. The survey found that:

66 Felix Dodds

- 6,416 local authorities in 113 countries had either made a formal commitment to Local Agenda 21 or are actively undertaking the process.
- National campaigns were underway in 18 countries accounting for 2,640 processes.
- Formal stakeholder groups existed in 73 percent of municipalities with Local Agenda 21 processes.
- In 59 percent of responding municipalities the Local Agenda 21 process had been integrated into the municipal system.
- Water resource management was the common priority issue for municipalities in all world regions and regardless of economic situation.
- Local authorities in all regions and regardless of economic situation list lack of both financial support and national government political commitment as key obstacles to greater success (UNDESA, 2002).

In Sweden and the United Kingdom,100 percent of local authorities conducted a LA21 process by WSSD. LA21 was the largest community engagement in local planning processes the world had ever seen. It may, we hope, be surpassed by what happens with localizing the SDGs, but at this point it is an example of what to do and what not to do.

Local Agenda 21 was also a great example of local stakeholder democracy while it lasted. It didn't try to replace representative democracy at the local level. Instead, it worked to ensure that local political leaders were able to better understand the interests in their community and to plan accordingly. For the stakeholders that participated, it succeeded in changing their community and for a time brought them into a positive and reinforcing relationship with their local authorities.

In countries such as Germany, there has also been a lot of investment and work with local government on addressing climate, mostly through the national climate initiative. Citizen and stakeholder participation are significant components, and a formal requirement for government funding. This builds on the previous work in Germany on LA21.

World Summit on Sustainable Development, continued

There is no question that the access to member states that had become the norm at the CSD is now accepted as the "new normal," at least for the sustainable development agenda. We have already looked at the preparatory process for WSSD, and we will look more closely at the work on partnerships in Chapter 7. One of the aims for stakeholders at WSSD, but also moving forward to the next ten years of CSDs, was making the CSD even more stakeholder-friendly in the development of policy and in its implementation.

Stakeholder Forum and their Vice Presidents who were the former Chairs of the Commission on Sustainable Development (CSD) convened a meeting during WSSD. This meeting, which was attended by key governments and major

The emergence of stakeholder democracy 67

stakeholders, was to review the CSD and what changes should be made to improve it.

Out of that meeting, a questionnaire was produced by the Stakeholder Forum and its results went on to serve as a major input to the 2003 CSD institutional meeting, at which the programme of work and modalities for the CSD were established for the next ten years. This was important because it summarizes what stakeholders and governments, including former chairs of the CSD, wanted to see. This built on the extensive experience in the process and of course their assessment of their constituencies' wishes and capacities. The relevant recommendations for this chapter included having the CSD become a two-year process, with year one used for review. In addition, as far as recommendations relating to stakeholder engagement it suggested:

Stakeholder Participation: In terms of policy discussions, stakeholders generally agreed on the need for greater participation and indicated a particular preference for the proposal of holding JOINT ministerial and stakeholder roundtables. In the implementation processes, the most popular preference was for the CSD to PROMOTE GOOD PRACTICE in partnerships and initiatives. Along the same lines as policy discussion, a larger group of respondents selected the option of holding JOINT reviews by stakeholders and governments in order to monitor progress. A majority of respondents also agreed that the CSD should encourage COMMON PRINCIPLES for stakeholder participation at all levels, and that all stakeholder processes should use SKILLED FACILITATORS.

Institutional Mechanisms: *Issue-Focused Commissions or Task Forces* – In general, the majority of respondents preferred the option of convening JOINT government and stakeholder commissions for both policy discussions and monitoring, rather than simply some form of inter-governmental forum.

Resources: Respondents generally preferred that the policy, implementation and monitoring process (facilitated by the CSD) should be mainly supported by sufficient government and intergovernmental funds as opposed to stakeholder funds.

Independent Review: Respondents supported the option of using independent non-governmental review bodies to monitor progress in implementation and policy.

National Bodies: The majority of respondents agreed that national, regional (sub- national) and local sustainable development commissions (or councils) [multi-stakeholder] required additional financial support from governments and intergovernmental bodies to follow-up Johannesburg commitments from the World Summit on Sustainable Development (Stakeholder Forum, 2003).

At the same time the survey was being conducted, the Stakeholder Forum produced a paper called "Post Johannesburg: The Future of the CSD." In the section "Involving Stakeholders," it said:

68   *Felix Dodds*

The Johannesburg Summit process was inadequate in addressing two important areas of stakeholder involvement:

- Participation in decision-making.
- Collaborative stakeholder action (partnerships with or without government or agency involvement).

The CSD will have to face up to these challenges as it moves forward toward supporting effective implementation. The key components of progress will need to include stakeholder involvement in political debate, policy making on emerging issues, and the effective use of implementation tools, of which partnership initiatives are but one approach (Stakeholder Forum, 2003).

Beyond WSSD – The end of dialogues at the CSD

By 2005, the CSD had given up the multi-stakeholder dialogue as a mechanism to engage stakeholder views. Megan Howell, whose PhD thesis we quoted earlier, explains:

> The Dialogues were a "small moment" of transformation, affecting the understanding of how intergovernmental processes on sustainable development operate, who may be legitimately included, what may be legitimately discussed, and how that discussion may proceed. The Dialogues achieved a great deal in simply establishing multi-stakeholder dialogue as a "tradition" of the CSD [UNCSD, 1999] and propelling the practice out into other intergovernmental meetings. Even the choice of title of the Dialogues was significant. Compared to the range of other descriptions regularly employed in such events, such as roundtables, hearings, panels and forums, the use of "The Multi-Stakeholder Dialogues" (for all its awkwardness) drew attention to the communicative, dialogical possibilities of exchange and interplay between diverse participants.
>
> The CSD Dialogues demonstrated that ... dialogue between stakeholders can make a constructive contribution to sustainable development. As an encounter among different "others", the Dialogues made significant headway in exposing participants to diverse worldviews and experiences; building new relationships, tolerance and understanding between Major Groups and with member states; educating participants on the possibilities and limitations of a dialogical approach; and revealing the immanent possibilities of a more sustainable world. Participants further elaborated the discourse of sustainable development within the intergovernmental sphere, had some influence on policy decisions, diversified the range of perspectives reflected in the official record, and established a more visible presence for civil society as part of intergovernmental deliberative processes on a varied range of economic, social, economic and political issues (Howell, 2004).

The CSD had provided opportunities for Major Groups (stakeholders) to develop relationships with member states, the United Nations at levels seldom seen before and amongst each other. Each year the level of involvement of Major Groups in the CSD process increased. Some of this progress was due to the increased involvement of Major Groups in the implementation of other UN Conference agreements, particularly the Habitat II Conference (1996).

The need for greater reform in stakeholder participation was underscored in the challenges that the Secretary-General had outlined in his report to the 2nd Summit WSSD Preparatory Committee, saying that the CSD stakeholder dialogues were an important mechanism but suffered two main shortcomings: (1) a lack of participation of women and representatives from developing countries (para 169), and (2) that "stakeholder participation is rarely allowed in actual decision making" (para 170).

The lessons of these events, as well as experience in other forums such as the Bonn Freshwater Conference in 2001, highlighted the common elements of successful stakeholder participation in multi-stakeholder dialogues:

- Sufficient preparation time.
- Face-to-face meetings between stakeholder representatives before the dialogue to agree the framework for the multi-stakeholder dialogue.
- Use of a trained facilitator.
- Relatively equal time division for debate between governments and stakeholders.
- The chair/facilitator empowered to draw some of the key conclusions from the multi-stakeholder dialogue into the official text and/or using other predetermined mechanisms of linking stakeholder contributions into intergovernmental decision-making.
- Ensuring predictable funding for effective participation, and a transparent nomination mechanism for the allocation of such funding.

The absence of these key elements from the MSDs in the Summit process led to deep concern about the validity of the MSDs. Many had put an enormous amount of work into consultation within their respective groups and then into the dialogues themselves without seeing much impact on the Summit outcome documents. The establishment of appropriate processes of engagement will give a clear indication of the degree to which the UN and governments take stakeholder participation as seriously as they have frequently stated – and as the Secretary-General's Report on UN reform has challenged them to do (Dodds et al., 2002).

It's clear that there wasn't the enthusiasm in the UN Secretariat for developing the MSDs beyond 2002, and some would even say there was active obstruction. Opposition was also reflected within the Major Groups. In part there had been a passing of the old order and those who had engaged most directly with the MSDs had moved on. Meanwhile, the new Major Group coordinators in many cases didn't see that the MSDs were delivering. This is because in 2001 and 2002 they hadn't delivered.

70   Felix Dodds

But perhaps the biggest impact was that there had developed a viewpoint by 2005 that ALL stakeholders should engage in ALL of the chances for speaking.

One of the reasons why the MSDs had worked had been the focus on the most relevant stakeholders for a particular issue. This had resulted in only three or four stakeholder groups per session with member states. This made it much easier for an interactive dialogue to be had. The idea of nine stakeholder groups all speaking meant that dialogue gave way to a set of disjointed statements.

The issue of equity of each stakeholder group on every issue was a standardization approach that showed over time that it delivered few benefits and often obstructed the ability to move forward and innovate. It became the death of MSDs at the CSD.

The MSDs had played a vital role for the years they were used to enable, in a domain that is clearly member state, stakeholders to express their views and discuss issues as part of the formal CSD process and not just through the discussions in the corridor. Member states did integrate the views of stakeholders during the 1998–2000 CSDs after hearing the dialogue. This helped to legitimize the outcome of MSDs, as we would see in the development of the Sustainable Development Goals (SDGs) fifteen years later.

Cardoso Panel

In response to the growing engagement of stakeholders in the UN, Secretary-General Kofi Annan in his September 2002 report on UN Reform – "Strengthening of the United Nations: An Agenda for Further Change" – put forward the idea of a panel of eminent people to review the relations between the UN and civil society. The Panel of Eminent Persons on United Nations–Civil Society Relations [Note 2.2 for Members of the Panel] was established in June 2003, and issued its report in June 2004. It was known as the Cardoso Report after its chair, former Brazilian President Fernando Henrique Cardoso (1995–2003).

Today it is difficult to even find a copy of the Cardoso Report on the Internet. One could imagine that it is as if it has been systematically destroyed. It reminds me a little of the books *Shadow of the Wind* or *Inkheart*. In both of these stories, the antagonists are searching out copies of the books to destroy them while the heroes are trying to find a copy.

The Cardoso Report became the center of one of the first fights between civil society discourse and multi-stakeholder discourse. What had started as a discussion between civil society and the UN ended as an endorsement for the emerging multi-stakeholder approach. Upon launching the Cardoso Report, the UN reported:

> Highlighting the report's proposals, Mr. Cardoso, who was accompanied by fellow panel members Kumi Naidoo of South Africa and Mary Racelis of the Philippines, emphasized the need to expand the idea of multilateralism to include multiple actors, from civil society and business as well

The emergence of stakeholder democracy 71

as central and local governments, who had helped draw up and implement global agreements. He also underscored the importance of multi-stakeholder partnerships in a world where networking was no longer limited by national borders. 'The world has changed, and the United Nations must change too,' he said.

Other recommendations included forging stronger links between the local and global levels. Cardoso believed that this would help overcome democratic deficits in global governance. Cardoso said. The Panel had also proposed that the General Assembly, rather than the Economic and Social Council (ECOSOC), become the entry point for non-governmental organizations to the United Nations, in an accreditation process that depended less on politics and more on skills and expertise. In addition, it had suggested ways of reducing the imbalance between civil society groups in the North and South, including a fund to assist southern NGOs in attending United Nations activities (UN, 2004).

This recognition of the importance of stakeholders and the role that multi-stakeholder partnerships might play in implementing global decisions reflected the progress made since the 1992 Earth Summit. This included, as has been mentioned above, the LA21 actions, which for the first time engaged local and sub-national actors in the implementation of a UN agreement.

The panel promoted the idea of a two-way street of learning from the local and national experience while also developing global policy proposals then feeding back down to the national and local level for implementation and lessons learned. This idea represents an attempt to address a "democracy deficit," to which discussions at the UN have been prone.

Let's look at some of the recommendations numbered as they were in the report:

Proposal 1: In exercising its convening power, the United Nations should emphasize the inclusion of all constituencies relevant to the issue, recognize that the key actors are different for different issues and foster multi-stakeholder partnerships to pioneer solutions and empower a range of global policy networks to innovate and build momentum on policy options. Member States need opportunities for collective decision-making, but they should signal their preparedness to engage other actors in deliberative processes.

Proposal 2: The United Nations should embrace an array of forums, each designed to achieve a specific outcome, with participation determined accordingly. The cycle of global debate on an issue should include:

- Interactive high-level roundtable meetings to survey the issues.
- Global conferences to define norms and targets.
- Multi-stakeholder partnerships to put the new norms and targets into practice.
- Multi-stakeholder hearings to monitor compliance, review experience, and revise strategies.

72 *Felix Dodds*

Proposal 5: The Secretariat should foster multi-constituency processes as new conduits for discussion of United Nations priorities, redirecting resources now used for single-constituency forums covering multiple issues. The Secretariat, together with other relevant bodies of the United Nations system, should convene public hearings to review progress in meeting globally-agreed commitments. Being technical and concerned with implementation rather than the formulation of new global policies, such hearings could be convened by the Secretary-General on his own authority. Proceedings should be transmitted through the Secretary-General to the relevant intergovernmental forums.

Proposal 6: The General Assembly should permit the carefully planned participation of actors besides central Governments in its processes. In particular, the Assembly should regularly invite contributions to its committees and special sessions by those offering high-quality independent input. The participation arrangements should be made in collaboration with the relevant constituency networks. The Secretariat should help to plan innovative and interactive sessions linked to but outside the formal meetings.

Proposal 7: In order to mainstream partnerships (with the UN), the Secretary-General should, with the approval of Member States and donor support:

- Establish a Partnership Development Unit headed by a high-level staff member to help incubate and decentralize the partnership approach, guide the needed management shifts, ensure sound evaluations and provide support services throughout the United Nations.
- Identify partnership focal points throughout all United Nations organs and agencies.
- Review partnership issues in such coordination forums as the United Nations System Chief Executives Board for Coordination and its High-Level Committee on Programmes.
- Provide training in partnership development to Governments, civil society and other constituencies, as well as to United Nations staff.
- Periodically review the effectiveness of those efforts.

The Global Policy Forum (GPF), a think tank based in New York and Bonn, was very critical of the Cardoso Report:

The Cardoso Report is based on a new concept of global governance that has been gaining ground in international discourse. It underlines the role played in international politics by "multi-stakeholder approaches" and policy networks of public and private actors. The new paradigm of international cooperation sees in "global partnerships" (Kofi Annan), "coalitions for change" (James Wolfensohn), or in "global public policy networks" a mode of future international cooperation beyond the traditional multilateralism of nation-states.

The emergence of stakeholder democracy   73

Advocates of the new concept (who are largely conservative intellectuals and politicians in the United States and Europe) argue that global problems have reached dimensions that go beyond the competences and capacities of national governments. Governments and international organizations alone are no longer able to address ever-more-complex global policy issues. Therefore, argue the advocates, the business sector and civil society must be actively engaged in global governance (Global Policy Forum, 2004).

Note that the GPF incorrectly labeled the multi-stakeholder approach as conservative, missing its roots in the New Left and the Port Huron Statement, or at the very least the intent of the statement to enhance representative democracy through engaging other actors in the discourse. The criticism that came from some also echoed the criticism that was leveled by the Old Left in the 1960s in the drive for participatory democracy. The Old Left did not seek a broadening of participation in democracy, but rather a vanguard approach to political change. The Cardoso Report was welcomed by other stakeholder groups.

The UN started to produce material with and for different stakeholder groups more broadly. CIVICUS, a large global civil society network, found most of the report acceptable except the sections on industry and business. CIVICUS said:

> Some civil society representatives at the UN have immediately voiced concern that incorporating the Global Compact into the proposed OCEP may create confusion about the essential nature and identity of civil society vis-à-vis the for-profit sector. This may in turn become a distraction from the real issues concerning relations between the UN and civil society and unintentionally create an atmosphere of further distrust between civil society and large multinational corporations (LMC). Furthermore, some representatives believe that the proposed arrangement may actually reduce the space of civil society at the UN given the considerable asymmetries between it and LMCs (CIVICUS, 2004).

None of the recommendations of the Cardoso Panel were endorsed by governments. The report was never debated at the UN other than to be noted that it exists. Some of its recommendations and analyses did find their way into UN Agencies and Programmes.

After WSSD, the multi-stakeholder approach to policy-making had solidified in a number of UN bodies. Below are a few examples of where the stakeholder approach has taken root, some of which we will revisit at more depth in Chapter 6.

1 Convention on the Elimination of All Forms of Discrimination against Women (CEDAW)

The Convention on the Elimination of All Forms of Discrimination against Women was originally adopted by the UN General Assembly in 1979 as a kind of bill of rights for women. In 2000, the Optional Protocol to [that] Convention included Article 2:

74   *Felix Dodds*

Communications may be submitted by or on behalf of individuals or groups of individuals, under the jurisdiction of a State Party, claiming to be victims of a violation of any of the rights set forth in the Convention by that State Party. Where a communication is submitted on behalf of individuals or groups of individuals, this shall be with their consent unless the author can justify acting on their behalf without such consent (UN, 1999).

Stakeholders can submit documentation to CEDAW describing their country's adherence to (or lack of adherence to) the Convention. There is a template for those who want to do this, and submissions can be confidential. Any submission that isn't sufficiently substantiated will be seen as inadmissible. The State Party must within six months give a written explanation or statement clarifying the matter raised. If the accused party has not taken appropriate action, then CEDAW will investigate the party.

This involvement of stakeholders in the monitoring of a State Party's actions with respect to a UN Convention is unique, but represents a model that could also be used elsewhere.

2 United Nations Environment Programme (UNEP/UN Environment)

The idea of engaging with stakeholders spread also to UNEP. In 2004, it changed the name of one of its branches from "the NGO Branch" to the "Major Groups and Stakeholders Branch" recognizing the importance and impact of a stakeholder approach. UNEP also upgraded the leadership of the branch to the level of director (D1).

UNEP worked with different stakeholders to help them address relevant environmental issues. UNEP would over the coming years instigate a Major Group and stakeholder approach to Ministerial Round Table Dialogues, offering stakeholder seats to different participants. It wasn't always a full dialogue approach but more of a stakeholder representative approach. It differed from the CSD by just enabling a small number of stakeholders to be part of each of the Ministerial Round Table Dialogues. Some would represent their stakeholder group, others their own organization's view, and others just their own views. What was limited was capacity-building and long-term preparation to engage in the roundtables, because selection was done at the UNEP meeting and not before.

This meant that those participating were required to be highly confident individuals who understood how to engage in a free-flowing dialogue and not just read something out that had been prepared before. Too often this would be the case, although there were the exceptions to this. For example, in the 2009 Ministerial Dialogue, where stakeholders put forward the idea of Rio+20 supporting Brazil's call. This helped build momentum for the Summit which was agreed to be the UN General Assembly in December 2009. UNEP recognized that Major Groups and other stakeholders had a number of key roles:

The emergence of stakeholder democracy   75

- the perspectives they bring to the table.
- the valuable research and advocacy functions they perform.
- their capacity to raise public awareness and role in helping foster long-term, broad-based support for UNEP's mission.
- their role in disseminating relevant information effectively.
- their capacity to implement UNEP's work programme far beyond UNEP's capabilities.
- their capacity to adapt the global UNEP work programme to national or local realities.
- their role as watchdogs to foster accountability.

3 Strategic Approach to International Chemicals Management (SAICM)

SAICM was developed as a multi-stakeholder and multi-sectoral outcome of WSSD to address the sound management of chemicals throughout their life cycle. It was adopted at the First International Conference on Chemicals Management (ICCM1) on February 6, 2006, in Dubai. Its objectives are grouped under five themes: risk reduction; knowledge and information; governance; capacity-building and technical cooperation; and illegal international traffic.

SAICM planners note that

> The Declaration and Strategy are accompanied by a Global Plan of Action that serves as a working tool and guidance document to support implementation of SAICM and other relevant international instruments and initiatives. Activities in the plan are to be implemented, as appropriate, by stakeholders, according to their applicability (SAICM, 2018a).

Consistent with the multi-stakeholder and multi-sector approach, the Bureau for the Conferences has one member state from each UN region and four representatives of different stakeholder groups – in this case NGOs, Trade Unions and Industry.

The approach for this UN Conference is to see stakeholders as partners. As they prepare for the 2020 Conference, the instructions issued by the Secretariat are clear:

> In providing input to the Intersessional Process, stakeholders are encouraged to provide their views on SAICM and the sound management of chemicals and waste beyond 2020. Input is encouraged from all stakeholder groups and across sectors. Based on the inputs received, a further elaborated document will be prepared under the guidance of the Co-Chairs of the Intersessional Process to support the preparations for and inform discussions at the Second Meeting of the Intersessional Process, which is scheduled to take place in March 2018. All SAICM stakeholders will have opportunities, on multiple occasions, to provide input through an open, transparent and online consultative process (SAICM, 2018b).

76 *Felix Dodds*

In preparation for the 2020 Conference, an independent evaluation underlined the importance of a multi-stakeholder approach, noting that SAICM

> is unique in its ambition as an inclusive multi-stakeholder, multisector voluntary global policy framework on sound chemicals management. It has provided the space and opportunity for government and non-government actors alike, to discuss and deliberate on the management of chemicals throughout their life cycle in an atmosphere of trust and cooperation. The achievement of the level of cooperation, coordination and trust was reflected by all stakeholder groups (SAICM, 2018c).

SAICM has shown that governments and stakeholders can work together on serious contentious issues and come up with joint approaches that engage them all in making chemicals safer.

4 UN Committee on World Food Security

The reform of the Committee on Food Security (CFS) from an FAO standing committee to an intergovernmental, interagency, multi-stakeholder policy platform (Committee on World Food Security) was the product of a tough fight to wrest global food security governance from the Rome-based agencies (FAO, IFAD, WFP) by the World Bank, certain UN actors and the G20 in 2008 after the food crisis. The reformed institution now ensures that other stakeholders are heard in the general debate on food security and nutrition.

The CFS is made up of Members, Participants and Observers. The membership of the Committee is open to all member states of the Food and Agricultural Organization (FAO), the International Fund for Agricultural Development (IFAD) or The World Food Programme (WFP) and non-member states of FAO that are member states of the United Nations.

The CFS allows for structured input from stakeholders at the global, regional and national levels. Member states are encouraged to participate in CFS sessions at the highest level possible and agree to full inclusion of civil society and private sector actors through the Civil Society Mechanism (CSM) and Private Sector Mechanism (PSM). Participants in CFS processes include representatives of UN agencies and bodies, civil society and non-governmental organizations and their networks, international agricultural research systems, international and regional financial institutions, and representatives of private sector associations and private philanthropic foundations

The High-Level Panel of Experts on Food Security and Nutrition (HLPE) was created in October 2009 as an essential part of CFS to provide independent, scientific knowledge-based analysis and advice. HLPE reports are requested by CFS, and their findings and recommendations serve as a basis for CFS policy discussions.

The HLPE has two components. The first is a Steering Committee made up of internationally recognized experts in a variety of food security and nutrition-related fields. The second is a roster of experts that is used to build teams that

The emergence of stakeholder democracy 77

act on a project-specific basis to analyze and report on issues related to food security and nutrition. The Steering Committee includes experts from the CSM and PSM and has been co-chaired by a stakeholder representative (recently an expert from among Indigenous Peoples).

The CFS structure allows input from all stakeholders at global, regional and national levels. It is comprised of a Bureau and Advisory Group, a Plenary, the HLPE and the Secretariat. The Advisory Group includes representation of the CSM and PSM and for CFS workstreams agreed to under a Multi-Year Program of Work (MYPOW) and technical task teams (TTT) are formed representing various CFS actors. The Committee reports to the UN General Assembly through the Economic and Social Council (ECOSOC) and to FAO Conference.

The CFS Bureau and Advisory Group

The Bureau is the executive arm of the CFS. It is made up of a Chairperson and twelve member countries: two each from Africa, Asia, Europe, the Near East and Latin America and one each from North America and South West Pacific.

The Advisory group is made up of representatives from the 5 different categories of CFS participants. These are:

- UN agencies and other UN bodies.
- Civil Society Mechanism (Civil society and non-governmental organizations, particularly organizations representing smallholder family farmers, fisherfolks, herders, landless, urban poor, agricultural and food workers, women, youth, consumers and Indigenous Peoples).
- International agricultural research institutions.
- International and regional financial institutions such as the World Bank, the International Monetary Fund, regional development banks and the World Trade Organization.
- Private Sector mechanisms (Private sector associations and philanthropic foundations).

The Advisory Group helps the Bureau advance the Committee's objectives, in particular to ensure linkages with different stakeholders at regional, sub-regional and local levels and to ensure an ongoing, two-way exchange of information (CWFS, 2018).

The Committee had an independent review in 2016, the findings of which were published early in 2017. This is something that wasn't undertaken for the multi-stakeholder dialogues associated with the CSD. The fivefold purpose of the evaluation was to:

- Produce evidence regarding whether CFS, as a multi-stakeholder forum, is achieving the vision outlined in the Reform Documents and its expected outcomes.
- Assess the extent to which CFS is performing its roles outlined in the Reform Document, efficiently and effectively, and if so, with what impact.

78 *Felix Dodds*

- Review the working arrangements, including the multi-year programme of work of CFS, in order to assess how the decision-making processes and planning may be impacting effectiveness.
- Propose forward-looking recommendations to enable CFS to respond effectively to the emerging food security and nutrition challenges, to further strengthen its comparative advantages, and to enhance its leadership role in improving global food security and nutrition.
- Educate about multi-stakeholder collaboration, for which the CFS represents a possible model to be replicated (CFS, 2017).

The Committee on Food Security, like SAICM, has developed a formal process for engaging with stakeholders in policy development.

4 United Nations Framework Convention on Climate Change (UNFCCC)

Interest in engaging in the work of the UNFCCC grew from a relatively small base of 234 accredited organizations in 2001 (Conference of the Parties [COP] 7th session) to 960 accredited organizations by the time of the Copenhagen Climate Summit in 2009 (COP 15). The stakeholder groups recognized by the UNFCCC were the same ones as those identified in Agenda 21, but they had slightly different abbreviations:

- BINGO – Business and Industry NGOs
- ENGO – Environmental NGOs
- FANGO – Farmers and Agriculture NGOs
- IPO – Indigenous Peoples Organizations
- LGMA – Local Government and Municipal Authorities
- RINGO – Research and Independent NGOs
- TUNGO – Trade Union NGOs
- WGC – Women and Gender Constituency
- YOUNGO – Youth NGO

This was broadened out after 2016 to include additional stakeholders called "informal NGO groups." As of this writing, informal NGO groups include the following:

- Faith Based Organizations (FBOs).
- Education and Capacity-Building and Outreach NGOs (ECONGO).
- Parliamentarians.

There is a difference in the privileges of the nine groups relative to these new (since 2016) stakeholders. For the nine groups, benefits in belonging to one of the constituencies include the ability to provide input to joint statements/interventions and access to the plenary floor; office space at COPs, timely

The emergence of stakeholder democracy 79

information through constituency daily meetings, access to bilateral meetings with officials, and tickets for limited access meetings such as opening ceremonies.

New stakeholders were added to the original list because of the emerging recognition that the original nine stakeholders identified in 1992 in Agenda 21 were not the only stakeholders that should be engaged with. This point was raised by educators as far back as the third CSD so that the follow-up to adoption of Sustainable Development Goals expanded the number of stakeholders recognized by the new High-Level Political Forum.

The role of these stakeholder groups has also been underlined by the UN Secretary-General in his Climate Summit in 2014 and the planned summit in 2020 which will focus on enhancing the role of stakeholders in addressing climate change either singularly or with other stakeholders and governments in partnership. This was also reflected in the 2018 California Global Climate Action Summit.

> The Global Climate Action Summit will bring leaders and people together from around the world to "Take Ambition to the Next Level." It will be a moment to celebrate the extraordinary achievements of states, regions, cities, companies, investors and citizens with respect to climate action.
>
> It will also be a launchpad for deeper worldwide commitments and accelerated action from countries—supported by all sectors of society— that can put the globe on track to prevent dangerous climate change and realize the historic Paris Agreement.
>
> The decarbonization of the global economy is in sight. Transformational changes are happening across the world and across all sectors as a result of technological innovation, new and creative policies and political will at all levels.
>
> States and regions, cities, businesses and investors are leading the charge on pushing down global emissions by 2020, setting the stage to reach net zero emissions by midcentury (Global Climate Action Summit, 2018).

5 UN General Assembly Hearings

As the CSD was moving away from MSDs, the UN General Assembly was experimenting with civil society and the private sector hearings which were called "informal interactive." The first one was held on June 23 and 24, 2005, in preparation for the World Summit 2005. It reviewed the implementation of the Millennium Development Goals (MDGs).

Because this process was happening in the development arena where the stakeholder approach had not yet taken root, the hearings were considered a venue for national governments, civil society, and industry. This tripartite approach excluded local government and academia. It also funneled all other stakeholders together, reducing the potential impact of their individual voices.

80 *Felix Dodds*

By the 2008 High-Level Meeting (HLM) on AIDS the hearings were integrated into the meeting taking place on the first day of the HLM, and there was much more stakeholder involvement in preparation. The Office of the President of the General Assembly requested that UNAIDS set up a Civil Society Task Force "to support effective and active participation of civil society organizations and industry." It was a similar approach to the one used for the high-level AIDs review two years previously. Six months before the event, UNAIDS put out a global tender to establish a Civil Society Support Mechanism (CSSM) to support the participation of the CSOs.

> The Terms of Reference (TOR) outlined a series of criteria for taking part in the CSSM including the ability "to network widely and involve a range of groups including their key stakeholder groups".
>
> Six months before the HLM, the CSSM was won by a coalition of organisations based in the North and South and led by the International Council of AIDS Service Organisations (ICASO) and the International Women's Health Coalition (IWHC). In turn, the Civil Society Support Mechanism established an International Support Group which was composed of a core sixteen civil society advocates representing different constituencies, issues and regions of the world who were asked to oversee the activities of the Support Mechanism on a voluntary basis.
>
> Together, the Support Mechanism and the Support Group helped decide on the selection criteria for the Task Force, which included the following: two representatives of networks of people living with HIV; three representatives from marginalised communities (drug users, sex workers, and men who have sex with men); a representative of the UNAIDS PCB NGO delegates; a representative from the Civil Society Support Mechanism; and one representative from each of the following: labour sector, private/business sector, women's organisation, youth organisation, and faith based organisation. The Task Force TOR also stipulated that lead civil society organisations would need to be able to demonstrate their ability to network widely (Stakeholder Forum, 2009).

The outcome from the hearing was a summary report drafted by the President of the General Assembly. Although presented as a CSO process, it actually became a multi-stakeholder process because meeting attendees wanted to hear the different voices. On the positive side, stakeholders were able to choose their own representatives and to shape the theme and topics that the hearing addressed. The summary of the meeting reflected key messages and recommendations of the stakeholders, such as specifying that the definition of vulnerable groups should include "migrants, youth, prisoners, indigenous peoples and most at risk populations, as well as 'sex workers, men who have sex with men, and injecting drug users'" (Stakeholder Forum, 2009).

What was disappointing was the engagement by governments. As one of the NGOs interviewed by Emily Benson for the Stakeholder Forum Stakeholder Empowerment Project said: "Most important Governments walked around but

The emergence of stakeholder democracy 81

didn't participate meaningfully in dialogue. It looked like 'NGOs, speak between yourselves'" (Stakeholder Forum, 2009).

In reviewing the impact of the hearings, Stakeholder Forum suggested in its report that:

- Hearings are susceptible to a number of externalities such as the low participation of decision-makers and clashes with other events on the programme and clear follow-up strategies.
- Hearings can be prone to overly-generic topics and themes.
- Hearings need to be entrenched in a wider engagement strategy involving six-month preparatory process, repeated opportunities to meet decision-makers.
- Require clear communication strategy to non-participating stakeholders.
- Require clear links to the decision-making process.
- Require a clear civil society coordination process before the meeting (Stakeholder Forum, 2009).

In reviewing the different options for stakeholder engagement with the UN, Stakeholder Forum suggested a Stakeholder Standard (Box 3.1) to help synthesize the lessons learned over the last fifteen years.

Box 3.1 The Stakeholder Standard (Stakeholder Forum, 2009) authors

1 Allow at least six months for stakeholder coordination and consultation prior to an intergovernmental meeting.
2 Clearly define "civil society" into groups, constituencies or stakeholders who will be affected by the outcome of the intergovernmental meeting.
3 Ensure all civil society coordinators represent a wider network or stakeholder group and have the resources and mechanisms to reach out to those networks.
4 Involve a combination of stakeholders in the initial design and preparatory processes for an intergovernmental meeting.
5 Identify and publish a set of criteria for the appointment of key civil society partners and coordinators. Involve stakeholders to define those selection criteria.
6 Ensure that summaries of all meetings with key civil society partners and coordinators are made publicly available.
7 Cover the costs for travel and accommodation for key civil society partners and coordinators.
8 Include capacity building and training initiatives as part of the civil society engagement strategy.
9 Provide all civil society coordinators with the same information and the same documents at the same time.
10 Allow time and resources for the engagement strategy to be evaluated and assessed after the meeting has ended.

82 *Felix Dodds*

Rio+20 and stakeholders

In 2006 President Mbeki of South Africa, addressing the UN General Assembly, called the Johannesburg Plan of Implementation (JPoI) a "forgotten piece of paper."

It seemed as if sustainable development was still dead at the subsequent UN General Assembly on September 25, 2007. President Luiz Inácio Lula da Silva of Brazil, addressing the UN General Assembly at the opening of its annual leaders' week, called for a new sustainable development Summit (UN News, 2007). The concept note that Brazil had released suggested the following:

- Review high-level political commitments to sustainable development.
- Provide the opportunity to seek consensus on areas of sustainable development that have evolved considerably in the last decade such as international governance and the production and use of renewable energy.
- Address gaps in the implementation of Agenda 21 and Multilateral Environmental Agreements.
- Strengthen the role of governments, Major Groups and other stakeholders such as the private sector through partnerships of the sustainable development agenda (Brazil, 2008).

Brazil recognized the role of Major Groups and other stakeholders and would be a champion for them throughout the process.

At the same time, the Stakeholder Forum organized a three-day multi-stakeholder workshop with member states and UN Agencies and Programmes on November 11–13, 2008, in Donostia, Spain. The outcome was the Donostia Declaration. It suggested a Summit that would address the following:

- Green Economy.
- New and emerging issues.
- Review of commitments.
- Institutional reform at the UN level (Stakeholder Forum, 2008).

The Donostia Declaration also started to map out the role that stakeholders might play in the development and implementation of a new Summit.

> To address the challenges, UN agencies, national governments, stakeholders and the general public need to engage in a new partnership for sustainable development – a blueprint for sustainable development, looking forward to 2030. These challenges also require an empowered mandate and an activist agenda by the international community tasked with monitoring and encouraging sustainable development.
>
> Moving instead to an integrated summit process could not only bring the new ideas needed, but also bring energy and commitments from stakeholders to play an active and critical role in shaping and implementing agreements as they evolve (Stakeholder Forum, 2008).

The emergence of stakeholder democracy 83

Writing in 2008, Donastia Declaration signatories asserted that an Earth Summit in 2012 offers the platform for global stakeholders to work towards common goals that transcend national boundaries.

> It cannot and should not be built without broad and grassroots public support. If Earth Summit 2012 is to be a watershed, it requires a communications strategy that addresses and involves "real" people. The realities of the globalized world and the opportunities presented by the revolution in global communications allow groups of people with common concerns and interests to link up and mobilise to push for change.
>
> Earth Summit 2012 should be more than an intergovernmental process – it should be a focal point for mass mobilisation of a broad range of stakeholders around the world, from regional and local governments, to cities, businesses, trade unions, NGOs and all other Major Groups identified by Agenda 21 and other stakeholders.
>
> These constituencies need to be engaged and involved not just as lobbyists but as actors in their own right, capable of making their own proposals for, and pledges to, the sustainable development of the future – this allows innovations to arise that complement and reinforce international obligations. It offers a chance over the next three years to explore and create new partnerships for sustainable development to become a driver for real change in implementing agreements (Stakeholder Forum, 2008).

The UN General Assembly resolution in December 2009 had twenty-nine paragraphs, of which eight dealt with the presence of Major Groups and other Stakeholders. This included:

> Encourages the active participation of all Major Groups, as identified in Agenda 21 and further elaborated in the Johannesburg Plan of Implementation and decisions taken at the eleventh session of the Commission, at all stages of the preparatory process, in accordance with the rules and procedures of the Commission as well as its established practices related to the participation and engagement of Major Groups (UN, 2009).

For the Rio+20 Stakeholder Forum would play the role that the Centre for Our Common Future played for the 1992 Earth Summit minus the Global Forum. It facilitated:

- Training sessions for new Major Group and other stakeholder delegates.
- A daily multi-stakeholder newsletter.
- Translating relevant capacity building materials for international, regional and national NGOs participating in Rio+20 advocacy.
- Working with civil society actors and stakeholder organizations to support the dissemination of the Major Groups work around Rio+20.

84 Felix Dodds

- Providing organizational support for civil society representatives attending Rio+20 and the preparatory meetings facilitating the morning meetings of Major Groups and stakeholders.
- Identifying common advocacy positions between Civil Society Organizations by conducting analysis on Major Group's position papers and the zero-draft compilation document.
- Conducting town hall meetings with local governments, NGOs and UN agencies to discuss the Rio+20 themes.
- Creating websites and webpages to share background information and coverage of the Rio+20 processes.
- Creating participation guides for civil society actors to get involved in the political processes feeding into Rio+20 (Stakeholder Forum, 2012).

64th NGO Conference: "Sustainable Societies; Responsive Citizens"

The United Nations Department of Public Information (UNDPI) has held an annual UNDPI NGO Conference since 1947. In August 2010, the then-Director for Outreach Division of UNDPI, Eric Falt, approached Felix Dodds, Executive Director of Stakeholder Forum, to ask if he would consider chairing the 2011 UNDPI NGO Conference. Eric – who left UNDPI in late 2010 to become Assistant Secretary-General at UNESCO – had revolutionized the outreach work of UNDPI on a number of fronts.

The UNDPI 64th NGO Conference was held in Bonn, on September 3 to 5, 2011.

The conference was unique in its approach and timing to influence Rio+20 and subsequently the Sustainable Development Goals (SDGs). It brought together 2,000 stakeholders from around the world, as well as a number of key governments and all the top UN Agencies and Programmes, some at Executive Director level.

The conference happened two months after Paula Caballero had first proposed the idea of SDGs at the informal government meeting in Solo, Indonesia.

In light of the proposal from Colombia the DPI NGO conference outcome document was re-centered around the idea of Rio+20 adopting a set of SDGs. The conference agenda was a mix of high-level panels, workshops, training, capacity-building and networking. The central outcome was to be a Chair's text.

The production of the Chair's text was undertaken by drafts being sent out on stakeholder list servers in the month leading up to the conference. At the conference an expert group would collect input during the conference day sessions and integrate it overnight into the outcome document.

The DPI NGO conference Chair's text included seventeen SDGs – they weren't the same as those that were agreed by Heads of State in September 2015, but they covered most of the same areas. I have left in capitals the names of the goals but have grouped them where they appear in the same goal that was agreed in 2015.

SUSTAINABLE DEVELOPMENT GOALS

To achieve the goals of Rio + 20 in an ambitious, time-bound and accountable manner, we call upon governments in accordance with human rights, the principle of common but differentiated responsibilities, and respective capabilities to adopt the following draft Sustainable Development Goals together with the sub-goals, reasons and clarifications relating to each goal:

The goals below are aspirational. While some of these are based on commitments already made by governments and other stakeholders, others are proposed on the basis of advanced thinking among civil society organizations.

1 Sustainable Agriculture (SDG 2).
2 Basic Health (SDG 3).
3 Sustainable Livelihoods, Youth & Education (SDG 4).
4 Water (SDG 6).
5 Clean Energy (SDG 7).
6 Subsidies and Investment (SDG 8).
7 Green Cities (SDG 11).
8 Sustainable Consumption and Production (SDG 12).
9 Climate Sustainability (SDG 13).
10 Healthy Seas and Oceans: Blue Economy (SDG 14)
11 Biodiversity (SDG 15).
12 Healthy Forests (SDG 15).
13 Access to Redress and Remedy (SDG 16).
14 Access to Information (SDG 16).
15 Public Participation (SDG 16).
16 Environmental Justice for the Poor and Marginalized (SDG 16).
17 New Indicators of Progress (SDG 17) (UNDPI, 2011).

Much of the DPI NGO Chair's Text outcome document was then reflected in stakeholder submissions to the Zero Draft for Rio+20. Another indication of the changing nature of the relationship between the UN, governments and stakeholders was that the briefings produced for member states by the Rio+20 Secretariat included the recommendations from the UNDPI NGO Conference. This was helped by the fact that the event was a UN conference though it was the first time that this conference had been used in this way to influence a UN conference and an ongoing process.

Preparatory sessions for Rio+20

As we move towards current times, we'll look in more depth at the last two significant engagements with stakeholders, which are Rio+20 and the development of the Sustainable Development Goals.

86 *Felix Dodds*

The Rio+20 process generally operated in a similar way to the Commission on Sustainable Development in its engagement with stakeholders. The formal process did not go well, and in the end needed to be rescued by Brazil. Following the Rio+20 Summit, Brazil completed what had seemed impossible for the Bureau of the Conference and its co-chairs.

Stakeholders used a number of mechanisms to engage with member states outside the formal process of reading a 1–2-minute statement, usually at the end of a negotiating session. These included:

- Being on a member states delegation and feeding in directly to that member state's position.
- Organizing or participating in workshops with member states.
- Contributing as an expert for the numerous "Friends" groups that had grown up in New York as informal places for member states to discuss issues that they have a common interest in.
- Side events in the meetings.
- Organizing conferences on topics and inviting member states to attend.
- Informal dinners with member states to discuss a particular issue.
- Bilateral meetings in corridors and coffee bars (as is traditional).

One of the critical alliances that developed between a number of member states and stakeholders was over the idea that the SDGs would be an outcome of Rio+20, and, if not that, then they would be part of the review of the Millennium Development Goals (MDGs).

Rio+20 *and the stakeholder Dialogue days*

There were over 10,000 accredited and participating stakeholders at Rio+20 (in 2012) and over 82 million people connected to the Summit virtually, making it the first real Internet Summit.

Parallel to the formal final negotiations, Brazil initiated the Sustainable Development Dialogues with the support of the United Nations. These were held between June 16 and 19 prior to the High-Level Segment of Rio+20.

Some people felt that these Dialogues were the backup plan if the Rio+20 negotiations failed. The design of these Dialogues was conducted with representatives from the nine Major Groups, as well as other stakeholders such as foundations, academics and philanthropic organizations and parliamentarians. This was very much in the tradition of what had happened for the UN Habitat II Conference in 1996, while building new ICT capacity. The ten topics were chosen by the Brazilian government, in the last few months before Rio+20, in consultation with stakeholders.

To enable input from around the world, UNDP launched a set of online platforms creating a democratic public space for discussion on the ten themes of the Dialogues. The online Dialogues were facilitated by key academics from renowned academic institutions around the world.

The Dialogues aimed to have a set of concrete recommendations for each area. They were viewed and voted for in a public website.

Although the Dialogues would be too late to have an impact on the negotiations, the top three recommendations from each of the ten Dialogues were presented at the four High-Level Roundtables. This acted as a key resource and another input to what would be negotiated after Rio+20 in the new Sustainable Development Goals. The ten Dialogues and their top three recommendations, abridged for the readers' benefit – and aligned with the future SDGs – were shared with member states.

The other key initiative of Rio+20 were Voluntary Initiatives (VI) – not partnerships, but commitments by organizations to contribute something to deliver the future we want. Although no real oversight for VIs was envisioned, the commitments, it was hoped, would represent a "bottom-up," self-policing and peer-reviewed re-examination of the voluntary initiatives.

"Next to the negotiated outcomes, over 730 voluntary commitments were announced, with an estimated value of about US \$530 billion" (Seth, 2013).

Worried about the lack of any system of accountability for VI's NRDC and Stakeholder Forum their publication *Fulfilling the Rio+20 Promises* raised concerns very similar to those that were raised after the 2002 World Summit on Sustainable Development in relation at that time to multi-stakeholder partnerships, i.e., that there needed to be "mechanisms that facilitate accountability and transparency [for both types of commitment] ... in order to encourage the support, drive, and ownership of all actors and to ensure that the promises made at Rio+20 are [kept]" (NRDC, 2013).

"The Future We Want," the main outcome document for Rio+20, left no doubt about how member states saw the role that stakeholders had played in Rio+20:

> We, the Heads of State and Government and high-level representatives, having met at Rio de Janeiro, Brazil, from 20 to 22 June 2012, with the full participation of civil society, renew our commitment to sustainable development and to ensuring the promotion of an economically, socially and environmentally sustainable future for our planet and for present and future generations (UN, 2012a).

The outcome document also identified increasing roles and responsibilities for Major Groups and other stakeholders. It started to identify which "other stakeholders" should be involved:

> Sustainable development requires the meaningful involvement and active participation of regional, national and sub-national legislatures and judiciaries, and all Major Groups: women, children and youth, indigenous peoples, non-governmental organizations, local authorities, workers and trade unions, business and industry, the scientific and technological community, and farmers, as well as other stakeholders, including local communities,

88 *Felix Dodds*

volunteer groups and foundations, migrants, families as well as older persons and persons with disabilities. In this regard, we agree to work more closely with Major Groups and other stakeholders and encourage their active participation, as appropriate, in processes that contribute to decision making, planning and implementation of policies and programmes for sustainable development at all levels (UN, 2012a).

Rio+20 also set up the process for negotiating the Sustainable Development Goals.

Sustainable Development Goals

There is no question that without Rio+20 the process to replace the MDGs would have taken a different path, and it is clear that stakeholders played a critical role in this – though not all of them. There was continuous opposition at the beginning by government development agencies and initially most of the development NGOs, with Save the Children Fund being the last one to accept the idea of the SDGs during one of the last negotiating sessions (July 2014). After Rio+20 it was still not a done deal that the MDGs would be replaced by the SDGs.

It is important to remember that the development of the MDGs had no stakeholder engagement, they were set behind closed doors by an Inter-Agency UN Committee. Because of this the MDGs were initially condemned by many stakeholders. The development of the SDGs would be a model of how to not only engage in the development of the outcome document but also to therefore inspire the involvement of them in helping to deliver the final outcome document.

The UN Secretary-General's Report of June 2012, "Realizing the Future We Want," suggested the way forward to replace the MDGs includes:

> 125. The United Nations Development Group has taken steps to initiate outreach on several levels: (i) supporting at least 50 national level post-2015 dialogues in developing countries to complement the active debates already ongoing in developed countries; (ii) convening nine global thematic consultations; and (iii) stimulating and supporting citizen and stakeholder engagement with the post-2015 agenda, including through an interactive web portal, crowd-sourcing of views, and submission of video testimonies, meeting summaries and artwork (UN, 2012b).

The SDG processes would have a large number of inputs, ALL of which stakeholders were engaged in.

With Rio+20 happening back to back with the development of the SDGs the government officials in most cases were the same people as were many of the stakeholders that they already had built a relationship with.

The original nine stakeholder groups (Major Groups) were added to, due to the outcome from the Rio+20 document, to include the education community, people with disabilities, older people, and volunteers. In addition, some multi-stakeholder coalitions like Beyond 2015 were given space. This resulted in a real weakening of the Major Group organizations that were contributing to multi-stakeholder coalition but not the Major Group. Organizations didn't know where to put their energy and their lobbying (into the coalition or into the Major Groups).

The Beyond 2015 coalition had been set up by the big UK NGOs and other northern NGOs and had initially focused their input to the High-Level Panel of Eminent Persons on the Post-2015 Development Agenda set up by the UN Secretary-General. As Beyond's own evaluation confirmed, there was "initial dominance by Northern NGOs, particularly from the UK" (Beyond 2015, 2015: 9).

Unlike the development of the MDGs there were a number of ways to engage in the development of the SDGs for stakeholders and individuals.

National consultations

There were over 100 national consultations about what priorities for SDGs should be. These were facilitated in developing countries in most cases by UNDP.

These were the weakest of the outreach processes. The main reason for this was the timeline to enable effective input to the thematic consultations and then into the High-Level Panel just didn't work because they overlapped. The national consultations reached out to a wide range of stakeholders including governments at all levels, NGOs, women's groups, youth, trade unions, the private sector, media, universities and think tanks.

It was hoped that these national consultations would also contribute to positions articulated by governments in New York. The reality is that very few outcomes had impact, and, in many cases, government representatives in New York didn't even know they had happened.

Eleven thematic consultations

All the eleven thematic consultations would become SDGs or parts of an SDG. They were coordinated by two countries, one developed and one developing, and backed up by the relevant UN bodies and played an important role in soliciting expert opinion and early input which was shared with member states.

The MY World survey

The Rio+20 Conference had been a tryout for how to engage the general public using social media. The "MY World" survey claimed 10 million respondents,

90   *Felix Dodds*

though in reality it was closer to 7 million, because they forgot to stop the counter in 2014.

The MY World project was developed as a partnership between United Nations Development Programme, the UN Millennium Campaign, the Overseas Development Institute, the World Wide Web Foundation, and over 230 supporting stakeholder organizations around the world.

The survey asked people to vote for six out of sixteen priority areas for development and showed real-time results in an interactive graph on its website. According to the evaluation after the event: "70 percent of those responding had come from only five countries" (MDF, 2016: 18).

The survey below does show some similarities to issues taken up as SDGs but one of the major criticisms of the MY World survey was that there were "no real advocates for the outcomes within the negotiating chamber. The UN did pass on the outputs to the UN Task Team, but these was seldom picked up by stakeholders in their lobbying of member states" (Dodds et al., 2016).

Outcomes from the survey were funneled to the UN's Technical Support Team that developed the twenty-nine issue briefs for member states.

The survey at the beginning had a slot that was labeled "other," enabling new issues to be put in. This was stopped due to a very successful campaign by the World Society for Animal Protection (WSPA, now World Animal Protection). WSPA persuaded their members around the world to add "Animal Protection" in the "other" field in the survey. At one point, this "astroturfing" effort made Animal Protection the second most popular SDG issue, with only Health having more support. Then "other" was taken out and those votes were disallowed.

That highlights one of the problems with a participatory online approach: it can and often is a vehicle for particular views and positions to be highlighted not by the citizens but an effective political campaign machine.

Two High-Level Panel Reports (2011 and 2013) – with stakeholder consultations around the world

To support preparations for Rio+20, the UN Secretary-General had set up a High-Level Panel on Global Sustainability. The Panel report, "Resilient People, Resilient Planet: A future worth choosing," had extensive stakeholder consultation and the report supported the idea of SDGs.

The second High-Level Panel set up by the Secretary-General was the High-Level Panel of Eminent People on the Post-2015 Development Agenda, co-chaired by President Susilo Bambang Yudhoyono of Indonesia, President Ellen Johnson Sirlef of Liberia and Prime Minister David Cameron of the United Kingdom. The Panel membership was drawn from world leaders and stakeholders. Its report, "A New Global Partnership: Eradicate Poverty and Transform Economies Through Sustainable Development," had three meetings which were preceded by consultations with stakeholders enabling the members of the Panel to hear additional views. Panel members also met with stakeholders individually or collectively as did the secretariat of the Panel, which accepted written input. The final report suggested twelve SDGs.

The emergence of stakeholder democracy 91

1 End Poverty (SDG 1).
2 Empower Girls and Women to Achieve Gender Equality (SDG 5).
3 Provide Quality Education and Lifelong Learning (SDG 4).
4 Ensure Health Lives (SDG 3).
5 Ensure Food Security and Good Nutrition (SDG 2).
6 Achieve Universal Access to Water and Sanitation (SDG 6).
7 Secure Sustainable Energy (SDG 7).
8 Create Jobs, Sustainable Livelihoods and Equitable Growth (SDG 8).
9 Manage Natural Resource Assets Sustainably (SDG 15).
10 Ensure Good Governance and Effective Institutions (SDG 16).
11 Ensure Stable and Peaceful Societies (SDG 16).
12 Create a Global Enabling Environment and Catalyse Long-Term Finance
    (SDG 17).

Thirteen sessions of the Sustainable Development Goals Open Working Group

The Rio+20 outcome document, "The Future We Want," called for the establishment of an Open Working Group to develop a set of SDGs through a process that would be open to all stakeholders:

> 248. We resolve to establish an inclusive and transparent intergovernmental process on sustainable development goals that is open to all stakeholders, with a view to developing global sustainable development goals to be agreed by the General Assembly. An open working group shall be constituted no later than at the opening of the sixty-seventh session of the Assembly and shall comprise 30 representatives, nominated by Member States from the five United Nations regional groups, with the aim of achieving fair, equitable and balanced geographic representation. At the outset, this open working group will decide on its methods of work, including developing modalities to ensure the full involvement of relevant stakeholders and expertise from civil society, the scientific community and the United Nations system in its work, in order to provide a diversity of perspectives and experience. It will submit a report, to the sixty-eighth session of the Assembly, containing a proposal for sustainable development goals for consideration and appropriate action (UN, 2012a).

The establishment of the SDG-OWG turned out to be more difficult than people expected as it was so popular seventy countries had to share the thirty seats. This was a unique approach in the intergovernmental arena. The negotiations would be co-chaired by Ambassadors Macharia Kamau (Kenya) and Csaba Korosi (Hungary).

The first eight sessions of the SDG-OWG were broken down into issue clusters that might become areas for the SDGs. Each issue had a panel of experts, in most cases from stakeholders, present. This enabled member states to get a better understanding of the state of particular issues and the challenges they

92 Felix Dodds

faced. This also enabled a set of stakeholder experts to present their ideas for member states to consider.

Throughout the process, stakeholders had a chance at the end of sessions to make a short intervention. Meanwhile, co-chairs met with the stakeholders for an hour every day before the sessions started, and invited member states to attend. The OWG process featured workshops, Friends of different issue government sessions, side events and intense daily bilateral meetings between different stakeholders and governments to share ideas and views. What was built over the period of Rio+20 and the SDG negotiations was a community of member states, UN officials and stakeholders seeking the best ideas for a roadmap to address the critical issues in front of the global community.

A Secretary-General Report – The Road to Dignity by 2030: Ending Poverty, Transforming All Lives and Protecting the Planet Synthesis Report of the Secretary-General on the Post-2015 Agenda (2014)

As the SDG-OWG finished its final session recommending 17 SDGs and 169 targets, there was still lobbying from a number of governments led by the USA and UK to reduce the number of SDGs and targets. This created a strong reaction particularly from developing countries and stakeholders who made it clear to the UN Secretary-General that they did not expect his report to change anything the SDG-OWG had agreed to.

This solid support from the vast majority of governments and stakeholders ensured that nothing changed in the report as far as the SDGs and their targets. It also at last closed down the discussion on if there would be another set of MDGs in addition to the SDGs. The resulting Secretary-General's Report underlined there was just one process.

Eight Intergovernmental Negotiations Sessions (INS) – with active stakeholder engagement in all the meetings

The formal negotiations for the 2030 Agenda for Sustainable Development started in January 2015. Ambassador Kamau of Kenya was again a Co-Chair, this time with Ambassador Donoghue of Ireland. Again, the approach was one of engaging with stakeholders in all the sessions of the INS. Following the approach of the SDG-OWG, the ambassadors would meet with stakeholders prior to each session. The stakeholders also had a chance in each session to communicate their views in short statements.

Perhaps the most effective approach was that both the SDG-OWG and the INS member states were available to stakeholders throughout for bilateral meetings. The final outcome document, the "2030 Agenda for Sustainable Development," has at its center the SDGs and their targets that had gone through the OWG the previous year, but it also put those into a framework of values, and emerging issues that the process had not been able to address.

The emergence of stakeholder democracy 93

Finally, it enabled an institutional roadmap to help with the implementation of the whole agenda.

After the SDGs

This chapter has tried to show that engagement of stakeholders in the policy development at the UN since the Rio Earth Summit in 1992 has been extensive. The development of the SDGs is the best example to date of how engaging stakeholders in the policy development has resulted in energizing them to become advocates helping to execute on and deliver policies.

Stakeholders have been reorganizing their priorities around helping to deliver the SDGs on the ground. This has included the major foundations through "SDGfunders.org" where they are reporting their funding along the SDGs and their targets. They are also creating national platforms of funders in diverse places like the Arab Region, Indonesia, Nigeria, Ghana and Kenya. By doing so they are bringing in foundations which are for the first time ever aligning their priorities to helping to fund an international agreement, the Sustainable Development Goals.

In the area of industry, a coalition of Global Reporting Initiative (GRI), the UN Global Compact and the World Business Council for Sustainable Development (WBCSD) have developed the SDG Compass – A Guide for Business Action to Advance the Implementation of the SDGs and their Targets to support companies in aligning their strategies with the SDGs and in measuring and managing their contributions.

In addition to individual stakeholders, you can find the large NGOs such as Worldwide Fund for Nature, Oxfam, Article 19 and "even" Save the Children Fund reorganizing around the SDGs. What has been surprising is that you are also finding groups such as Donkey Sanctuary focusing on what their contribution to helping to deliver the SDGs can be. They see in many developing countries, particularly in Africa, that donkeys play a critical role in enabling the local economy, helping to empower women and assisting with disaster relief in difficult terrains.

Local and sub-national councils are organizing their own "homegrown" implementation of the SDGs through their own stakeholders. After all, over 60 percent of the SDGs will be delivered at the local level.

Conclusion

We live in a time where there is widespread uncertainty about the foundations on which a democracy is built. This requires even more than before for stakeholders to take up their responsibility to work with governments to strengthen and stabilize democracy.

Winston Churchill's well-known appreciation for democracy bears repeating:

> Many forms of Government have been tried, and will be tried in this world of sin and woe. No one pretends that democracy is perfect or all-wise.

94   *Felix Dodds*

> Indeed, it has been said that democracy is the worst form of Government except for all those other forms that have been tried from time to time ... (Churchill, 1947).

In this chapter and the previous chapter, we have tried to show how stakeholder democracy has built on other forms of democracy and most importantly how it can be seen as an evolution of representative democracy. It is not an attempt to replace representative democracy; it is a way of strengthening representative democracy.

The path from representative democracy to participatory democracy is, and will be, perhaps longer than some of us had hoped. But the authors of this book do believe that it is the right path.

In the last two decades, we have seen the evolution of tools that enable individual voices to be heard. We have at the same time witnessed attacks on facts, science and truth.

In many countries, instead of working with stakeholders, governments have been reducing the space for them. They often see them as an opposition to their policies rather than as potential experts helping to develop those policies or partners in delivering them. In Chapter 5 we will look at examples such as National Councils for Sustainable Development as a mechanism to embed stakeholder democracy as a means not only for delivering the SDGs but for helping the development of representative democracy.

In August 2018, former New York Mayor Rudy Giuliani said: "truth is relative." Counselor to the President Kellyanne Conway has called out "alternative facts." All this has been fueled by the President of the United States, who has clocked in the 649 days of his Presidency as of November 2, 2018 – according to the *Washington Post*: "President Trump has made 6420 false or misleading claims" (Washington Post, 2018).

That's an average of nearly 9.9 false or misleading claims a day according to their fact checking.

The promise, as the new century matured, has dissipated into one of the most challenging and potentially dangerous periods for humanity.

As the 1992 Rio Earth Summit ended and governments left with what had been called the "Blueprint for the Twenty-First Century" (Agenda 21) hope for a climate and biodiversity agreement was in the air.

Many of those critical issues that were identified in 1992 have not been addressed, not least because many thought that there was more time and that they could be dealt with tomorrow, but tomorrow is today. Time is running out.

The agreement in 2015 on the Sustainable Development Goals and the Paris Climate Agreement perhaps gave humanity the last chance to choose a path that would ensure equity, fairness and sustainability for all.

This path is one that has been designed and created by governments, the UN and stakeholders, meaning ultimately all of us. Both these major agreements are testimony to a positive engagement with stakeholders in the policy agreement.

The emergence of stakeholder democracy   95

Because of this there is a level of stakeholder engagement in helping to implement these agreements that has not been seen before. In the following chapters, we deal with some of the key elements that make multi-stakeholder partnerships such a critical part of the sustainable development ecosystem.

References

Abzug, B. (1992) Speech at UN. Available online at: https://www.brainyquote.com/a uthors/bella_abzug

Armstrong, N. (1969) Speech from the Moon. Available online at: https://en.wikipedia. org/wiki/Neil_Armstrong

Beyond 2015 (2015) Beyond 2015 Campaign Final Evaluation. Available online at: http://beyond2015.org/final-evaluation-beyond-2015

Brazil (2008) Concept Note on Rio+20. Brasilia: Government of Brazil.

Centre for Our Common Future (1990, December) *Brundtland Bulletin*. Geneva: Centre for Our Common Future.

Churchill, W. (1947) The Worst Form of Government. The International Churchill Society. Available online at: https://winstonchurchill.org/resources/quotes/the-worst-form-of-government/

CIVICUS (2004) Too Close for Comfort: Should Civil Society and the Global Compact Live Under the Same UN Roof?Washington: CIVICUS. Available online at: https://www.globalpolicy.org/component/content/article/226/32334.html

Commission on Global Governance (1995) *Our Global Neighbourhood*. Oxford: Oxford University Press.

Committee on Food Security (CFS) (2017) Evaluation of the Committee on World Food Security. Rome: CWFS. Available online at: http://www.fao.org/fileadmin/templates/cfs/Docs1617/Evaluation/CFS_Evaluation_Draft_Report_version5_31Jan2017-clean.pdf

Committee on World Food Security (CWFS) (2018) CFS Structure. Rome: CFS. Available online at: http://www.fao.org/cfs/home/about/structure/en/

CSD NGO Steering Committee (1994) Terms of Reference. New York.

Dodds, F., Gardiner, R., Hales, D., Hemmati, M. and Lawrence, G. (2002) Post Johannesburg: The Future of the UN Commission on Sustainable Development. London: Stakeholder Forum.

Dodds, F., Strong, M. and Strauss, M. (2012) *Only One Earth: The Long Road via Rio to Sustainable Development*. London: Routledge.

Dodds, F., Donoghue, D. and Roesch, L. R. (2016) *Negotiating the Sustainable Development Goals: A Transformational Agenda for an Insecure World*. London: Routledge.

ELCI (1991) Agenda ya Wananchi. Nairobi: Environment Liaison Centre International.

Global Climate Action Summit (2018) About the Summit. San Francisco: GCAS. Available online at: https://www.globalclimateactionsummit.org/about-the-summit/

Global Policy Forum (2004) Comments by Global Policy Forum on the Cardoso Panel Report. New York: Global Policy Forum. Available online at: https://www.globalpolicy.org/images/pdfs/08gpf.pdf

Gore, A. (1995) Quote from a letter from Vice President Gore to UNED-UK reproduced in the UNED-UK Annual Report 1995/1996. London: Stakeholder Forum.

Harding, N. (1992) *The Marxist-Leninist Detour in Democracy: The Unfinished Journey*. Edited by John Dunn. Oxford: Oxford University Press.

96 Felix Dodds

Howell, M. (2004) A thesis submitted in fulfillment of the requirements for the degree of Doctor of Philosophy in Planning: Sustaining Dialogue, A Study of the Multi-Stakeholder Dialogues at the United Nations Commission on Sustainable Development, The University of Auckland.

Kaul, I. and Menoza, U. (2003) Advancing the Concept of Global Public Goods in Kaul, I., Conceircao, P., Le Goulven, K. and Mendoza, R. U. (eds.), *Providing Global Public Goods: Managing Globalization*. New York: Oxford University Press.

Lawrence, G. (1998) The Future of Local Agenda 21 in the New Millennium. London: Stakeholder Forum. Available online at: http://www.stakeholderforum.org/mediafiles/UNED%20millenium%20paper2.pdf

Lerner, S. (1992) *Earth Summit: Conversations with Architects of an Ecologically Sustainable Future*. Bolinas, CA: Common Knowledge Press.

Lindner, C. (1992a, November) The Centre for Our Common Future: Rio Reviews. *Network*. Geneva: Centre for Our Common Future.

Lindner, C. (1992b) Interview with Chip Lindner in Lerner, S., *Earth Summit: Conversations with Architects of an Ecologically Sustainable Future*. Bolinas, CA: Common Knowledge Press.

Litsios, S. (1994) Comments at the UNED-UK Round Table on Health and Environment as republished in the UNED-UK Annual Report 1993/1994. London: Stakeholder Forum.

MacKenzie, B. M. (1997) Comments in the UNED-UK Annual Report 1996/1997. London: UNED-UK.

MDF (2016) Outcome Evaluation Report: Building the Post 2015 Development Agenda – Open and Inclusive Consultations for the United Nations Development Group. Ede: MDF.

Merriam-Webster (2018) Definition of Globalization. Available online at: https://www.merriam-webster.com/dictionary/globalization

Moore, F. (2001) Comments made on the Bonn 2001 Multi-Stakeholder Dialogue found in the Annual Report of Stakeholder Forum 2001/2002. London: Stakeholder Forum. Available online at: http://www.stakeholderforum.org/sf/mediafiles/sf_annual_report_02.pdf

Morganthau, H. (1944) Quote in What are the Bretton Woods Institutions?Washington, DC: Bretton Woods Project. Available online at: https://www.brettonwoodsproject.org/2005/08/art-320747/

NRDC (2013) Fulfilling the Rio+20 Promises: Reviewing Progress since the UN Conference on Sustainable Development. Washington, DC: NRDC and Stakeholder Forum. Available online at: https://www.nrdc.org/sites/default/files/rio-20-report.pdf

Seth, N. (2013) Foreword in Fulfilling the Rio+20 Promises: Reviewing Progress since the UN Conference on Sustainable Development. Washington, DC: NRDC and Stakeholder Forum. Available online at: https://www.nrdc.org/sites/default/files/rio-20-report.pdf

Stakeholder Forum (2003) The Future of the CSD Survey Report. London: Stakeholder Forum.

Stakeholder Forum (2008) Donostia Declaration. London: Stakeholder Forum.

Stakeholder Forum (2009) Stakeholder Forum Empowerment Project. London: Stakeholder Forum.

Stakeholder Forum (2012) The Nature of Stakeholder Engagement at Rio+20. London: Stakeholder Forum.

Strategic Approach to International Chemicals Management (SAICM) (2018a) SAICM Overview from their website. Available online at: http://www.saicm.org/About/SAICMOverview/tabid/5522/language/en-US/Default.aspx

The emergence of stakeholder democracy   97

Strategic Approach to International Chemicals Management (SAICM) (2018b) SAICM Call for Input to the Intersessional Process on SAICM and the Sound Management of Chemicals and Waste Beyond 2020. Available online at: http://www.saicm.org/Resources/ SAICMStories/Cochairssummarycallforinput/tabid/5918/language/en-US/Default.aspx

Strategic Approach to International Chemicals Management (SAICM) (2018c) Draft Report: Independent Evaluation of the Strategic Approach from 2006–2015. Geneva: SAICM. Available online at: http://www.saicm.org/Portals/12/documents/meetings/ IP2/IP_2_4_Independent_Evaluation.pdf

Strong, M. (1972) Opening Speech to the UN Conference on Human Environment. Available online at: https://www.mauricestrong.net/index.php/opening-statement

Tebbit, N. (1981, October 15) Speech to the Conservative Party Conference. Available online at: https://en.wikiquote.org/wiki/Norman_Tebbit

UNCSD (1999). Report on the Seventh Session 1 May and 27 July 1998 and 19–30 April 1999. New York: UN Economic and Social Council. E/CN.17/1999/20.

United Nations (1946) United Nations Charter Article 71. New York: UN. Available online at: http://www.un.org/en/charter-united-nations/

United Nations (1968) ECOSOC Resolution 1296 (XLIV). New York: UN. Available online at: https://www.globalpolicy.org/component/content/article/177-un/31832.html

United Nations (1992) Agenda 21. New York: UN. Available online at: https://sustaina bledevelopment.un.org/content/documents/Agenda21.pdf

United Nations (1993a) UNGA Resolution 47/191: Institutional Arrangements to Follow up the United Nations Conference on Environment and Development. Available online at: http://www.un.org/documents/ga/res/47/ares47-191.htm

United Nations (1993b) Mandate for the Commission on Sustainable Development. New York: UN. Available online at: https://sustainabledevelopment.un.org/intergovernm ental/csd/mandate

United Nations (1997) Overall Progress Achieved since the United Nations Conference on Environment and Development Report of the Secretary-General Addendum Role and Contribution of Major Groups. New York: UN. Available online at: http://www. un.org/ga/search/view_doc.asp?symbol=E/CN.17/1997/2/Add.22%20&Lang=E

United Nations (1999) Optional Protocol to the Convention on the Elimination of All Forms of Discrimination against Women (A/54/L.4). New York: UN. Available online at: https://documents-dds-ny.un.org/doc/UNDOC/GEN/N99/774/73/PDF/N9977473. pdf?OpenElement

United Nations (2004) Press Briefing by Panel on UN – Civil Society Relations. New York: UN. Available online at: http://www.un.org/press/en/2004/Cardoso062104.doc.htm

United Nations (2009) Implementation of Agenda 21, the Programme for the Further Implementation of Agenda 21 and the Outcomes of the World Summit on Sustainable Development. New York: UN. Available online at: https://documents-dds-ny.un.org/ doc/UNDOC/LTD/N09/632/68/PDF/N0963268.pdf?OpenElement

United Nations (2012a) The Future We Want. Rio de Janeiro: UN. Available online at: http://www.un.org/disabilities/documents/rio20_outcome_document_complete.pdf

United Nations (2012b) Realizing the Future We Want. New York: UN. Available online at: http://www.undp.org/content/undp/en/home/librarypage/poverty-reduction/realizing-th e-future-we-want/

United Nations Department of Economic and Social Affairs (UNDESA) (2002) Second Local Agenda 21 Survey: Background Paper No 15, produced by ICLEI. New York: UN.

98 *Felix Dodds*

United Nations Department of Public Information (UNDPI) (2011) Declaration of the 64th Annual UN DPI/NGO Conference Chair's Text Sustainable Societies; Responsive Citizens. Bonn: UNDPI. Available online at: http://www.stakeholderforum.org/filea dmin/files/Bonn%20Declaration%202011.pdf

UNED-UK (1993) UNED-UK Aims and Objectives in Annual Report 1993–1994. London: Stakeholder Forum.

United Nations Environment Programme (UNEP) (1972) Constitution of UNEP. Nairobi: UNEP. Available online at: http://web.unep.org/exhibit/

UN News (2007) President Lula of Brazil Proposes 'Rio + 20' to Follow on Earth Summit. Available online at: http://www.un.org/apps/news/story.asp?NewsID= 23952&Cr=general&Cr1=debate#.UX4MtcoteVerdia

Washington Post (2018, November 2) President Trump Has Made 6,420 False or Misleading Claims over 649 Days. *Washington Post*. Available online at: https://www.wa shingtonpost.com/politics/2018/11/02/president-trump-has-made-false-or-misleading-claims-over-days/?utm_term=.659a8d63bd85

Young, R. O. (1997) *Global Governance: Drawing Insights from the Environmental Experience*. Cambridge, MA: MIT Press.

4   Civil society discourse

Introduction

> Civil society has become a notoriously slippery concept, used to justify radically different ideological agendas, supported by deeply ambiguous evidence, and suffused with many questionable assumptions (Edwards, 2004).

As mentioned in Chapter 3 there have been two different (and rival) discourses at play around the best way to develop and implement policy, particularly at the global level. The first is a stakeholder discourse which is inclusive of everyone and the second is a civil society discourse which excludes key actors in society and which tries to create one voice for all the others.

Chapter 3 dealt with how the stakeholder approach to policy development and partnerships has developed and detailed its strengths and weaknesses. This chapter examines three different theories within the civil society discourse along with the pros and cons of its use at the global level. It explores questions such as:

- Are advocates and practitioners of civil society actually reducing space for non-state actors and excluding significant actors by doing so?
- Is there a set of core beliefs and values that are consistent across civil society actors and advocates?
- Are civil society actors, advocates and academics in the northern hemisphere dictating the terms of global discourse?
- How can Non-Governmental Organizations (NGOs) be part of civil society if they are basically acting as service agents for governments?
- How can NGOs be critical of certain companies if they are accepting funding from companies that arguably contribute to the problems they are working to address?
- Why do some Civil Society Organizations (CSOs) obstruct the participation of others?
- Whom or what does civil society truly represent?

100   Felix Dodds

Michael Edwards is the former Director of the Ford Foundation's Governance and Civil Society Program. The quote from him above emphasizes the reality of contemporary discourse about civil society. We would be remiss if we did not note that while Edwards was still optimistic about civil society when he made the observation above, he also went on to say to say that it was also tempting to dismiss the concept of civil society as "hopelessly compromised."

Edwards found a glimmer of hope in the realization that civil society, if subject to a rigorous critique, could "re-emerge" (his word) to offer "significant emancipation potential, explanatory power, and practical support to problem solving in both established and emerging democracies."

Civil society as a term derives from the phrase *koinōníapolitikḗ*, which Aristotle coined for his book *Politics* in the fourth century BC. Aristotle viewed civil society as citizens living in a particular community and participating in a set of shared interests.

"Community" in this context can mean either a geographical community or a community of interest. J. Bartram (2018) points out that in one sense, "community" serves as a synonym for settlement, a piece of geographical space with human habitants that is manifestly distinct from other adjacent spaces. In this usage, there is no suggestion of interaction or social capital [*meaning economic resources obtained from interactions between businesses and individuals or networks of individuals*], although social capital is likely to be created in some types of settlements. "Community" can also mean a group of people who are associated by a common interest or means of communication. They may or may not reside in a single settlement, but if they're part of a settlement, they're generally a subset of the inhabitants there. Communities of interest resemble what we tend now to call "networks."

Chapter 2 noted the hypothesis that, over time, representative democracy progresses slowly towards participatory democracy. For a participatory democracy to exist, a number of key elements need to be in place, not least people having a level of respect and civility for each other that seems to be farther away today than it was at the beginning of the twenty-first century.

Some history may be helpful: Prior to the eighteenth century, civil society was thought of as a "social contract." Two of the most prominent thinkers of the Enlightenment, John Hobbes and John Locke, didn't see civil society as separate from the state. To them, it represented the move from absolute monarchy to a new dynamic with the increasing political rights of parliaments and other representative bodies.

"Those who are united into one body and have a common established law and judicature to appeal to, with authority to decide controversies between them and punish offenders, are in civil society one with another," Locke wrote in 1690.

In the late eighteenth and early nineteenth century, the definition of "civil society" began to encompass the market. Friedrich Hegel is credited with helping to develop this new meaning (Hegel, 1820).

Karl Marx offered an alternative to the Hegelian conception of civil society as a stage of difference that properly intervenes between the family and the state. He believed that civil society helped the survival of capitalism.

In the Marxist view, the state is an agent of the bourgeois class, and a pernicious actor that confines civil society to a competition between private interests. Contemporary academic Jichang Wen argues that, for Marx, the development of civil society is the same as the process by which individual interests become class interests, because civil and political society (different but related concepts) are derived from "social division" (Wen, 2015).

Hegel's ideal is metaphysical, and Marx's is societal, but there is still a massive problem with this kind of thinking, in that it arguably negates or dilutes human agency by seeing everything as following from forces beyond our control.

In the 1980s, intellectuals challenging the Soviet occupation of Eastern Europe based some of their opposition on a renewed appreciation for civil society. As President Václav Havel commented nearly a decade after leading a coalition called the Civic Forum and becoming the first freely elected president of Czechoslovakia:

> While a totalitarian system of the Communist type could now and then coexist with private ownership, and sometimes even with private enterprise, it could, as a matter of principle, never coexist with a developed civil society. Genuine civil society is the truest fundamental of democracy, and totalitarian rule can never, by definition, be reconciled with that. It was therefore no coincidence that one of the most intense and possibly the most fateful attack that accompanied the installation of Communist power was an attack on civil society (Havel, 1999).

The Civic Forum under Havel's leadership was a key actor while it opposed the Communist regime. After the fall of Communism, it split along traditional political and ideological lines, with the largest portion becoming the right-of-center Civic Democratic Party. Other examples might be the fall of the Berlin Wall, the rise of the successful Solidarity movement in Poland, the short-lived "Arab Spring" of 2010–2012, and the so-called "Ukrainian Revolution" of 2014.

Outside Europe at approximately the same time, intellectuals in Latin America used musings about civil society as part of the rationale from which to challenge right-wing dictators. In short, civil society as a concept has often been used as a rallying call from which to question both totalitarian regimes and intransparent multilateral organizations. Nigel Martin and Rajesh Tandon of the Montreal International Forum addressed this second usage:

> Although citizens around the world are being increasingly governed by multilateral institutions such as the WTO or the World Bank, there are no elected officials overseeing these bodies and consequently, no electorate to whom they would be truly accountable (Martin and Tandon, 2014).

102   *Felix Dodds*

That said, some people in developing countries regard civil society as a concept imposed on them by intellectuals in the northern hemisphere. Alex Awiti, for example, points out that

> Africans must deal with the fact that civil society in Africa is dominated by a legion of development NGOs funded by foreign donors. These NGOs are large transnational organizations which are seen as institutions of transnational governance ... capable of challenging the state's legitimacy and/or undermining national sovereignty (Awiti, 2016).

We will return to this issue later. First, let's review the three main interpretations of civil society: the school of associational life, the school of the good society, and the school of the public sphere.

Civil society as associational life

Civil society as associational life builds on European political theory from the nineteenth and early twentieth centuries. Key figures include Alexis de Tocqueville, Proudhon and Duguit. Tocquville's *Democracy in America* promotes the importance of associations among its citizens. Tocqueville referred not only to political associations, but also to non-governmental groups such as recreational leagues, clubs and professional organizations. A more recent example would be the Rotary organization.

By joining such clubs, participants generate social capital in their respective communities. This school of thought stresses the role of volunteerism and community action as a balance against dominance by the state. In doing so, it offers a level of accountability and has been equated with a more liberal individualism while facilitating social cooperation at the same time. Associational life does not include family, industry or the state, which are, of course, major components of any society.

Within this civil society discourse are elements of mutualism and cooperative pluralism.

"Mutualism: the doctrine or practice of mutual dependence as the condition of individual and social welfare" (Merriam-Webster, 2018).

"Cooperative Pluralism: the process of negotiation between the government and two opposing interest groups" (McFarland, 1993).

At the center of association life is voluntary action, often through well-established NGOs and civic organizations. The building of social capital in a society is critical to reducing political ghettos whether they be left or right wing. Increasingly in 2018, we see people operating in social and traditional media platforms that reinforce their own views. Associational life can break some of this self-segregation up, at least theoretically enabling debate or discussion that would not otherwise happen.

While associational life is generally applauded, it's not always helped by platforms that claim to enable association. The ubiquity of the Internet and the

Civil society discourse   103

concomitant rise in the use of social media has fostered much divisiveness. Any "association" can now be done both in a community of place and in a community of interest, but social capital generated that way does not necessarily benefit everyone in a given community.

Looking specifically at right-wing networks (although much the same could be said of their left-wing networks), Arthur Bradley (2018) describes the problem of inaccurate information as a function of the fact that on social media platforms, "anyone – irrespective of credentials – can take it upon themselves to be a journalist, essayist, political agitator, or publisher of information." Moreover, he notes with respect to a study of "fake news" on Twitter

> Because fake stories are often deliberately inflammatory and are specifically designed to provoke an emotional reaction, they are shared more quickly and more widely by Twitter users – meaning that they end up on more people's newsfeeds than real stories.

One consequence of this ease of publication, Bradley says, is that

> If false stories relate to a subject like immigration – already a politically-sensitive issue which can evoke emotive and sometimes ill-informed opinion (most Europeans vastly overestimate the population of Muslims in their country, for example) – then they are sure to encourage radicalisation and political polarisation.

Moreover, Bradley's "amicus brief in favor of professional gatekeeping" notes that "Many internet users do not think to question the reliability of the content that they read online."

Association life can be romanticized, so it is important to realize that it can also be exclusive where you find particular clubs and associations based on religion, class or gender. The voluntary, state-free (e.g., unregistered) and spontaneous nature of associations also ensures that most of them have internal accountability but not external accountability, although their adherents typically regard this as a strength rather than weakness.

Associations are not necessarily neutral politically. There are many instances of governments offloading responsibilities to the nonprofit sector but not working to ensure that those organizations are equipped for success. This is irresponsible but looks good on the balance sheet. This shuffling of responsibility ultimately weakens the ability of governments to provide critical social services. Moving services from democratic oversight to voluntary oversight is often problematic, as is moving public sector services to the private sector. In both cases, measures undertaken to reduce costs can adversely affect service levels and oversight mechanisms.

104 Felix Dodds

Civil society as the good society

There are a variety of views of what a "good society" looks like, just as there are a variety of views of what "civil society" means. One school of thought suggests that the two terms are synonymous and work in tandem to enrich modern liberal democratic states.

This school of thought holds that a "good society" recognizes human rights, democracy, equality and freedom. At its heart would be Karl Popper's theory of democracy, which is not based on who should rule, but rather on how to remove a bad ruler without using violence. To achieve this, the theory goes, the state would need to embrace transparency, accountability and justice as fundamental principles.

Popper argued for open societies and against closed societies, or – as he called them – "tribal societies." Today he would see the centralization of information into political ghettos through traditional or social media platforms as incompatible with an open society, because that centralization reduces transparency and accountability.

Might Popper even extend his criticism to look at how civil society organizations themselves operate? He did warn us (in his seminal 1945 book, *The Open Society and Its Enemies*) that the road would not be easy, writing that a civilization that

> might perhaps be described as aiming at humanness and reasonableness ... has not yet recovered from the shock of its birth — the transition from the tribal or "enclosed society," with its submission to magical forces, to the "open society" which sets free the critical powers of man (Popper, 1945).

Popper also speculated that the shock of that transition was one of the factors that contributes to the rise of reactionary movements "which have tried, and still try, to overthrow civilization and return to tribalism."

Common notions of what is good have changed over the years – in part because of the growing interaction of people with each other, beginning with local communities and progressing to regions, countries, continents and even the planet. Those interactions provide a glimpse of the core values that might comprise a good society.

Many civil society organizations advocate supporting liberal democratic values, but are not themselves democratic. Even as advocates for democratizing the multilateral space, they often do not embrace the values they fight for in their own structures and interactions. For example, many nonprofit organizations do not let their staff join trade unions. This constraint includes the well-publicized charges of union-busting at the Los Angeles office of Greenpeace (Blake, 2002).

The "good society" school of thought includes business and industry in its understanding. Over the past twenty-five years, for instance, a growing number of businesses and industries have embraced the concept of corporate social

Civil society discourse 105

responsibility (CSR). This development has been supported by the emergence of tools to help monitor company activity in environmental, social and governance (ESG) reporting.

We have seen stock exchanges around the world introduce mandatory reporting on their activity in ESG realms as a listing requirement for companies. The publishing of sustainable development strategies and the reporting on companies' environmental impacts using tools such as those of the Global Reporting Initiative (GRI) are among the ways individuals and communities can now judge companies and their contributions to be part of a "good society."

An important step was taken in increasing transparency for multinational companies in 2016 with the publication of the Corporate Benchmarking on Human Rights. This is a method of benchmarking companies based on the delivery of standards outlined in the UN Guiding Principles on Business and Human Rights. The Principles are not legally binding, but have been endorsed by many stakeholders including Oxfam (2013) and the United States (in 2014 for international business).

Some on the political left are critical of this rights-based approach:

> The United Nations Guiding Principles locate human rights at the centre of the corporate social responsibility agenda and provide a substantial platform for the development of business and human rights policy and practice. The initiative gives opportunity and focus for the rethinking and reconfiguration of corporate accountability for human rights. It also presents a threat: the danger, as we see it, is that the Guiding Principles are interpreted and implemented in an uncritical way, on a 'humanitarian' model of imposed expertise. The critical and radical democratic communities have tended to be, perhaps rightly, suspicious of rights talk and sceptical of any suggestion that rights and the discourse of human rights can play a progressive role (Li and McKernan, 2016).

A November 2018 blog entry by Felix Dodds and Gaston Ocampo pointed out that several UN Global Compact companies were producing voluntary reports suggesting they were delivering on the Ruggie Human Rights Principles, even though examining their records in light of Corporate Human Rights Benchmarking reveals this to be untrue. With respect, for example, to household names that have been active in the UNGC for many years and have taken leadership roles, Dodds and Ocampo wrote that PepsiCo Inc (23 percent) and Starbucks (25 percent) "have not engaged in a dialogue with the CHRB on the data and how they will address the situation making their delivery against the CHRB to be so low."

In a recent report filed with the UNGC, PepsiCo Inc claimed that its complex value chain allows it to ensure positive human rights impacts through direct operations while using corporate leverage to encourage positive change in its indirect chain of operations. Because it operates across national borders, PepsiCo claims that whenever issues arise, it seeks to follow the higher standard –

106 *Felix Dodds*

no matter whether that standard is based on local or international laws. Finally, when addressing Due Diligence, PepsiCo asserted that it had programs in place to assess adverse human rights impacts, implement remedies as necessary and carry out external consultation to ensure an effective and "well-grounded respect for the human rights of 300,000+ employees" (Dodds and Ocampo, 2018).

In a similar way, the World Benchmarking Alliance (WBA), established in 2017, benchmarks companies on their delivery of the Sustainable Development Goals (SDGs). The theory is that by publishing this data, a race to the top will develop among companies as they increasingly try to distinguish themselves from their competitors. As this race to the top gains steam, it could become much clearer which companies are actually serious about contributing to a "good society" (assuming that the SDGs are part of the definition of "good society"). This school of thought posits that more companies might become responsible members of civil society, in a demonstration of Edwards' insight (from 2004) that "The good society tries to build a positive relationship between the market, government and the voluntary sector."

Notwithstanding recent growth in the number of metrics meant to help track and codify positive social impact, the optimism of the late 1990s and early 2000s towards the idea of "civil society" has dampened since Mary Kaldor gave the Martin Wright memorial lecture in 2003, where she theorized that

> the growing interconnectedness of states, the emergence of a system of global governance, and the explosion of the movements, groups, networks and organizations that engage in the global or transnational public debate, have called into the question the primacy of states (Kaldor, 2003).

Kaldor and thinkers like her made the case for a global civil society separate from local, state and the national civil society. Michael Edwards' book *Future Positive* and David Held's writing on "cosmopolitan democracy" both share Kaldor's optimism.

> If democracy is about self-determination, globalization about trans-border processes and cosmopolitanism about universal principles which must shape and limit all human activity, together they help us understand that the fate of humankind can no longer be disclosed merely by examining self-enclosed political and moral communities, and that the principles of democracy and cosmopolitanism need to be protected and nurtured across all human spheres (Held, 2010).

Civil society as a public sphere

> The value of a public sphere rooted in civil society rests on three core claims: first, that there are matters of concern important to all citizens and to the organization of their lives together; second, that through dialog, debate and cultural

creativity citizens might identify good approaches to these matters of public concern; and third, that states and other powerful organizations might be organized to serve the collective interests of ordinary people – the public – rather than state power as such, purely traditional values, or the personal interests of rulers and elites. These claims have become central to modern thinking about democracy and about politics, culture, and society more generally (Calhoun, 2011).

The third school of thought on civil society centers around the "public sphere." As with other aspects of civil society, you can trace the original ideas back to Aristotle, where he argued that people should pursue the common good. Perhaps the greatest modern advocate for the public sphere approach is Jurgen Habermas. In characteristically dense style, Habermas theorized in 1962 that private people who come together as a public "soon claimed the public sphere regulated from above against the public authorities themselves" (Habermas, 1962). This was ostensibly to engage those authorities "in a debate over the general rules governing relations in the basically privatized but publicly relevant sphere of commodity exchange and social labor."

Habermas was an advocate for "critical theory" as a way of enabling the public sphere to be an effective space for critiquing and changing society. "Critical theory" includes several elements. It's oriented towards critiquing and changing society as a whole, in contrast to traditional theory that attempts only to understand or explain society.

Max Horkheimer of the Frankfurt School of Sociology wanted (in 1937) to distinguish critical theory as a radical, emancipatory form of Marxian theory, critiquing both the model of science put forward by logical positivism and what he and his colleagues saw as the covert positivism and authoritarianism of orthodox Marxism and Communism. For Horkheimer, a theory was critical insofar as it sought "to liberate human beings from the circumstances that enslave them" (Horkheimer, 1982).

Another advocate of the public sphere school of thought was John Keanes. He approached civil society as a space to meet and to challenge dictators, and as an area where the market did not play a significant role. Public space and public debate have been cornerstones to any successful democratic government. Coming together to freely debate ideas is a profound way to advance ideas and to hopefully develop better policies and outcomes for people.

There have been many examples where the public sphere has been effective in channeling the people's voice to governments, but there have also been instances where it has not. A good example where the government listened in this regard might be the issue of civil rights, although this took a long time and required a great deal of sacrifice by a countless number of individuals. An example where the government did not listen, however, can be found in the UK on the issue of the Iraq War in 2003. Over 85 percent of people in the UK wanted a UN resolution before going to war, but the Prime Minister – Tony Blair – ignored this. In both cases, there was public debate.

108   *Felix Dodds*

Other examples might include town hall meetings in the United States, and some of the global forums at intergovernmental conferences of the last twenty-five years. These are all public spaces where political conversations are encouraged.

The 1990s was a decade of UN conferences and summits that set new global norms, in part to help counterbalance rapid globalization. Around these events were global forums of civil society or stakeholders, depending on whether they were following the development events (civil society – a subset of stakeholders) or the sustainable development events (all relevant stakeholders).

There is clearly an overlap between development and sustainable development but it's important to realize that argument had to be won from the 1980s onwards. Not all development by any means takes consideration of the environment.

These events and processes offered real opportunities for a broad range of stakeholders to learn from each other and to create transnational campaigns. They also shared ideas which could positively transform their local communities.

Social movements

Social movements first became part of the political and media landscape for many people through what the media too often called the anti-globalization movement, which might be better described as a global justice movement. Activists focused on the expansion of world markets by what they saw as the ruling elites – institutions like the WTO and IMF – and the developed country clubs such as the G8. These movements highlighted the perception that global elites and institutions were undermining local decision-making, the development of local markets and the increased use of natural resources.

"Corporations Rule the World" was one of the slogans coined during this period. This sentiment materialized in the campaigns to change the rules on trade and development at the multilateral level. Demonstrations around the meeting of the World Trade Organization (WTO) in 1999 in Seattle and the G8 in Genoa in 2001 were perhaps the most well-known and violent manifestations of this ethos.

David Korten and other advocates of these campaigns could be said to have a romanticized view of the past as a golden age when "rich and poor alike ... shared a sense of national and community interest" (Korten, 1995). Noam Chomsky tried to clear up the mess of the anti-globalization narrative when he asserted in 2002 that the term "globalization" had been "appropriated by the powerful to refer to a specific form of international economic integration" that was based on "investor rights" and rendered "the interests of the people incidental." Citing the *Wall Street Journal*, Chomsky observed that "the business

Civil society discourse 109

press, in its more honest moments, refers to the 'free trade agreements' as 'free investment agreements.'" Accordingly, he went on to say, "advocates of other forms of globalization are described as 'anti-globalization,' though it is a term of propaganda that should be dismissed with ridicule," because (Chomsky opined) "no sane person is opposed to globalization, that is international integration" (Chomsky, 2002).

In the early 2000s, at the same time as the World Economic Forum meetings in Davos, Switzerland, and in response to the growth of globalization, the World Social Forums meeting and other international social forums took place.

These forums were initially in Brazil, but Canada, India, Kenya, Senegal and Tunisia also hosted them. These were gathering places for those who saw themselves as part of either civil society or (among the especially optimistic) the vanguard of a new global citizens movement.

Wikipedia (2018) descriptions of the World Social Forum (WSF) note that it prefers to define itself as "an opened space – plural, diverse, non-governmental and non-partisan" that stimulates decentralized debate, reflection, proposal-building, and alliances that encourage a more "democratic and fair world."

It's also important to distinguish social movements from other types of gatherings.

> A social movement is a particular form of collective behavior in which the motive to act springs largely from the attitudes and aspirations of members, typical acting within a loose organizational framework. Being part of a social movement requires a level of commitment and political activism rather than formal or card-carrying membership above all, movements move ... A movement is different from spontaneous mass action such as an uprising or rebellion in that it implies a level of intended and planned action in pursuit of a recognized social goal (Abragan, 2018).

As mentioned earlier in this chapter, critics from Africa and other parts of the developing world have questioned conventional wisdom about social movements, and also assumptions often made about civil society as a whole. Comments recorded at the WSF in Nairobi, Kenya, included this one:

> To describe only the diversity would be to miss the real, and perhaps more disturbing, picture. The problem was that not everyone was equally represented. Not everyone had equal voices. This event had all the features of a trade fair – those with greater wealth had more events in the calendar, larger (and more comfortable) spaces, more propaganda – and therefore a larger voice. Thus, the usual gaggle of quasi donor/International NGOs claimed a greater presence than national organisations – not because what they had to say was more important or more relevant to the theme of the WSF, but because, essentially, they had greater budgets at their command. Thus, the WSF was not immune from the laws of (neoliberal) market

110   *Felix Dodds*

forces. There was no levelling of the playing field. This was more a World NGO Forum than an anti-capitalist mobilisation, lightly peppered with social activists and grassroots movements (Manji, 2007).

Counterintuitive as it may seem, the Internet has shrunk the amount of public space that can host true debate between people of differing views. You can now exist in a community of people where your views are not challenged, and there develop a set of "truths" for that group alone. This phenomenon is very worrying for the creation of a rational and fact-based conversation. Evidence-based discussion has been subsumed by the echo chambers that social media platforms help facilitate.

Civil society, trust in government and the devolution of power

In 2018, belief in government's ability to make a positive difference in people's lives is perhaps at its lowest level since the 1920s and 1930s. This is largely due to the economic crisis of 2008.

According to Special Inspector General for the Troubled Assets Relief Program (SIGTARP), Christy Goldsmith Romero, only thirty-five American bankers (Office of the Special Inspector General, 2016) were put in jail following the 2008 financial crisis. None of these thirty-five were from the major Wall Street financial houses that caused the crisis. Iceland, on the other hand, prosecuted their Prime Minister and jailed thirteen bank chairmen or presidents. Matthew Oxenford from Chatham House reviewed the impact of the financial crisis in a January 2018 report, noting that "The crisis required a write-down of over $2 trillion from financial institutions alone, while the lost growth resulting from the crisis and ensuing recession has been estimated at over $10 trillion (over one-sixth of global GDP in 2008)" (Oxenford, 2018).

Underneath these figures are people's jobs, homes and livelihoods that had been impacted by, as former Speaker of the US House of Representatives Newt Gingrich put it, "casino capitalism."

Historically in the US, public trust in government – according to the Pew Trust in Government polls – was over 50 percent up until the end of the Nixon Presidency. It wasn't until 2001 that public trust in government rose for the first time since the early 1970s to over 50 percent, rising to 54 percent after the "9/11" attacks. This had been a continuation of an upward trend under the Clinton administration, which was at 44 percent when he left office. After the financial crisis in October 2008, however, public trust in government fell to 24 percent. As of this writing under President Donald Trump, it has fallen to a record low of 18 percent.

An important question we all face is what needs to be done to bring back citizens' confidence in the institutions of government? There are clearly some actions that could be taken, such as removing the influence of money in politics, ending gerrymandering, enabling proportional representation for voting (*numbering your choice of candidate and that the winning candidate would need over 50 percent of the vote with those at the bottom being reallocated to their second preference, etc.*) so that all views can be represented, and breaking up what in too many countries has become a two-party system into one offering real choice. Introducing better fact-checking systems on both social and traditional media platforms, and reducing the unsettling blend of entertainment and news, might also help address this issue.

To understand how false news spreads, Vosoughi et al. (2018) used a data set of rumor cascades on Twitter from 2006 to 2017. About 126,000 rumors were spread by approximately 3 million people. False news reached more people than the truth; the top 1 percent of false news cascades diffused to between 1,000 and 100,000 people, whereas the truth rarely diffused to more than 1,000 people. Falsehood also diffused faster than the truth. Summarizing the study results in 2018, Vosoughi noted that "The degree of novelty and the emotional reactions of recipients may be responsible for the differences observed."

The past twenty years has seen the trend to devolve power from central government to sub-national and local governments. This has often been undertaken without adequate funding or ensuring that appropriate governance structures are in place to support that devolution. On the positive side, devolution lends increased agency to local stakeholders with an oftentimes deeper understanding of their community than central governments and national stakeholder organizations.

As this devolution continues, we may see increased trust in public institutions accompanied by more local stakeholder groups emerging with solutions specifically tailored for their communities.

What role does civil society play in all of this?

Most countries in the world are now democracies. With this being the case, however, have we seen too many people move to the nonprofit sector as opposed to engaging directly in politics and serving in government? Are the present leaders a result of this phenomenon? Society needs government no matter what some may say, and the contributions that we all make to strengthen the effectiveness of government at every level will arguably strengthen the backbone of the quest for a "good society."

Civil society in the twenty-first century

Of the myriad definitions of civil society, the one that perhaps defines it most clearly is from the London School of Economics Centre for Civil Society. They define the term as follows:

1   Civil society refers to the arenas of uncoerced collective action around shared interests, purposes, and values.
2   In theory, its institutional forms are distinct from those of the state, family and market, though in practice, the boundaries between states, civil society, family and market are often complex, blurred, and negotiated.

3   Civil society commonly embraces a diversity of spaces, actions and institutional forms, varying in their degree of formality, autonomy and power (LSE, 2006).

Many people assume that civil society has a set of core beliefs such as eradicating poverty, promoting sustainable development or advancing human rights. The lack of any clear accepted definition of who should be included or excluded in civil society makes it an imprecise theory.

Too often when civil society is being discussed, the term becomes, in effect, a synonym for NGOs. It's true that NGOs dominate the space, and at least at the global level, these are often northern NGOs or their southern partners – which are sometimes regarded as northern clients.

There are some serious questions around even the term NGOs, because large international NGOs that receive most of their funding from developed country governments often deliver services without much local accountability, knowing that what little accountability they have is to the entity funding them.

Local NGOs that serve particular communities understandably have a better form of local accountability.

There are also GONGOs (Government-Organized NGOs), which are not technically part of government but do advocate for the people in government who helped to organize them.

Membership-based NGOs have their members set policy and hold the staff of the organization accountable, but as an organizational model, this one is too often the odd one out.

Some NGOs receive funds from industry and can be seen to align with the concerns of their funders.

Neither this chapter nor this book is about NGO accountability, but a rough taxonomy of the NGO landscape is offered here by way of emphasizing that accountability needs to be addressed by civil society actors.

Apart from the temptation to equate civil society with the actions or portfolios of NGOs, the other classic mistake is to equate civil society with one or more of the stakeholder groups in it. The definitions below show that theorists of civil society can't agree on which stakeholders are even included in the term.

What is obvious is that significant stakeholders aren't included. In a typical approach of government, industry and civil society leave these significant stakeholders with no room to express their perspectives.

How we classify industry also affects thinking about civil society, because industry ought not be regarded as monolithic. In the climate change negotiations, for example, there are at least three groupings of industry: carbon-based industry, renewable industry and the finance sector. A stakeholder approach would map these out and give space for all these voices to be heard.

So, let's look at some of the perspectives on this particular issue.

The World Bank argues that

Civil society discourse 113

There has been a deliberate shift away from use of the term nongovernmental organization (NGO), which refers more narrowly to professional, intermediary and nonprofit organizations that advocate and/or provide services in the areas of economic and social development, human rights, welfare, and emergency relief.

While the Bank traditionally focused on NGOs, it now notes

> a general acceptance that the Bank must reach out more broadly to CSOs [civil society organizations] including not just NGOs, but also trade unions, community-based organizations, social movements, faith-based institutions, charitable organizations, universities, foundations, professional associations, and others (World Bank, 2007).

At present the World Bank seems to have a catchall definition of civil society on their website, describing it as including "the wide array of nongovernmental and not for profit organizations that have a presence in public life [and] express the interests and values of their members and others, based on ethical, cultural, political, scientific, religious or philanthropic considerations" (World Bank, 2018).

The UN Guiding Principles for Reporting Framework define civil society organizations (CSOs) as: "Non-state, not-for-profit, voluntary entities formed by people in the social sphere that are separate from the State and the market" (UN, 2018).

The European Union considers CSOs to include: "all non-State, not-for-profit structures, non-partisan and non–violent, through which people organize to pursue shared objectives and ideals, whether political, cultural, social or economic." They can be "membership-based, cause-based or service-oriented." Its list of examples of CSOs includes "community-based organizations, non-governmental organizations, faith-based organizations, foundations, research institutions, gender and LGBT organizations, cooperatives, professional and business associations, and the not-for-profit media." In addition (says the European Union), "Trade unions and employers' organizations, the so-called social partners, constitute a specific category of CSOs" (EEUISSS, 2010).

The African Development Bank Framework for Enhanced Engagement with Civil Society Organizations states rather comprehensively that "the CSO comprises the full range of formal and informal organizations within society."

According to the bank's official definition,

> civil society encompasses a constellation of human and associational activities operating in the public sphere outside the market and the state. It is a voluntary expression of the interests and aspirations of citizens organized and united by common interests, goals, values or traditions, and mobilized into collective action either as beneficiaries or stakeholders of the development process. Though civil society stands apart from state and market

114   *Felix Dodds*

forces, it is not necessarily in basic contradiction to them, and it ultimately influences and is influenced by both (ADB, 2008).

In his preface to "The Future Role of Civil Society," Klaus Schwab, the founder and executive chairman of the World Economic Forum, made a point of noting that "NGOs, labour leaders, faith-based organizations, religious leaders and other civil society representatives play a critical and diverse set of roles in societal development." He further suggested that "In the last two decades these roles have shifted as the external environment for civil society has changed" (Schwab, 2013).

Schwab thanked "The Forum's NGO, labour and faith communities, as well as the cross-sector Project Steering Group and members of the network of Global Agenda Councils" for "contributing extensive support and guidance to the development of [the aforementioned] publication" (Schwab, 2013).

Although the World Economic Forum is clearly interested in the views of stakeholders, mixing up the various discourses makes them harder to understand.

Threats to civil society

The assumption often is that civil society, if it has a political position, often falls on the left side of the political spectrum. However, this doesn't have to be the case, as we saw with the example of the Civic Forum.

Consider the National Rifle Association, which has been a UN NGO accredited organization since 1996. Most religions have supporting organisations accredited to the UN as NGOs. Even the Heritage Foundation, a major right-wing think tank, has UN accreditation (2003). The Cato Institute, a libertarian think tank, promotes civil society. Their founder, Edward H. Crane, said "In a civil society, you make the choices about your life. In a political society, someone else makes those choices" (Crane, 1993).

Impacts of the 2008 financial crisis spawned a growth of both left- and right-wing populism built on different views of what a "good society" is. Does a "civil society" include refugees or migrants, for example? Is it built on a free press? Is it built on facts? Are there facts anymore?

Much of the approach of civil society has been picked up by those on the right. It also has enabled it to be highjacked as an organizing method by what some would call less "civil" parts of society.

In a time of increasing inequality, some wealthy people are approaching policy development utilizing their own version of "civil society" with the intent of keeping more of their wealth.

In the past, this might have been done through right-wing dictatorships. Now it can be done through voter suppression, gerrymandering (though the left has used this too) and creating their own facts. Economist James McGill Buchanan has identified public choice theory as a main driver of thinking on the right. Recently Shughart explained this very well:

"Public choice" is "politics without romance." The wishful thinking it displaced presumes that participants in the political sphere aspire to promote the common good. In the conventional "public interest" view, public officials are portrayed as benevolent public servants who faithfully carry out the "will of the people." In tending to the public's business, voters, politicians, and policymakers are supposed somehow to rise above their own parochial concerns.

In modeling the behavior of individuals as driven by the goal of utility maximization – economics jargon for a personal sense of well-being – economists do not deny that people care about their families, friends, and community. But public choice, like the economic model of rational behavior on which it rests, assumes that people are guided chiefly by their own self-interests and, more important, that the motivations of people in the political process are no different from those of people in the steak, housing, or car market. They are the same human beings, after all. As such, voters "vote their pocketbooks," supporting candidates and ballot propositions they think will make them personally better off, bureaucrats strive to advance their own careers, and politicians seek election or reelection to office. Public choice, in other words, simply transfers the "rational actor" model of economic theory to the realm of politics (Shughart, 2018).

The right wing has also started using Alinsky's *Rules for Radicals* and applying those (historically leftist) tools to their work. After all, Alinsky did say:

> What follows is for those who want to change the world from what it is to what they believe it should be. "The Prince" was written by Machiavelli for the Haves on how to hold power. "Rules for Radicals" is written for the Have-Nots on how to take it away (Alinsky, 1971).

This can be used as a strategy anywhere on the political spectrum and now is being utilized on both the left and the right.

The lack of an accepted set of core principles underpinning civil society has resulted in much of the approach behind civil society being practiced by those supporting right-wing populist parties worldwide. That isn't to say there haven't been suggestions on what the principles for civil society might be. For example, Box 4.1 includes suggestions from the World Movement for Democracy:

Box 4.1 International principles protecting civil society

To protect civil society organizations (CSOs) from the application of the legal barriers, the following principles seek to articulate what governs and protects CSOs from repressive intrusions by government.

116 Felix Dodds

Principle 1:
The Right to Entry (Freedom of Association)

1   International law protects the right of individuals to form, join and participate in civil society organizations.

- (a) Broad scope of right. Freedom of association protects the right of individuals to form trade unions, associations, and other types of CSOs.
- (b) Broadly permissible purposes. International law recognizes the right of individuals, through CSOs, to pursue a broad range of objectives. Permissible purposes generally embrace all 'legal' or 'lawful' purposes and specifically include the promotion and protection of human rights and fundamental freedoms.
- (c) Broadly eligible founders. The architecture of international human rights is built on the premise that all persons, including non-citizens, enjoy certain rights, including the freedom of association.

2   Individuals are not required to form a legal entity in order to enjoy the freedom of association.
3   International law protects the right of individuals to form a CSO as a legal entity.

- (a) The system of recognition of legal entity status, whether a "declaration" or "registration/incorporation" system, must ensure that the process is truly accessible, with clear, speedy, apolitical, and inexpensive procedures in place.
- (b) In the case of a registration/incorporation system, the designated authority must be guided by objective standards and restricted from arbitrary decision making.

Principle 2:
The Right to Operate Free from Unwarranted State Interference

1   Once established, CSOs have the right to operate free from unwarranted state intrusion or interference in their affairs. International law creates a presumption against any regulation or restriction that would amount to interference in recognized rights.

- (a) Interference can only be justified where it is prescribed by law and necessary in a democratic society in the interests of national security or public safety, public order, the protection of public health or morals or the protection of the rights and freedoms of others.
- (b) Laws and regulations governing CSOs should be implemented and enforced in a fair, apolitical, objective, transparent and consistent manner.

Civil society discourse 117

- (c) The involuntary termination or dissolution of a CSO must meet the standards of international law; the relevant government authority should be guided by objective standards and restricted from arbitrary decision making.

2 CSOs are protected against unwarranted governmental intrusion in their internal governance and affairs. Freedom of association embraces the freedom of the founders and/or members to regulate the organization's internal governance.

3 Civil society representatives, individually and through their organizations, are protected against unwarranted interference with their privacy.

Principle 3:
The Right to Free Expression

1 Civil society representatives, individually and through their organizations, enjoy the right to freedom of expression.

2 Freedom of expression protects not only ideas regarded as inoffensive or a matter of indifference but also those that offend, shock or disturb, since pluralism and the free flow of ideas are essential in a democratic society. CSOs are therefore protected in their ability to speak critically about government law or policy, and to speak favorably about human rights and fundamental freedoms.

3 Interference with freedom of expression can only be justified where it is provided by law and necessary for respect of the rights or reputations of others; or for the protection of national security or of *public ordre*, or of public health or morals.

Principle 4:
The Right to Communication and Cooperation

1 Civil society representatives, individually and through their organizations, have the right to communicate and seek cooperation with other representatives of civil society, the business community, and international organizations and governments, both within and outside their home countries.

2 The right to receive and impart information, regardless of frontiers, through any media embraces communication via the Internet and information and communication technologies (ICTs).

3 Individuals and CSOs have the right to form and participate in networks and coalitions in order to enhance communication and cooperation, and to pursue legitimate aims.

Principle 5:
The Right to Freedom of Peaceful Assembly

1 Civil society representatives, individually and through their organizations, enjoy the right to freedom of peaceful assembly.

118 *Felix Dodds*

2 The law should affirm a presumption in favor of holding assemblies. Those seeking to assemble should not be required to obtain permission to do so.

- (a) Where advance notification is required, notification rules should not be so onerous as to amount to a requirement of permission or to result in arbitrary denial.
- (b) The law should allow for spontaneous assembly, as an exception to the notification requirement, where the giving of notice is impracticable.

3 The law should allow for simultaneous assemblies or counter-demonstrations, while recognizing the governmental responsibility to protect peaceful assemblies and participants in them.
4 Interference with freedom of assembly can only be justified where it is in conformity with the law and necessary in a democratic society in the interests of national security or public safety, public order, the protection of public health or morals or the protection of the rights and freedoms of others.

Principle 6:
The Right to Seek and Secure Resources

Within broad parameters, CSOs have the right to seek and secure funding from legal sources, including individuals, businesses, civil society, international organizations, and inter-governmental organizations, as well as local, national, and foreign governments.

Principle 7:
State Duty to Protect

1 The State has a duty to promote respect for human rights and fundamental freedoms, and the obligation to protect the rights of civil society. The State's duty is both negative (i.e., to refrain from interference with human rights and fundamental freedoms), and positive (i.e., to ensure respect for human rights and fundamental freedoms).
2 The State duty includes an accompanying obligation to ensure that the legislative framework relating to fundamental freedoms and civil society is appropriately enabling, and that the necessary institutional mechanisms are in place to ensure the recognized rights of all individuals (World Movement for Democracy, 2018).

Values in society change over time, and it was thought by many progressives with the election of President Obama that the United States had accepted a set of values that included tolerance, stewardship of the planet, fairness and justice for all.

Civil society discourse 119

However, the United States elected a President in 2016 who wants to build a wall (supported by only 45 percent Americans, Axios, 2018a) to keep people out, and to remove people who have arrived, often as economic migrants, based principally on the color of their skin. This is at the same time as opinion polls (Axios, 2018a) show that there are still 61 percent of Americans who support Deferred Action for Childhood Arrivals (DACA), a legal path for children who came to America with their parents as illegal immigrants.

Has Trump tapped a reservoir of ill feeling so that we now see the growth of an "uncivil society," inspired by what some people used to call the leader of the free world?

Karl Popper warned us about confirmation bias, sagely observing that

> If we are uncritical, we shall always find what we want: we shall look for, and find, confirmations, and we shall look away from, and not see, whatever might be dangerous to our pet theories. In this way it is only too easy to obtain what appears to be overwhelming evidence in favor of a theory which, if approached critically, would have been refuted (Popper, 1957).

The lack of a robust set of definitions, principles and values makes the civil society concept at its best a set of disjointed ideas, and at its worst a mechanism to diminish the views of key stakeholders in society and to exclude others from policy-making and the machinery that executes decisions.

More can be done to strengthen the voices of individual stakeholders, including those that are traditionally left out of "civil society" schools of thought. Effective stakeholder mapping helps to ensure that all relevant stakeholders are included in particular decisions and projects.

> In most cases, asking civil society scholars to distill policy and practice from their theories is like seeking help on plumbing from the local vicar. An embarrassing silence, followed by the sound of pairs of shuffling feet, is the usual accommodation to the obvious question – so what should we do? (Edwards, 2004)

Conclusion

This chapter may not have convinced those who believe in the civil society discourse that it is, at best, imperfect as a tool for addressing our social problems. The chapter does try to honor the enormous successes and actions that activists have used to challenge dictators wherever they are in the world.

The civil society discourse has a vital role to play in mobilizing diverse groups against totalitarian regimes, but as far as developing and implementing policy, it has proved to be limiting.

As argued in this chapter, civil society has no unified definition of who it does and does not include. It clearly excludes important stakeholders and reduces the space and voices in any process down to a single voice. A tripartite

120   *Felix Dodds*

approach in engaging government, industry and civil society alone is one where within the civil society those unique voices are muffled by the need to compromise with other stakeholders.

The tripartite approach also reduces industry to a single voice. It is also important that other voices be heard. In contrast, a stakeholder approach, for example, can distinguish between old polluting industries and new greener industries, creating a space where both could voice their inputs.

The late Ralf Gustav Dahrendorf, class conflict theorist extraordinaire, was less than sanguine about how quickly change might yield common acceptance of a context for conversation about what is good for countries: "It takes six months to create new political institutions, to write a constitution and electoral laws. It may take six years to create a half-way viable economy. It will probably take sixty years to create a civil society" (Dahrendorf, 1990), he opined.

Despite the absence of a definition to which everyone can subscribe, however, the role civil society plays in the context of associational life is a vital one, because the clubs and societies that are created in its wake or under its auspices contribute to the social capital in a community. By doing so, civil society even in nascent and imperfect form improves quality of life, and may reduce the ghettoization of information to at least a small degree.

Civil society space at the global level tends to be dominated by northern NGOs. It's fair to say that whatever discourse is in play, those involved should work to ensure that the coordinating mechanism isn't dominated by northern NGOs. When that happens, you can get gatekeepers that control the space as opposed to creating an open, democratic, transparent, accountable and enabling environment.

The stakeholder approach, however, makes it very clear that unique voices (a gender perspective, a trade union view, a next-generation input, etc.) need to be heard. And, of course, any stakeholders who are actually excluded from civil society discourse also need to be heard.

A civil society discourse can compromise or dilute unique voices by attempting to bring them together into one voice, so those who advocate for the merger of unique voices need to be asked why that is a good idea.

Finally, the journey of democracy is often not a straight one. In 2018, we are living in dangerous times where facts and science are being challenged and representative democracy is under threat. We are living in a time when 72 percent of Americans say that traditional outlets (media) report news they know to be fake, false or purposely misleading (Axios, 2018b).

This is a time for supporting representative democracy and working to build a more stable and dynamic version of it for future generations.

The movement towards participatory democracy focuses on a long-term goal. It requires a society comprised of people who respect one another and who welcome debate based on facts and not opinions. What we have seen in recent years is that the tools that many hoped would build a more equitable, fair and just society can just as easily be used as tools against these goals. Time is not on our side. We know now what needs to be done on critical issues such as climate change. The 2015 agreements on climate change and the Sustainable Development Goals gave humanity a roadmap, but at the time of writing this book, the impetus for following that roadmap with the appropriate policy changes and urgent actions has not materialized. In a different context, Martin Luther King, Jr., reminded us that:

> We are now faced with the fact that tomorrow is today. We are confronted with the fierce urgency of now. In this unfolding conundrum of life and history there is such a thing as being too late. Procrastination is still the thief of time. Life often leaves us standing bare, naked and dejected with a lost opportunity. The "tide in the affairs of men" does not remain at the flood; it ebbs. We may cry out desperately for time to pause in her passage, but time is deaf to every plea and rushes on. Over the bleached bones and jumbled residue of numerous civilizations are written the pathetic words: "Too late" (King, 1967).

References

Abragan, R. (2018) Civil Society & Social Movements. Available online at: https://www.scribd.com/document/335023279/Civil-Society-Social-Movements

African Development Bank (ADB) (2008) Framework for Enhanced Engagement with Civil Society Organizations. Tunis-Belvedère: African Development Bank. Available online at: https://www.afdb.org/fileadmin/uploads/afdb/Documents/Policy-Documents/Framework_for_Enhanced_Engagement_with_Civil_Society_Organizations-06_2015.pdf

Alinsky, S. (1971) *Rules for Radicals*. New York: Vintage Books.

Awiti, A. (2016) Time to Re-Imagine the Role of Civil Society in Africa. Seoul: International Policy Digest. Available online at: https://intpolicydigest.org/2016/07/26/time-re-imagine-role-civil-society-africa/

Axois (2018a) Exclusive Poll: Trump's Iron Wall of Defense. Available online at: https://www.axios.com/immigration-midterms-2018-support-trump-daca-border-wall-5d633f9a-8857-4eaa-b141-5378603f20f9.html

Axios (2018b) How Often Do You Think That Traditional Media News Sources Report News They Know To Be Fake, False or Purposely Misleading? Available online at: https://drive.google.com/file/d/1iLiKlECoMHmA2QiOj06sRPM7t68iUX9i/view

Bartram, J. (2018, August 31) Email exchange with Felix Dodds.

Blake, J. (2002) L.A. Greenpeace Office Closed Suddenly by Parent Company. *Daily Bruin.* Available online at: http://dailybruin.com/2002/03/04/la-greenpeace-office-closed-su/

Bradley, A. (2018) Why Radical Right-Wing Networks Thrive on Social Media. London: PS21. Available online at: https://projects21.org/2018/04/04/why-radical-right-wing-networks-thrive-on-social-media/

Calhoun, C. (2011) Civil Society and the Public Sphere in Edwards, M. (ed.), *The Oxford Handbook of Civil Society.* Oxford: Oxford University Press.

Chomsky, N. (2002) On Escalation of Violence in the Middle East. Split: The Croatian Feral Tribune. Available online at: https://chomsky.info/20020507/

Crane, H. E. (1993) Defending Civil Society. Cato Institute Speech. Available online at: https://www.cato.org/publications/speeches/defending-civil-society

122 Felix Dodds

Dahrendorf, R. (1990) Has the East Joined the West? *New Perspectives Quarterly*, 7. 2.

Dodds, F. and Ocampo, G. (2018) Time for the UN Global Compact to Evolve into the UN Due Diligence Mechanism? A Real Chance with the 2018 Partnership Resolution. Available online at: https://blog.felixdodds.net/2018/11/time-for-un-global-compact-to-evolve.html

Edwards, M. (2004) *Civil Society*. Cambridge: Polity Press.

EEUISSS (2010) The Role of Civil Society in Global Governance. Brussels: European Union.

Habermas, J. (1962) Quoted in Halverson, D.Jurgen Habermas and the Public Sphere. Available online at: https://partiallyexaminedlife.com/2016/03/02/jurgen-habermas/

Havel, V. (1999) Speech at Vaclav Havel's Civil Society Symposium. Prague: Czech Government. Available online at: http://eng.yabloko.ru/Publ/Archive/Speech/gavel-260499.html

Held, D. (2010) *Cosmopolitanism: Ideals and Realities*. Cambridge: Polity Press.

Hegel, W. F. G. (1820) Elements of the Philosophy of Right. Available online at: https://www.marxists.org/reference/archive/hegel/works/pr/prcivils.htm

Horkheimer, M. (1982) Critical Theory: Selected Essays. Continuum Pub Corp. Available online at: https://philpapers.org/rec/HORCTS-3

Li, Y. and McKernan, J. (2016) Human Rights, Accounting, and the Dialectic of Equality and Inequality. *Accounting, Auditing & Accountability Journal*, 29. 4, pp. 568–593, https://doi.org/10.1108/AAAJ-07-2015-2142

Locke, J. (1690) An Essay Concerning the True Original, Extent and End of Civil Government. Available online at: http://www.let.rug.nl/usa/documents/1651-1700/john-locke-essay-on-government/

London School of Economics (LSE) (2006) Centre for Civil Society: Report on Activities July 2005–August 2006. London: LSE. Available online at: http://eprints.lse.ac.uk/29398/

Kaldor, M. (2003) The Idea of Global Civil Society. London: International Affairs. Available online at: http://eprints.lse.ac.uk/29398/1/CCSReport05_06.pdfhttp://www.lse.ac.uk/globalGovernance/publications/articlesAndLectures/theIdeaofGlobalCivilSociety.pdf

King, M. (1967) Sermon Beyond Vietnam: A Time to Break Silence. Riverside Church in New York City. Available online at: http://www.hartford-hwp.com/archives/45a/058.html

Korten, D. (1995) *When Corporations Rule the World*. Boulder, CO: Kumarian Press.

Manji, F. (2007) World Social Forum: Just Another NGO Fair. *Pambazuka News: Voices for Freedom and Justice*. Available online at: https://www.pambazuka.org/governance/world-social-forum-just-another-ngo-fair

Martin, N. and Tandon, R. (2014) Preface in *Global Governance, Civil Society and Participatory Democracy*. New Delhi: Academic Foundation.

McFarland, S. A. (1993) *Cooperative Pluralism: The National Coal Policy Experiment*. Kansas: University Press of Kansas.

Merriam-Webster (2018) Mutualism Definition. Available online at: https://www.merriam-webster.com/dictionary/mutualism

Office of the Special Inspector General (2016) Report to Congress. Washington, DC: US Government. Available online at: https://www.sigtarp.gov/Quarterly%20Reports/January_28_2016_Report_to_Congress.pdf

Oxenford, M. (2018) The Lasting Effects of the Financial Crisis Have Yet to Be Felt. London: Chatham House. Available online at: https://www.chathamhouse.org/expert/comment/lasting-effects-financial-crisis-have-yet-be-felt

Popper, K. (1945) *The Open Society and Its Enemies*. London: Routledge.

Popper, K. (1957) Chapter 29, The Unity of Method in Popper, K., *The Poverty of Historicism*. London: Routledge.

Schwab, K. (2013) Preface in The Future Role of Civil Society. Geneva: World Economic Forum. Available online at: http://www3.weforum.org/docs/WEF_Future RoleCivilSociety_Report_2013.pdf

ShughartII, F. W. (2018) Public Choice. Carmel: The Library of Economics and Liberty. Available online at: https://www.econlib.org/library/Enc/PublicChoice.html

United Nations (2018) UN Guiding Principles Reporting Framework. New York: UN. Available online at: https://www.unglobalcompact.org/library/3761

Vosoughi, S., Roy, D. and Aral, S. (2018) The Spread of True and False News Online. *Science*. Available online at: http://science.sciencemag.org/content/359/6380/1146

Wen, J. (2015) Study on Marx's Theory of Civil Society and Alienation. Beijing: Canadian Social Science. Available online at: http://www.cscanada.net/index.php/css/article/viewFile/6543/pdf_253

Wikipedia (2018) World Social Forum. Available online at: https://en.wikipedia.org/wiki/World_Social_Forum

World Bank (2007) Consultations with Civil Society: A Sourcebook Working Document. Washington, DC: Word Bank. Available online at: http://siteresources.worldbank.org/CSO/Resources/ConsultationsSourcebook_Feb2007.pdf

World Bank (2018) Overview from the World Bank Website. Washington, DC: World Bank. Available online at: http://www.worldbank.org/en/about/partners/civil-society#2

World Movement for Democracy (2018) International Principles Protecting Civil Society. Washington, DC: World Movement for Democracy. Available online at: http://www.defendingcivilsociety.org/en/index.php/principles

5 Literature review

Carolina Duque Chopitea

Introduction

This chapter synthesizes research and current discourse on stakeholder democracy, shedding light on the academic discourse and the political debate. The literature review undertaken in this section relies on normative and empirical studies that highlights the strengths and weaknesses, the opportunities and risks of the role of stakeholders and multi-stakeholder partnerships (MSPs) in decision-finding, decision-making and implementation. Hence, this review brings to the forefront pressing questions regarding the viability of stakeholder democracy and, subsequently, multi-stakeholder partnerships, as a form of participatory, deliberative democracy, to improve policy and implementation, especially focusing on matters of global governance and sustainable development. Despite our emphasis on global governance, the material selected for this chapter focuses on stakeholder democracy at all levels, and mostly on the course of development of stakeholder democracy and multi-stakeholder processes since 2002, the post-Johannesburg World Summit on Sustainable Development (WSSD) period.

Despite the growing trends towards national protectionism, a mounting share of political decisions are taken and debated through international mechanisms, especially regarding environmental multilateralism and now sustainable development. Those decisions are impacting people and politics within states all around the world. Advocates of stakeholder democracy argue that stakeholders such as NGOs, private sector companies, industry associations, worker unions and other stakeholders may better represent people affected by global decisions than elected governments (Agné et al., 2015). And, they can contribute a diversity of knowledge, expertise and perspectives that governments are not able to feed into debates or mobilize for action. The issue of representation, however, is a controversial one that we will look at more closely. The rise of stakeholder democracy deserves attention and scrutiny if its strengths and weaknesses are to be better understood so that integrating stakeholders in decision-finding, decision-making and policy implementation can be conducted in the best possible ways.

The present review focuses firstly on the underlying political and academic discourse especially around stakeholder democracy and multi-stakeholder partnerships. Secondly it looks at its capacity to deliver legitimacy, accountability and representation in global governance. Thirdly this chapter addresses the role of multi-stakeholder partnerships in decision-finding, decision-making and implementation. Finally, this chapter suggests areas that need further consideration and research in order to develop a more comprehensive understanding of stakeholder democracy and multi-stakeholder partnerships in global governance.

Stakeholder democracy, academic discourse and political debate

For the past decades there have been debates on whether and how to increase democracy in global governance in ways that would address three deficits, namely the implementation deficit, the governance deficit and the participation deficit. At first the debate was dominated by cosmopolitan and federalist ideas that democratic institutions like a parliament, constitution and citizenry should be established at the global level (Agné et al., 2015). However, such an approach is utopian, probably unrealistic and based on state-centric notions of democratic legitimacy and accountability (Bäckstrand, 2006a). Scholars and politicians have turned away from this idea and rather emphasize the democratic merits of stakeholder engagement in global governance (Agné et al., 2015). This is based on the normative principle that people significantly or potentially affected by decisions should be included or represented in the making of those decision (Agné et al., 2015). Advocates of stakeholder democracy argue that stakeholding as a strategy for democratization of global governance is more attractive than general global elections for example, as it allows people who perceive they will be affected by a global decision ("that is, not all people") to be self-organized and to participate in finding, making and implementing those decisions ("that is, not all global decisions") (Agné et al., 2015).

The ideas of stakeholder democracy and stakeholder engagement are not new. However, since the establishment of the Nine Major Groups (Women, Children and Youth, Indigenous Peoples, NGOs, Local Authorities, Workers and Trade Unions, Business and Industry, Scientific and Technological Community, and Farmers) during the 1992 Rio Summit, and even more since the WSSD in Johannesburg, these terms and concepts have drawn significant attention. With the intention to build a more inclusive framework there have been attempts to expand the Major Groups to include local communities, volunteer groups and foundations, migrants and families, the elderly and people with disabilities (Adams and Pingeot, 2013). Critics insist that expanding the major groups would be "opening a Pandora box" as it may become too broad and jeopardize the progress done in multi-stakeholding since 2002. Other stakeholders were eventually invited to participate in UN processes related to sustainable development which can be done in close partnership with Major Stakeholders (UN-DESA, 2018).

Scholars and politicians have branded stakeholder democracy and multi-stakeholder processes as a form of global governance that have the potential to bridge multilateral norms and local action as they draw on several different

126   *Carolina Duque Chopitea*

actors (Bäckstrand, 2006a). A successful example of how stakeholder democracy can bridge global multilateral norms and local action was the implementation of Local Agenda 21. Local governments alongside stakeholders worked together at the local level to push for a global agenda that had at its core sustainable development. Moreover, it is currently widely accepted in the international community that multi-stakeholder processes and partnerships have become an essential part of international development to advance for the 2030 Sustainable Development Agenda (UNU-IAS and ESCAP, 2018). The idea underpinning these partnerships is that responsibility for implementing the complex and often "wicked" issues in sustainable development cannot rely solely on government, but must be undertaken collaboratively by diverse actors from across sectors of society. The rationale was therefore that multi-stakeholder partnerships were an important tool to forward Agenda 21, and are now an important tool to implement the Sustainable Development Goals (SDGs). However, recent evaluations of the Johannesburg partnerships that emerged from the World Summit on Sustainable Development (WSSD) in 2002 suggest that partnerships can benefit from a "clearer linkage to exiting institutions and multilateral agreements, measurable targets and timelines, effective leadership, improved accountability, systemic reviews, reporting and monitoring mechanism" (Bäckstrand, 2006a). These insights should be considered for further improvement of multi-stakeholder partnerships. Nevertheless, regardless of such weaknesses dialogue and collaboration among multiple stakeholders is widely considered as essential for the implementation of sustainable development and other polices, and for such reason it is likely that development organizations and other actors will continue investing in multi-stakeholder initiatives (Kusters et al., 2017).

Moreover, stakeholder democracy can help close the implementation gap by connecting local action and global rules in a context-specific, flexible and decentralized manner (Bäckstrand, 2006a). As it was seen in the case of Local Agenda 21 and hopefully will be seen through the implementation of the SDGs, stakeholder democracy and especially multi-stakeholder partnerships can decrease the governance gap by complementing multilateral treaty-making with voluntary initiatives that mobilize additional resources and capacities. Finally, they can reduce the participation gap in global governance as it has the potential to include an array of diverse stakeholders and actors can be included (Bäckstrand, 2006a).

It seems that scholars have recognized the capacity of stakeholder democracy in bridging the global governance deficit. Nonetheless, the political and academic debate regarding stakeholder democracy continues to focus on its capacity to be able to deliver legitimacy, accountability and representation, especially in the context of multi-stakeholder partnerships for sustainable development.

Multi-stakeholder partnerships and liberal environmentalism

The 1992 Rio Summit consolidated norms of liberal environmentalism (Bernstein, 2001), in which sustainable development is viewed as compatible with capitalism and liberal trading order, and liberal democracy and "good governance" are depicted as the most viable political institutional frameworks for

Literature review 127

addressing sustainable development. Therefore, in this new policy paradigm, flexible, decentralized and voluntary market-oriented approaches to environmental and development problem-solving have been advanced as a crucial complement to the dominant top-down, state-centric decision-making (Bernstein, 2001; Bäckstrand, 2006a). Multi-stakeholder partnerships fit this description. Stakeholder democracy and the processes it advocates, such as multi-stakeholder partnerships, "starts from the premise that democracy is more about deliberation, reasoned argument and public reflection among affected stakeholders than voting and aggregation" (Bernstein, 2001; Bäckstrand, 2006a). Legitimacy emerges from an open and public process of deliberation among multiple members of society ranging from governments and business to NGOs and civil society (Bäckstrand, 2006a). Yet, whether stakeholder democracy and multi-stakeholder processes yield greater legitimacy in global governance structures has been disputed by some scholars as previously discussed. Therefore, the democratic quality of multi-stakeholder processes is an important academic and political debate. On the one hand, MSPs are seen as a way of democratizing global governance through a stakeholder democratic perspective aimed at fostering better implementation and decision-making, particularly in the context of the SDGs. On the other hand, critics also see these initiatives as a privatization of global governance reinforcing dominant neoliberal modes of globalization (Schouten et al., 2012).

Regardless of the perspective taken, it is correct to say that these partnerships emerged partly as a response to the demonstrated limits of multilateralism, where intergovernmental organizations alone cannot address the pressing and complex problems that sustainable development presents (Bäckstrand, 2006a). Stakeholder partnerships are especially important now as the liberal democratic order is in crisis and has lost legitimacy and thus, they may help restore some of the trust in the system. Hence, multi-stakeholder partnerships have been posed as ground-breaking forms of governance that can effectively bridge the three deficits in global governance, especially in environmental politics and sustainable development. Scholars argue that MSPs have been a way of increasing inclusion and legitimacy in terms of "broad ownership" of decisions in international problem-solving initiatives (Bäckstrand, 2006a). However, as MSPs lack a centralized authority and are not bound to an electorate questions of to whom they should be accountable become increasingly important. Critics argue that "the new participatory governance paradigm is just part of the neo-liberal regulatory models dressed in the language of participation, which privileges powerful actors and consolidates sovereign, capitalist and modern power structures" (Bäckstrand, 2006b). Thus, matters of representation, legitimacy and accountability are of vital importance, especially in the face of global inequality as MSPs have been mostly dominated by stakeholders from the North, who are often more equipped with resources to participate.

Legitimacy, representation and accountability

Agné et al. (2015) suggest that one of the underpinnings of stakeholder democracy theory is the premise that strengthening opportunities for involving

128   *Carolina Duque Chopitea*

stakeholders in decision-making as well as decision-finding and implementation enhances the democratic legitimacy of such decision-making procedures. One reason that this is so is because there are greater opportunities for involvement of self-organized stakeholders in global policy-making, hence contributing to experiences and perceptions among these actors that global policy-making is democratic (Agné et al., 2015). However, matters of legitimacy, accountability and representation of stakeholders involved in global governance are of concern, especially given that stakeholders often operate outside formal democratic procedures since most of them like NGOs, industry associations, and grassroot organizations are not formally elected by the people or often even their own supporters.

Legitimacy

Scholars and politicians have supported and opposed the legitimacy of stakeholder democracy, and it remains a heated debate. As mentioned before, stakeholder democracy advocates assert that involvement of stakeholders in the process of decision-finding, decision-making and implementation can lead to greater legitimacy of those decisions. Legitimacy in the stakeholder model is generated through democratic deliberation of a variety of societal actors, from governmental delegates, social movements, business and scientific communities. The democratic legitimacy hinges upon successful creation and institutionalization of global public spaces for deliberation (Bäckstrand, 2006b).

However, the idea that increased participation in global governance yields greater legitimacy has been contested. For instance, in their study, Agné et al. (2015) find that democratic legitimacy of international organizations among stakeholder organizations is not strengthened by opportunities for participation in intergovernmental organizations. Instead, the democratic legitimacy in international organizations is shaped by the level of democracy in the home countries of stakeholder organizations and their perceived influence over policy outcomes. Therefore, the authors argue stakeholder democracy appears ineffective for creating greater experiences of democracy in international organizations simply by strengthening opportunities for participation in global governance. They explained that if the reason why stakeholder involvement in global governance does not yield greater legitimacy on international organizations is due to the apparent lack of influence and power of stakeholders in global governance, then the principle of stakeholder democracy should persist since the normative ideal can be strengthened by increasing the influence of stakeholders. However, if the reason why it does not yield greater democratic legitimacy is because stakeholder organizations are unrepresentative, then the idea of creating democratic legitimacy through stakeholder involvement needs to be reconsidered (Agné et al., 2015).

Literature review   129

In addition, the discussion on increasing legitimacy of intergovernmental organizations is increasingly tied to the implementation gap. For instance, "ownership of outcomes and agreements by a wider range of stakeholders who are affected by issues and who may be partly responsible for policy implementation along with governments is desirable on grounds of efficacy of democracy" (Bäckstrand, 2006b). In other words, engaging stakeholders in the decision-making process is said to enhance their sense of ownership of the outcome which in turn will motivate them to play their part in implementing the decision (Dodds, 2018).

Representation

Representation is another important focus at the forefront of the debate on stakeholder democracy. Questions in this context include: What is the level of representation? Which stakeholders are included? Which stakeholders are leading multi-stakeholder partnerships in global governance? Are disenfranchised groups, stakeholders from all Major Groups, stakeholders from developing and developed countries equally represented? Is mere (equal) participation a sufficient indicator of representation or do we need to look at the quality of participation? Are all stakeholders contributing actively and successfully to a stakeholder process or partnerships?

For example, it has been widely criticized that multi-stakeholder partnerships have been mostly North driven, reflecting North–South inequalities in world politics (Pattberg and Widerberg, 2014). And therefore, it is imperative to ask if partnerships are open to public scrutiny and if they are representative and inclusive of different stakeholders and their interests. Given that stakeholders often operate outside formal democratic process and that social and political inequities may be reflected between stakeholders and stakeholder partnerships questions of representation become central to ensuring that various voices are heard. Stakeholder democracy scholars insist that "stakeholder representation beyond elections allows for the inclusion of varied and different perspectives, and more emphasis on deliberative features compensates for the relative absence of electoral bases" (Bäckstrand, 2006b). In this sense, stakeholder democracy is placed within less state-centric notions of global governance such as "governance from below." "This brings informal, participatory, non-electoral and non-territorial forms of democracy at the global level to the fore" (Bäckstrand, 2006b). The purpose of stakeholder democracy is not to replace representative democracy or to replace states and governments, but rather to find more effective and legitimate ways of overcoming the limitations of exclusive territorial governance and better understand the cross-boundary nature of environmental and social issues, and more broadly of sustainable development in a globalized world.

Accountability

A central topic of debate regarding accountability in stakeholder democracy is the extent to which stakeholder representatives are accountable to the community or collectives they are drawn from and speak for. To date, a mechanism to

130   *Carolina Duque Chopitea*

hold stakeholders accountable at the global level has not been fully realized. Critics point to the fact that many of these partnerships no longer exist but are still being listed on the UN website, calling them "zombie partnerships." There is a lack of accountability and effective monitoring of these partnerships and of the database where they are listed (Dodds, 2018). It would require capacities to demand regular reporting, and a system for delisting those that do not report. One of the issues with the multi-stakeholder partnerships that emerged from WSSD was then the lack of rules and procedures, defining what partnerships are and how they should interact with and report to the UN system and/or national governments (Dodds, 2018). These gaps are now being reflected in the lack of accountability relating to these partnerships and the database listing them.

Instead of exporting a domestic model of democratic legitimacy and accountability to global governance, these concepts should be redefined to fit these non-traditional forms of governance structures. We need to rethink notions of accountability and legitimacy and make them congruent with contemporary global governance structures (beyond state-centric) consisting of overlapping and competing authorities – sovereign, private as well as hybrid (Bäckstrand, 2006a). Again, the idea of furthering stakeholder democracy is not to replace current representative democracies, but to compliment them and fill the gap of current deficit and mistrust, especially in implementation and legitimacy. A "top-down" accountability approach or a purely top-down approach is neither suitable for stakeholder democracy nor for stakeholder partnerships since it does not fit to the decentralized and flexible nature of stakeholder self-organization. Therefore, partnerships need pluralistic accountability structures such as professional peer accountability, reputational accountability, market accountability and financial accountability and mutual accountability within multi-stakeholder partnerships (Witte et al., 2003).

Decision-finding, decision-making and implementation

As it has been mentioned throughout this literature review, increasing inclusion of stakeholders in global policy-making can result in the "ownership" of the outcomes, and hence such ownership may yield greater responsibility from those stakeholders to act. Though contested, the assumption underpinning the stakeholder democracy paradigm is that more participation and deliberation by affected groups, including "ownership" of outcomes and partial responsibility for policy implementation, will generate more effective collective problem-solving and action (Bäckstrand, 2006b). Nevertheless, the benefits of stakeholder democracy not only emerge in decision-making and policy implementation but way before; stakeholder democracy can better facilitate problem identification and decision-finding. Considering the complexity of policy-making at a global level for sustainable development a variety of perspectives need to be considered that will help to point out and gather information on issues that need to be addressed. And, since people on the ground are the ones truly facing the issues, they may be better equipped to point out problems and thus help find solutions.

Literature review 131

Hence, it is generally accepted that stakeholders have the capacity to move forwards essential perspectives and expertise to intergovernmental debates allowing for more robust decisions (Adams and Pingeot, 2013). Some of the value-added elements brought by stakeholder engagement to the sustainable development process include (Adams and Pingeot, 2013):

- New perspectives and expertise they bring to the table.
- Valuable research and advocacy functions.
- Capacity to raise public awareness and information dissemination.
- Capacity to adapt global policies to national or local realities.
- Watchdogs to foster accountability.

The underlaying ideas is that the direct input of people on the ground in global policy, for instance in the UN processes, is essential to ensure that the adopted policies and programs incorporate the perspectives and proposals of the people they intended to support in the first place. However, critics point out that participation by stakeholders such as grassroots organizations, civil society, smaller NGOs, and communities has often been difficult to achieve due to a lack of knowledge or interest on global policy-making, lack of funding and outreach, and the lack of explanation on how global policy-making can be translated into local action (Adams and Pingeot, 2013).

Another reason that has limited the political participation of stakeholders is the fact that it is difficult for them to measure whether their perspectives have been considered and have impacted decisions. If stakeholders rarely see the results from their inputs and fail to receive feedback, they may feel frustrated and abstain from further participating (Adams and Pingeot, 2013). Therefore, stakeholder democracy advocates insist that the role of stakeholders should go beyond that of perspective sharing and decision-finding. Stakeholder participation should be the "active presence of Major Groups and other stakeholders in the design, execution and monitoring of sustainable development follow up activities at all levels, going beyond the passive exchange of information" (Adams and Pingeot, 2013). As well, advocates of MSPs insist that for participants to be committed to the process, the purpose and expected outcomes of the partnerships should be clear. It is necessary that the participants understand the process thoroughly, its purpose, how the information is used for decision-making and implementation, and the potential follow-up measures (Kusters, et al., 2017). Major Groups, for example, have made it clear that meaningful participation means being engaged in all aspects throughout the whole process. This is in fact the most meaningful way to absorb all the benefits that come from multi-stakeholder partnerships, which will lead to proper problem identification, decision-making and implementation.

To allow for a comprehensive inclusion of perspectives to identify problems and come up with the best solutions and implementation plans, the commitment to stakeholder democracy and partnerships, in general, should be supported by funding as well as strengthening access to information and building

132   *Carolina Duque Chopitea*

the capacity of civil society to be able to engage. Supporting stakeholder participation both in terms of funding and providing information is essential since governments cannot make informed decisions on sustainable development without the expertise of those affected the most (Adams and Pingeot, 2013). The fact that stakeholders from the North have taken the lead can be reflected in the lack of funding and information to stakeholders in the developing world.

Looking ahead

This chapter attempted to review the most pressing issues surrounding multi-stakeholder partnerships and stakeholder democracy more broadly. This literature review found that despite the excitement around stakeholder democracy due to its capacity to bridge the three deficits in global governance (implementation deficit, the governance deficit and the participation deficit), there is still a lot of work to do if its potential is to be fully realized. Questions of legitimacy, representation and accountability have proven to be central in the debate and no consensus has been reached among scholars and politicians regarding these themes. However, such debate also reflects the need to clarify the role, standardized practices and come up with the appropriate mechanism for multi-stakeholder partnerships with the intention of improving the legitimacy, representativeness and accountability of MSPs.

Therefore, it can be concluded that despite increased efforts to forward stakeholder democracy at the global level by including and engaging multi-stakeholder partnerships in policy-making the lack of proper guidelines and an institutionalized framework to guide MSPs' actions persist. The lack of such framework limits the capacity of governments and stakeholders from groundbreaking decision-finding, decision-making and implementation of policies for sustainable development. Both critics and advocates of the partnerships insist that organizing large, complex multi-stakeholder groups requires sophisticated implementation structures for ensuring collaborative actions (Filho, 2018). It is crucial that scholars, politicians and the people themselves keep experimenting and researching with the aim of developing a multi-stakeholder partnership framework that is participatory; it entails added-value activities have clear objectives and contain specific targets and deadlines for the partnerships; basically, a comprehensive framework to guide the MSPs.

Without such framework to guide and monitor partnerships it will be impossible to properly employ and measure the effectiveness of stakeholder engagement in policy-making and of multi-stakeholder partnerships. Lack of measurements may in turn negatively impact participation from both stakeholders and governments due to lack of understanding of the impact from their input. Such a framework would allow to measure and possibly promote the legitimacy, representativeness and accountability of stakeholder democracy practices and provide a way to measure meaningful participation and its outcomes and impacts. In the context of this book, then, academics and those who have been engaged in discussions around MSPs proposed to set up an MSP

Charter. The hope is that it will help improve the quality of MSPs and establish a standard that partnerships can be measured by. In the context of the SDGs such a Charter may also be used to help quantify partnerships' impact on SDG implementation.

References

Adams, B. and Pingeot, L. (2013) Dialogue, Debate, Dissent, Deliberation: Strengthening Public Participation for Sustainable Development. UN DESA /DSD Major Groups Programme, 1–27.

Agné, H., Dellmuth, M. L. and Tallberg, J. (2015) Does Stakeholder Involvement Foster Democratic Legitimacy in International Organizations? An Empirical Assessment of a Normative Theory. *Review of International Organizations*, 10, 465–488.

Bäckstrand, K. (2006a) Multi-Stakeholder Partnerships for Sustainable Development: Rethinking Legitimacy, Accountability and Effectiveness. *European Environment*, 16, 290–306.

Bäckstrand, K. (2006b) Democratizing Global Environmental Governance? Stakeholder Democracy after the World Summit on Sustainable Development. *European Journal of International Relations*, 12(4), 467–498, doi:10.1177/1354066106069321.

Bernstein, S. (2001) *The Compromise of Liberal Environmentalism*. New York: Columbia University Press.

Dodds, F. (2018) Zombie Partnerships: Are We About to See the Multi-Stakeholder Partnership Bubble Burst? Could We Be Seeing upto 84% Failure? Available online at: http://blog.felixdodds.net/2018/07/zombie-partnerships-are-we-about-to-see.html

Filho, W. L. (2018) *Handbook of Sustainability Science and Research*. World Sustainability Series. Cham: Springer.

Kusters, K., Buck, L., Graaf, de M., Minang, P., Oosten, vam C. and Zagt, R. (2017) Participatory Planning, Monitoring and Evaluation of Multi-stakeholder Platforms in Integrated Landscape Initiatives. *Environ Manag*, 1–12, doi:10.1007/s00267–00017–0847-y.

Pattberg, P. and Widerberg, O. (2014) Transnational Multi-Stakeholder Partnerships for Sustainable Development: Building Blocks for Success. *IVM Institute for Environmental Studies*, 7–59, doi:10.13140/2.1.3172.0329.

Schouten, G., Leroy, P. and Glasbergen, P. (2012) On the Deliberative Capacity of Private Multi-Stakeholder Governance: The Roundtable on Responsible Soy and Sustainable Palm Oil. *Ecological Economics*, 83, 42–50.

Spiro, P. J. (2018) Stakeholder Theory Won't Save Citizenship in Bauböck, R. (ed.), *Democratic Inclusion*. Manchester: Manchester University Press.

UN-DESA (2018) Major Groups and Other Stakeholders. Sustainable Development Goals Knowledge Platform.

UNU-IAS and ESCAP (2018) Partnering for Sustainable Development Guidelines for Multi-stakeholder Partnerships to Implement the 2030 Agenda in Asia and the Pacific. United Nations, 1–70.

Witte, J. M., Streck, C. and Benner, T. (2003) The Road from Johannesburg: What Future for Partnerships in Global Environmental Governance? In Progress or Peril? Networks and Partnerships in Global Environmental Governance. Global Public Policy Institute.

6 Examples of successful multi-stakeholder policy development

International arena

Stakeholders have tried many different ways to influence policy development over the last twenty-five years. Much of the stakeholder impact has been shaped through conversations between people in the hallways or corridors of intergovernmental meetings. Aware of this history, global institutions and governments at all levels are increasingly seeking more formal processes to synthesize views in a way that policy makers can engage with and note to include in their deliberations.

The UN Conference on Human Settlement (Habitat II) benefited from the more open approach to stakeholders that had emerged from the Earth Summit process (1992) and the subsequent meetings of the UN Commission on Sustainable Development (CSD).

Two important developments in the preparatory process and the Habitat II Conference (1996) are worth looking at in depth.

The first development worthy of note was the engagement of stakeholders in the negotiation process itself. The Habitat II preparatory process had three formal sessions, with the first two in Nairobi and the final one in New York. At the second preparatory meeting in Nairobi, stakeholders had set up a multi-stakeholder body to engage with the negotiating process. Yet neither of the first formal meetings went well, so after each an informal meeting was added to the diary. The second of these informal meetings was held in Paris, and warrants further review.

In Paris, meeting participants were treated as relative equals in discussions regardless of whether they were governments, UN staff or stakeholders. As far as influencing the text, the approach taken by the meeting as the chair moved from paragraph to paragraph was that stakeholders could table suggestions for the text. If a government endorsed a stakeholder suggestion, it became a live amendment. This approach resulted in governments and stakeholders working together on amended text and even presenting that text together. A lot of suggestions from stakeholders were included in what would then be presented to the final preparatory meeting in New York. Governments found this a useful approach and adapted it for the Habitat II Conference itself. Even so, this

Examples of successful MS policy development   135

approach has not been repeated at any subsequent UN conference or negotiation.

The second innovation in the run-up to Habitat II was the development of Multi-Stakeholder Dialogues (MSD) for that conference. Habitat II was designed with two formal committees. Committee One negotiated over text, while Committee Two focused on this new idea of MSDs.

The Second Committee of the conference was unique for the way it hosted an interactive discussion space where the different stakeholder groups had to say what their contribution for implementing the Habitat Agenda would be.

Stakeholder groups identified in the Habitat II process were: local authorities, the private sector, parliamentarians, non-governmental organizations, foundations, labour unions, academics and professionals, wisdom seekers (older people) and the UN system. Half a day was assigned for each of the stakeholder groups to present their vision and activities for implementing the Habitat Agenda before a dialogue took place.

The outcome from these interactive half-day sessions with governments and other stakeholders was attached to the Habitat Agenda. At that time, it represented a significant recognition of the role that stakeholders could play in implementing global agreements. Although it did not influence the government-negotiated text, it did lay out an agenda that described the roles and responsibilities that the different stakeholders could play.

It is often forgotten that Habitat II had even gone as far as to suggest that in the follow-up to the conference, the Commission on Human Settlements

> might be expanded to include local authorities, non-governmental organizations (NGOs) and the private sector in the work of the Commission so as to help define the Centre's work programme in response to common priorities in the areas of shelter and sustainable urban development.

This [expansion] would "support Habitat's effort to strengthen and further develop its partnerships with local authorities, the private sector and NGOs established during the preparations for Habitat II" (UN, 1996).

While the suggested expansion never happened, it did show willingness by governments in the 1990s to consider more joint policy development.

Some people argued that governments didn't assign much importance to the Habitat issues and were, therefore, more relaxed as far as involving stakeholders. It's also true that the Habitat Agenda dealt with local and sub-national issues where stakeholders *should* be involved in helping to deliver them, so engaging them was a smart move.

As a process becomes more important, governments reduce the opportunity for stakeholder engagement, reasoning that softer forums can be experimental places but more developed approaches require other (more controlled) forums.

A final thought on Habitat II highlights something that is true for all inter-governmental processes, which is that particular individuals often play critical roles in becoming champions for new ideas.

136   Felix Dodds

In Habitat II, Ambassador for Pakistan Shafqat Kakakhel was Chair of the formal negotiations. The Ambassador was also the Chair of the Committee of Permanent Representatives in Nairobi and Chair of the Group of 77. These responsibilities gave Ambassasor Kakakhel a unique role, and made him and a unique representative who championed much of the advanced form of engagement. He would continue this in his role as Deputy Executive Director of UNEP later in the 1990s.

Global level: Commission on sustainable development Multi-Stakeholder Dialogues

Chapter 3 summarized the approaches to sustainable development at the CSD. Here we go into more depth on Multi-Stakeholder Dialogues (MSDs) as one of the best examples of a mechanism for engaging in policy development with member states.

The CSD played a critical role as an experimental space, particularly in the 1990s, for different forms of stakeholder engagement in policy development.

Learning from the Habitat II process, the CSD NGO/Stakeholder Steering Committee presented a similar organizing idea to the Second Committee of the UN General Assembly in October 1996. The General Assembly subsequently agreed that for the Rio+5 conference in 1997 (the review of Agenda 21), each of the Major Groups would again be given half a day to present their ideas for the further implementation of Agenda 21 and the roles and responsibilities that Major Groups and governments should take.

Meetings similar to those that had paved the way for Habitat II were held while governments were negotiating the outcome for Rio+5. Joke Waller-Hunter of the Netherlands, then the Director of the UN Division on Sustainable Development, worked with stakeholders to create a much more robust and impactful approach.

To come up with a new design, Ms. Waller-Hunter brought the co-chairs of the CSD NGO Steering Committee together with industry and trade union representatives for a two-day workshop in October 1997. The resulting approach was endorsed by the Bureau for the Commission on Sustainable Development, and the process is outlined in Box 6.1.

Box 6.1 Summary of the dialogue process (Howell, 2004)

Summary of the dialogue process (October to June)

Preparations

- Identification of Dialogue topic and themes, Secretariat and Bureau
- Identification of relevant Major Groups and focal points, Secretariat and Bureau

Examples of successful MS policy development 137

- Preparation of Starter Papers on each of the themes, Focal Points in consultation with Major Groups
- Phone Conferences on logistics and co-ordination, Secretariat and Focal Points
- Identification of opening statement speakers and Major Group teams, Focal Points in consultation with Major Groups

Sessions

- Opening remarks from the Chair
- Opening statements from each participating Major Group
- Response by one Southern and one Northern Government
- Floor is opened for Dialogue between participating Major Groups, Member States, IGOs, and other Major Groups
- Concluding Statements from each participating Major Group

Outcomes

- Chairman's Summary
- Impact on negotiations
- Independent Major Group initiatives

To address the common problem at Habitat II and Rio+5 of the dialogues being at the same time as formal negotiations, the CSD spent the first two days of meetings on four three-hour sessions presided over by the Chair of the CSD, with no negotiations scheduled simultaneously. Themes for the MSDs were proposed by the UN Secretariat and decided by that year's government Bureau.

UN Commissions operate with a Bureau composed of representatives, one from each of the UN groupings (Western Europe and Other Group, Eastern Europe, Africa, Asia and Latin America and the Caribbean).

Following those "dialogue days," the Secretariat and Bureau identified the most relevant Major Groups for each of the given topics, and invited the relevant Organizing Partners for those Major Groups to act as facilitators and identify the teams to participate.

The dialogues for the first year focused on Industry and Sustainable Development. NGOs, Trade Unions, and Industry were the three most relevant stakeholder groups to this topic invited to join the dialogue. Other stakeholders were prompted to work through those three stakeholder groups, each of which was asked to produce a paper addressing the following four themes:

- Responsible entrepreneurship.
- Corporate management tools.
- Technology cooperation and assessment.
- Industry and fresh water.

138   *Felix Dodds*

Cielito Habito, the Minister for the Environment in the Philippines, was the Chair of the CSD in 1998. The stakeholder papers had to be sent to the UN by February in preparation for a June CSD. This also gave the Secretariat time to produce a comparative analysis to help the Chair plan for each of the dialogues. In producing the papers, stakeholders were required to explain what their respective efforts at outreach had been. This was to ensure as wide an input as possible, and to help ensure that membership in each stakeholder team was balanced between developed and developing country participants. Habito was conscious of how groundbreaking this approach might be:

> I'd like to consider this just as a first step in the process that the Commission has been undertaking in increasing the role of the Major Groups in our work. And so, we hope that with this Industry Segment we can really set a tone for how we can bring in the Major Groups more closely and more directly into the deliberations of the Commission (Habito, 1998).

As a model of inclusion, this was revolutionary. Each stakeholder group made a short presentation of its paper. The presentation was followed by a debate among member states, in an opportunity for them to challenge what stakeholders were saying. This format inspired some interesting exchanges, and embarrassed the few stakeholder representatives who could not defend particular positions. Over the three most successful years of the dialogues, there was a rapid increase in the quality of the material produced and the choice of experts to be part of the dialogue teams.

Table 6.1 shows the participation of the different core stakeholders in the dialogues.

After the four dialogue sessions had finished in 1998, a very unusual incident occurred. Joke Waller-Hunter and Cielito Habito invited the co-chairs of the CSD NGO/Stakeholder Steering Committee, the Industry and Trade Union coordinators to review the Chair's summary and make any suggestions for changes before it was circulated to member states. This courtesy would not be repeated under the subsequent Director of the Division on Sustainable Development, who took a dimmer view of stakeholders.

One of the most significant, and most controversial, discussions was about whether industry voluntary initiatives or agreements work. This was based on the NGOs and the Trade Unions calling for a review saying that they didn't work and the industry group initially objecting. In the end the industry group split with surprisingly the more conservative grouping the International Chamber of Commerce supporting the call and the more moderate World Business Council for Sustainable Development objecting.

Subsequently in the negotiations, member states established the first multi-stakeholder working group to follow up on a CSD decision. The UN Division on Sustainable Development would facilitate this open-ended working group of stakeholders, UN Agencies and Programmes to examine voluntary initiatives and agreements.

Examples of successful MS policy development 139

Table 6.1 Number of interventions by Major Groups per session: Industry (Howell, 2004)

Session:	A	B	C	D	Total/group
Government	13	10	17	14	54
NGO	9	6	15	9	39
Industry	7	12	9	5	33
Trade Union	7	9	11	5	32
IGO	3	3	0	0	6
Youth	1	1	3	1	6
Indigenous	0	1	1	1	3
Women	0	0	0	1	1
Total/session	40	42	56	36	174

As reported in the daily *Earth Negotiations Bulletin*:

> At the close of the stakeholder Dialogues on Wednesday, there was consensus across a number of the participating major groups, government delegations and the CSD Secretariat that the Commission had finally produced a useful and productive forum for focused exchanges (ENB, 1998).

In the follow-up to the 1998 CSD decision on voluntary initiatives, the open working group on voluntary initiatives produced a report. The group identified nine elements that could be part of a more substantial review. Those elements were:

(i) Impetus and context

What are the conditions, events, considerations – for example, response to external pressures, policy gaps, social responsibility, desire to preempt or complement regulation and so forth – that led to the start of the voluntary initiative or agreement?

In what ways are stakeholders involved and what induced them to participate?

(ii) Purpose and design of the voluntary initiative and agreement

What are the goals and objectives of the voluntary initiative or agreement, and how do they relate to sustainable development?

How are the goals and objectives identified and by whom? What strategic mechanisms are selected to achieve the goals? What are the mechanisms for transparency and accountability?

What are the anticipated risks and benefits and how are they addressed in the design? What is the timetable of the initiative?

140   *Felix Dodds*

(iii) Multi-stakeholder participation

How are stakeholders identified and how is their participation ensured? Who takes the lead? Which groups play a supportive role? How do the varying interests secure representation?

What kinds of groups are involved – for example, government, business and industry, non-governmental organizations, trade unions – and what roles do they play? How are issues of the responsibility of different stakeholders dealt with?

(iv) Commitment to sustain the voluntary initiative or agreement

What generates stakeholders' commitment? How is commitment sustained in the face of changing circumstances?

(v) Mutual trust and respect

What working methods are used to build and sustain mutual trust and respect among the various stakeholders? How does mutual trust, once established, contribute to successful problem-solving and conflict mediation?

(vi) Monitoring and assessment

To what extent does the voluntary initiative or agreement meet its stated objectives and goals and how does it contribute to the goals of sustainable development?

Who assesses performance, results and impact of the voluntary initiative or agreement? How are assessment results to be shared and reported? What methodologies are used to measure the costs and benefits of the voluntary initiative or agreement?

(vii) Verification

What independent external involvement and expertise are helpful in reviewing and validating the assessment? How is verification to be structured in terms of finance, independence and credibility?

(viii) Communication

What types of information are generated and shared among the stakeholders and the public? Was the information provided adequate for full and informed stakeholder participation? How is this communication achieved so as to ensure transparency as well as respect for confidentiality?

How are learning and feedback used to promote continuous improvement?

(ix) Replication and capacity-building

How do voluntary initiatives and agreements contribute to capacity-building and broader replication and adoption so as to ensure continuous improvement? (UN, 1999)

Examples of successful MS policy development 141

The UN Report recommended that the Commission might want to continue work of this group, and that its work might include that it would "continue generating information about voluntary initiatives and agreements, including the most appropriate means for possible reviews." It also saw value in making that information widely available.

This issue of voluntary initiatives was then taken up by the CSD in 1999, and Decision 7/6 said:

(d) Also recognizes the potential value of processes which involve Governments and all relevant major groups and other stakeholders for addressing sustainable development issues, and encourages future work on voluntary initiatives and agreements.

(e) Encourages all relevant major groups and other stakeholders, in cooperation with relevant United Nations bodies, to continue generating information about voluntary initiatives and agreements, including the most appropriate means for possible reviews, and to make this information widely available, and requests its secretariat to facilitate these efforts, inter alia, through its Internet site.

(f) [The CSD] stresses the need for better understanding and analysis of the possible impact of voluntary initiatives and agreements on developing countries, and requests all relevant major groups and other stakeholders to report periodically, through the Commission's secretariat, on steps they have taken or progress they have made in assisting developing countries in understanding and making use of, as appropriate, the lessons to be learned from the use of voluntary initiatives and agreements (UN, 1999).

The focus for the next CSD dialogue in 1999 was tourism. In preparation, incoming Chair Simon Upton, Minister of Environment for New Zealand, instructed his Chief of Staff, David Taylor, to meet with the stakeholder groups in London. This was after their papers had been finished and the comparative analysis had been completed. He used this meeting to focus on the areas of agreement as far as he could prior to the dialogue sessions.

The tourism dialogue expanded the number of stakeholders groups from three to four:

- Business and Industry (World Travel and Tourism Council [WTTC], the International Hotel and Restaurant Association)
- Workers and Trade Unions (the International Confederation of Free Trade Unions/Trade Union Advisory Committee to the Organisation for Economic Cooperation and Development [OECD])
- Local Authorities (the International Council Local Environmental Initiatives [ICLEI])
- Non-Governmental Organizations (the CSD NGO Steering Committee)

142   *Felix Dodds*

Four themes (addressed for three hours each) highlighted important aspects of sustainable tourism. These themes were:

- Industry initiatives for sustainable tourism.
- Influencing consumer behavior.
- Promoting broad-based sustainable development while safeguarding the integrity of local cultures and protecting the environment.
- Coastal impact of tourism.

After the dialogue portion of the meeting, Chairperson Simon Upton experimented by introducing his summary of the key points as part of New Zealand's text for the outcome document. This procedural move meant that member states had to consider the points raised and then accept, amend or reject them, thus giving real weight to the dialogue outcome.

One of the critical issues the CSD tried to address was that of financial leakages. For instance, when someone buys a holiday from a developed country travel agent, often as much as 70 percent of the income from the holiday goes out of the country where the holiday is happening back to the country of origin or other developed countries. Leakage are from for example: goods and services, infrastructure, foreign investment, promotional expenditures, transfer pricing, tax exemptions and foreign workers. To address this, the CSD agreed in the follow-up process to set up an informal open-ended working group:

> 10. The Commission invites the United Nations Secretariat and the World Tourism Organization, in consultation with major groups and other relevant international organizations, to jointly facilitate the establishment of an ad hoc informal open-ended working group on tourism to assess financial leakages and determine how to maximize benefits for indigenous and local communities; and to prepare a joint initiative to improve information availability and capacity-building for participation, and address other matters relevant to the implementation of the international work programme on sustainable tourism development (UN, 1999).

Table 6.2 shows the participation of the different core stakeholders in the tourism dialogues.

The UN Secretariat's assessment of the final outcome included the observation that "80 percent of the international work programme on sustainable tourism development adopted by CSD in 1999 came from proposals made and discussed at the multi-stakeholder dialogue on tourism" (Clark and Aydin, 2003).

This illustrated the HUGE impact that this session of the MSDs had on government policy decisions.

Juan Mayr, the Environment Minister of Columbia, was elected as the new chair of the CSD for 2000. The dialogues in 2000 focused on agriculture.

Table 6.2 Number of interventions by Major Groups per session: Tourism (Howell, 2004)

Session:	A	B	C	D	Total/group
Government	9	8	7	9	33
NGO	11	16	11	15	53
Industry	15	12	13	16	56
Trade Union	12	12	15	14	53
Local Auth.	8	9	8	8	35
IGO	0	2	0	3	5
Youth	0	1	0	0	1
Indigenous	0	0	2	0	2
Total/session	55	60	57	66	238

Four of the most relevant Major Group stakeholders were again selected to join the dialogue:

- the International Agri-Food Network for Business and Industry
- the International Federation of Agricultural Producers and Via Campesina for Farmers
- the International Confederation of Free Trade Unions (through the Trade Union Advisory Committee Organisation for Economic Cooperation and Development, and the International Union of Food and Allied Workers' Associations) for Trade Unions and Workers
- the CSD NGO Steering Committee's NGO Caucus on Sustainable Agriculture and Food Systems for Non-Governmental Organizations

The four issues addressed in 2000 were:

- Choices in agricultural production techniques, consumption patterns and safety regulations: potentials and threats to sustainable agriculture.
- Best practices in land resources management to achieve sustainable food cycles.
- Knowledge: identifying and providing for education and training as keys to a sustainable food system.
- Globalization, trade liberalization and investment patterns: economic incentives and conditions for promoting sustainable agriculture.

As Megan Howell explained in her PhD thesis:

The Dialogues were largely abstracted from reality, with participants striking an easy resonance with the values, principles and ideals of a sustainable future. However, at those few moments when participants delved beneath the self-evident to reveal deeply held values, or to share their own

144   *Felix Dodds*

experiences and struggles (such as occurred with the Indian cotton farmer in the Agriculture Dialogues), one could sense the prospect that genuine, meaningful communicative engagement between diverse groups could indeed lead to the shifts in worldviews and the kinds of creative solutions that are sought in the discourse of sustainable development. It also suggested that the UN could be well placed to facilitate such transformative encounter amongst diverse others – potentially a more constructive contribution to catalysing sustainable action and implementation (Howell, 2004).

The follow-up to the agriculture dialogues led to the establishment of another process:

46. As part of the ongoing review of progress towards SARD and within existing structures and resources, FAO and the Commission secretariat, in consultation with Governments, relevant international organizations and all major groups, are invited to continue the stakeholder dialogue on SARD, including facilitating the adequate and meaningful participation of stakeholders from developing countries. In preparing for the tenth session of the Commission and the 10-year review of the outcome of the United Nations Conference on Environment and Development, this dialogue should emphasize the identification of specific examples and the development of case studies that illustrate or support the principles of SARD (UN, 2000).

Table 6.3 shows the participation of the different core stakeholders in the dialogues.

The UN report on voluntary initiatives to the 1999 CSD showed that very little progress had occurred. There hadn't even been a follow-up, face-to-face meeting due to a lack of funds, though one was planned during the CSD. The UN set up a web portal for interested parties to showcase examples and best practices. There was an unfunded proposal for the UN to work with the

Table 6.3 Number of interventions by Major Groups per session: Agriculture (Howell, 2004)

Session:	A	B	C	D	Total/group
Government	8	7	n/a	14	29
NGO	12	6	n/a	6	24
Industry	12	9	n/a	9	30
Trade Union	8	8	n/a	9	25
Farmers	11	10	n/a	8	29
IGO	0	0	n/a	2	2
Indigenous	0	2	n/a	3	5
Total/session	51	42	n/a	51	144

Examples of successful MS policy development 145

Technology, Business and Environment Program housed within the Center for Technology, Policy, and Industrial Development at the Massachusetts Institute of Technology (MIT) to "examine the potentials of voluntary initiatives and agreements in a selected number of developing countries and one country with an economy in transition" (UN, 2000).

There was no report on follow-up to the Tourism decision of 1999. Both these multi-stakeholder initiatives suffered from a near total lack of funds to support the work.

In preparation for the Millennium Summit, the UN Secretary-General prepared his Millennium Report – "We The People: The Role of the United Nations in the 21st Century." In the report, he recognized the increasing role that stakeholders were playing:

> Better governance means greater participation, coupled with accountability. Therefore, the international public domain – including the United Nations – must be opened up further to the participation of the many actors whose contributions are essential to managing the path of globalization. Depending on the issues at hand, this may include civil society organizations, the private sector, parliamentarians, local authorities, scientific associations, educational institutions and many others (UN, 2000).

In December 2000, the UN General Assembly agreed to include multi-stakeholder processes as an integral part of the Earth Summit 2002 process, including multi-stakeholder dialogues or panels at Regional PrepComms (PrepComm 1 and 2) and at the Summit itself.

The chair for the 9th session of the Commission on Sustainable Development was Professor Bedrich Moldan from the Czech Republic, who had been the first Minister of Environment of Czechoslovakia. The fourth multi-stakeholder dialogue focused on sustainable energy and transport. This time five key Major Groups were involved:

- the International Chamber of Commerce, the World Business Council for Sustainable Development and the World Energy Council for Business and Industry
- the International Confederation of Free Trade Unions (through the Trade Union Advisory Committee to the Organisation for Economic Cooperation and Development) for Workers and Trade Unions
- the NGO Caucus on Energy and Climate Change and NGO Caucus on Sustainable Transport of the CSD NGO Steering Committee for Non-Governmental Organizations
- the International Council for Local Environmental Initiatives for Local Authorities
- the International Council of Scientific Unions and the World Conservation Union for the Scientific and Technological Community

146   *Felix Dodds*

The four dialogue sessions addressed:

- Achieving equitable access to sustainable energy.
- Sustainable choices for producing, distributing and consuming energy.
- Public private partnerships to achieve sustainable energy for transport.
- Sustainable transport planning: choices and models for human settlement design and vehicle alternatives.

Unlike the previous CSD, no multi-stakeholder follow-up process was initiated. The two previous processes on voluntary initiatives and financial leakage in the tourism industry had petered out. According to stakeholders, this was due to a lack of interest in the UN Secretariat and their inability to find funds to enable these initiatives to grow and bear fruit.

Table 6.4 shows the participation of the different core stakeholders in the energy and transport dialogues.

There were a number of reasons why this session of the MSDs suffered from poor engagement by member states.

First, energy was a very politically sensitive issue, particularly in relation to climate change. Energy hadn't made it as an original chapter of Agenda 21 in 1992 because of opposition from OPEC countries and the United States under President George H. W. Bush.

Energy with transport and tourism were added in 1997 at Rio+5. This was achieved because of a more engaged US under President Bill Clinton and the urgency of preparations for the UN Framework Convention on Climate Change (UNFCCC) meeting in Kyoto in December 1997.

Second, there was to be an ongoing intersessional process set up by the CSD to prepare for a major outcome at the upcoming World Summit on Sustainable

Table 6.4 Number of interventions by Major Groups per session: Energy/Transport (Howell, 2004)

Session:	A	B	C	D	Total/group
Government	5	7	3	3	18
NGO	9	8	7	9	33
Industry	10	6	9	8	33
Trade Union	7	5	7	7	26
Local Auth.	5	4	4	5	18
Scientists	5	8	8	7	28
IGO	1	1	0	0	2
Youth	0	1	0	0	1
Indigenous	3	0	0	0	3
Total/session	45	40	38	39	162

Examples of successful MS policy development 147

Development (WSSD), and this allowed the energy issue to be kicked down the road until 2002.

Thirdly, there were too many Major Groups in each session to have a productive dialogue. It became clear that four was the maximum number of participating groups that a three-hour session with governments and UN could meaningfully support.

Finally, Chair Moldan did not shape the discussion by challenging the participants. Moldan, who had been the first Environment Minister for the newly independent Czechoslovakia in 1992, was now chairing the CSD as a representative of the Czech Republic, but had fallen out with the then Czech Environment Minister. This seriously weakened his ability to innovate, and he became more reliant on a conservative secretariat.

The multi-stakeholder dialogues (1997–2001) were recognized as a unique way to involve stakeholders in assessing progress in Agenda 21 implementation. They even helped to build consensus among the stakeholders in some areas. The dialogues also fostered a better understanding of why particular stakeholders held certain views and helped to build the foundations for generating new multi-stakeholder partnerships for sustainable development outlined in the ten-year review of Agenda 21 – the WSSD (see Chapter 7 for more on this).

In terms of policy impacts, the CSD decisions between 1998 and 2001 increasingly reflected much of what was discussed in the multi-stakeholder dialogue sessions and the key role stakeholders played in implementing session outcomes.

Such dialogues were considered an integral component of the preparations for the World Summit on Sustainable Development in September 2002. But an observation after the 2001 CSD by Megan Howell, on the staff of the CSD NGO Steering Committee at the time, turned out to be very accurate:

> Of course, a number of contextual factors contribute to this perceived decline – including the politicised nature of the energy issue, and the disinclination (verging on hostility) of some of the participants to engage with each other. Nonetheless, the change of character from 1998 to 2001 reveals a deeper failure of organisers and participants to learn from their experience over the years, and to enhance the quality of their communicative engagement. Perhaps as a consequence of the heavy time and resource demands of preparing for and participating in the Dialogues, significant questions about the objectives, processes and outcomes of the Dialogues went unasked and unanswered (Howell, 2004).

National level: Sustainable development councils and commissions

The United Nations World Commission on Environment and Development (1987), more commonly known as the Brundtland Commission, suggested that countries may "consider the designation of a national council, public

148 *Felix Dodds*

representative or 'ombudsman' to represent the interests and rights of present and future generations" (WCED, 1987).

The Earth Summit in 1992 underlined this in Chapters 8 and 38 of Agenda 21, which recommended the establishment of National Councils for Sustainable Development (NCSD) to ensure the development and implementation of strategies and policies on sustainable development.

> States may wish to consider setting up a national coordination structure responsible for the follow-up of Agenda 21. Within this structure, which would benefit from the expertise of non-governmental organizations, submissions and other relevant information could be made to the United Nations (UN, 1992).

The establishment of NCSD was a real opportunity to create national mechanisms that could help achieve more integrated long-term approaches to delivering sustainable development not dependent on national elections. As importantly, NCSD created a space to build trust, agree on a common vision and share knowledge. This fostered increased acceptance of policy decisions among the public. The 1990s were an experimental time, with stakeholder engagement at all levels. But at the same time, they were also engaged at those expanded levels with the different policy agendas as advocates or implementers.

This process built on a rich tradition initially set up after the Second World War where National Economic and Social Councils (NESCs) were established in Europe to bring together different stakeholders to help with post-war reconstruction. NESCs contributed to many diverse stakeholders working together, and by enabling a national platform to exist, they became the forerunners of the NCSD. In some cases, they were converted into NCSDs, or two bodies merged into one.

By the time of the World Summit on Sustainable Development (WSSD) in 2002, there were over 100 NCSDs (or equivalents) around the world. These were established through widely diverse mechanisms, such as:

- Presidential decree: Argentina and Vietnam
- Ministerial decree: Niger and Barbados
- Council of State decision: Finland
- National law: Mexico and Philippines
- Letter from the environment minister: Norway
- Cabinet resolution: Ukraine and Grenada

The structures of NCSDs differed from country to country but (per IIED in 2005) had common attributes such as focus on the following:

- consensus-building
- engagement and partnership

Examples of successful MS policy development 149

- fair process
- transparency.

A more recent review of the purpose and mandate on a number of NCSDs is reflected in Table 6.5 produced in 2018 by Stakeholder Forum (Nouhan et al., 2018).

In 2019, not many of these councils still exist, but those that do have become an accepted part of the national governance for sustainable development in their respective countries. The long-established NCSDs have been interesting. In particular, the German NCSD has developed some useful processes that other countries could learn from.

Germany produced its first strategy for sustainable development for the World Summit on Sustainable Development (WSSD) and has since then had its strategy peer group reviewed three times (in 2009, 2013 and most recently in 2018). The most recent review underlined some important lessons such as having the leadership of the council in the Chancellery (Prime Minister) convening meetings at the ministerial level.

Table 6.5 Examples of NCSDs supported by NSDSs (Nouhan et al., 2018)

National Councils for Sustainable Development (NCSD)	National Sustainable Development Strategies (NSDS)	NCSDs Role in Relation to NSDS
Bangladesh Sustainable Development Monitoring Council	National Sustainable Development Strategy 2010–21 (NSDS)	NCSD ensured effective implementation and monitors NSDS progress
Estonian National Commission on Sustainable Development	Estonian Sustainable Development Act and the Sustainable Development Strategy (SE21)	NCSD monitors progress towards SE21
Hungarian National Council for Sustainable Development	National Framework Strategy on Sustainable Development of Hungary	NCSD mandated by parliament to analyze NSCD implementation
Mauritian Maurice Ile Durable Commission (MID)	Maurice Ile Durable Policy, Strategy and Action Plan (MID SAP)	MID was created by the government to ensure compliance, monitoring and follow-up of the MID SAP
Tunisian National Commission for Sustainable Development	National Sustainable Development Strategy (NSDS)	NCSD developed the NSDS, analyzes and monitors its implementation, along with other national sustainable development policies (Indicators of Sustainable Development - National Agency for the Protection of the Environment)

150   *Felix Dodds*

The 2018 review made clear that there is still a need for more coordination because twenty-nine of the strategy's sixty-three indicators are off-track. This calls for a strong action plan for the State Secretaries' Committee and for departmental action plans that include accountability. Partnerships with stakeholders are also trending in the wrong direction. The strategy's indicator system suggests that challenges relating to agriculture, land use, and energy mean that targets would not be met on current trends. The review also identified the need for more progress on links ("interlinkages") between areas. The focus on interlinkages is something that the German government has been aware of and pioneered perhaps more than any other government. But even they have found it difficult to have people work across silos. Interestingly, the peer review endorsed performance auditing and recommended that the German Council for Sustainable Development be granted independent legal entity status:

> The oversight mechanisms provided by parliaments and national audit institutions are important globally in monitoring progress on sustainable development and ensuring accountability. The Peer Review recommended greater powers for the Bundestag's Advisory Committee on Sustainable Development. We also suggested that ways be found to reflect the Strategy in the Government's budget to enable monitoring. As well, we noted the decision of the International Organisation of Supreme Audit Institutions Congress in 2016 that the national institutions should undertake performance audits on SDG implementation, thereby contributing to ensuring accountability.
>
> The German Council for Sustainable Development was established in 2001 and is a well-respected convener of stakeholders and advisor of government on cross-cutting issues of sustainability. Consideration should be given to it having a legal entity status which befits its independent role (Germany, 2018).

This idea of an NCSD peer group review process is a very good way of ensuring that a country has a better chance of staying on track. But Guenther Bachmann, Secretary-General of the German Council for Sustainable Development, does raise some important issues in a recent paper:

> Germany has twice already invited eminent persons and experts from abroad to scrutinize the German approach to sustainability. We have tried to learn from review processes known within the OECD and the DAC. But for peer reviewing sustainability politics, we found that those processes must change. The selection of peers and working modality must ensure a multi-stakeholder perspective. This provides for serious debate on governance and mindsets during this selection process. How could governance support inter-linkages and integration and discourage fragmentation and bilateralism, double-structures and ineffectiveness? (Bachmann, 2018)

Examples of successful MS policy development 151

The paper focuses on the need for an 18th Sustainable Development Goal that better addresses and understands that shared responsibility and global citizenship is needed to address the challenges we will and are facing.

In the early 2000s, the French government made common cause with French-speaking countries in Africa to share experiences and establish knowledge management on issues of mutual interest.

Another interesting approach we could learn from was taken by UNDESA (2009). They reviewed how to strengthen national capacity for integrating sustainable development principles into development strategies in countries emerging from conflict. They found that "only two out of ten post-conflict countries in Africa and two out of ten post-conflict countries in Asia and the Pacific are taking an NSDS approach in their comprehensive development frameworks" (UN, 2009).

That review found some messages that are still relevant to the development of any NSDS. They include recommendations for:

- Integrating all relevant strategies into the NSDS.
- Using specialists to support specific issues.
- Ensuring that national sustainable development strategies are driven by countries rather than donors.
- Working towards effective data collection, transparent decision-making and timely monitoring of results.
- Addressing the interlinkages in national sustainable development strategy is critical to fostering stakeholder participation and maximizing local knowledge.

The NCSD in Lebanon also offers useful lessons to anyone paying attention. It has been described as follows by the UN:

> The Council of Ministers established a national committee to oversee and guide the roll-out of the SDGs. The committee is chaired by the prime minister and includes 50 state officials at director-general level, to facilitate the continuation of work regardless of political developments. The committee also includes civil society and the private sector representatives to promote an open, inclusive and participatory approach. It has four thematic groups organized around the "5Ps" (People, Planet, Prosperity, Peace, [and Partnerships], justice and strong institutions). The fifth "P," Partnerships, was considered a cross cutting issue [for implementing] the SDGs. The Office of the Prime Minister serves as the committee's secretariat (UN, 2018).

When undertaken well, the NCSDs are an important way to bring in all relevant government departments and stakeholders to approach the issues, discuss tradeoffs and increase the benefits of any policy.

There have been different approaches to the setting up of National Councils or National Stakeholder bodies. Broadly speaking, there have been three types

152 Felix Dodds

of National Councils set up since the 1992 Earth Summit. In the first type, representation is internal, meaning comprised solely of government or ministerial employees and other civil servants. The second type of national council has a mixed membership comprised of both government and stakeholder representatives. The final type of national council is comprised exclusively of stakeholders.

The United Kingdom had two multi-stakeholder bodies, one formed by stakeholders with government departments on it, and the other formed by the government with stakeholders on it.

For work related to the UN Commission on Sustainable Development, the government utilized an independent body, Stakeholder Forum for a Sustainable Future (then UNED-UK Committee). At the time, Stakeholder Forum (SF) had two UK government departments on its Executive Committee, Environment and Development, but those departments did not control its work or the funding for it. Stakeholder Forum also annually elected stakeholders from the different Major Groups to its executive committee.

In this case, SF conducted in the first ten years independent multi-stakeholder reviews of the UK government's implementation of Agenda 21 both domestically and internationally. The government of the United Kingdom frequently attached Stakeholder Forum's report to its own national report submission to the UN.

For domestic work focusing on what the UK should do more broadly for sustainable development, the UK government established the Sustainable Development Commission (SDC) in late 1999. This body was funded by the four key stakeholders invited to participate in it.

SDC in its heyday described itself as follows:

> For the UK Government, the SDC has an official watchdog function, scrutinising progress on implementing its sustainable development strategy [and] monitoring targets [associated with] the sustainable management of the Government estate and procurement. We combine this with providing policy advice and helping to build capability across a range of departments (SDC, 2011).

For the first few years, the Chair of both bodies was the same person, Jonathon Porritt. Following Mr. Porritt's turn at the helm, SDC included Stakeholder Forum Chair Derek Osborn as a member. The Commission made recommendations to the government on sustainable development policy from 1993 to 2011, when it closed down during preparations for Rio+20.

Charles Nouhan, the current Chair of Stakeholder Forum, outlined the strengths and weaknesses of each NCSD type in a paper that he produced for the Friends of Governance for Sustainable Development in September 2018 (see Table 6.6).

The Rio+20 outcome document, "The Future We Want," called on countries to "strengthen national, subnational and/or local institutions or relevant multi-stakeholder bodies and processes, dealing with sustainable development" (UN,

Examples of successful MS policy development 153

Table 6.6 Strengths and weaknesses of the three models of National Councils (Nouhan et al., 2018)

Strengths	Weaknesses
Government Representative Membership NCSDs	
*Greater influence over policy, even potentially having legislative powers *Stronger leadership *Greater resources to implement strategies *Higher public profile	*Potentially less independent and objective *Higher risk of being influenced by political interests *Not necessarily conducive to long-term thinking *Can result in lower levels of ambition
Associated with Mixed Membership NCSDs	
*Likely to be more representative *Can facilitate greater participation *Greater ability to draw on a wide range of opinions and expertise *Likely to lead in more progressive recommendations	*Avoiding dominance of government voices over those of stakeholders *Avoiding deadlock and producing coherent messages in a timely manner *Avoiding siloed thinking and keeping track of the larger picture
Outside Government Membership NCSDs	
*Their independence enables thorough scrutiny of government policy and speaking out about perceived unsustainable policies and practices *Likely to be very representative and have strong connections to substantial stakeholder networks at the subnational level *Can potentially call upon large public support base to provide legitimacy and help advocate for recommendations	*Influence over decision-makers and policy *Having representatives of a high enough status and standing *Ensuring interests and expertise that go beyond environmental issues *Securing long-term funding

2012). Unfortunately, the 2030 Agenda for Sustainable Development didn't underline this requirement.

Over the years, the NCSD model has achieved a number of successes. Such councils have proven to be effective mechanisms for governments to consult with stakeholders; in doing so they have helped to build support for potentially difficult legislation. They have also helped to produce national policies and strategies on sustainable development that have advanced parts of Agenda 21 and the WSSD Johannesburg Plan of Implementation (JPoI).

A key role in the first period, 1993 to 2002 that NCSD played was in developing national strategies for sustainable development. Some actually draft them [as in] Armenia, Croatia, Hungary, Mauritius, Panama and the Philippines … A smaller number have played a key role in implementing them – these have usually been [in] smaller countries and [where NCSD was] very much linked to the government, such as [in] Mauritius and Panama (Nouhan et al., 2018).

154   *Felix Dodds*

A key weakness is that any NCSD can easily be abolished if not created under a legal mandate as governments change hands or priorities change. Another key aspect of NCSDs is that they need to be adequately funded, and most have not been. Many of the most successful ones have been linked to the office of the prime minister (e.g., in Finland and the Philippines).

Those that are supported by strong political mandate have survived. As of 2018 there are no NCSDs in 110 countries. Thirty-five new ones have been established since the 2030 Agenda was promulgated in 2015, and twenty-eight pre-existing NCSDs continue to operate. At present there are fourteen NCSDs in the European Union, and the European Strategy on Sustainable Development (European Union, 2006) declares that

> Member States should consider strengthening or where they do not yet exist, setting up multi-stakeholder national advisory councils on sustainable development to stimulate informed debate in the preparation of National Sustainable Development Strategies and/or contribute to national and EU progress reviews.

Stakeholder Forum's Charles Nouhan observes that:

> NCSD have not however been universally adopted by countries as a means of promoting sustainable development. But several of the countries that have made the most progress on sustainable development have found that NCSDs have played a valuable part in achieving this progress. Conversely, where countries have discontinued their NCSDs this has often coincided with a marked decline in political ambition to achieve more sustainable patterns of development (Nouhan et al., 2018).

The first review of the 2030 Agenda in September 2019 will offer an opportunity to establish, reactivate and reinvigorate the national multi-stakeholder councils to help accelerate the implementation of the SDGs and to help deliver their 169 targets. The national voluntary reports that have been produced in the first cycle have in some cases been produced by governments without adequate involvement of stakeholders. The 2019 review will offer the chance to give guidance to governments to again establish NCSD as a core part of their implementation, monitoring and review process.

With the SDGs being universal, the 2030 Agenda offers a real chance for every country to conduct national conversations on what the best way might be to deliver the SDGs.

The sub-national and local level: Think global, act local

As mentioned in Chapter 3, the Earth Summit (1992), through Chapter 28 of Agenda 21, was the first time that local governments were really given a role in helping to deliver a global agreement. "By 1996, most local authorities in each

Examples of successful MS policy development   155

country should have undertaken a consultative process with their populations and achieved a consensus on 'a local Agenda 21' for the community," as the final Agenda 21 text put it.

It is important to note that most environmental challenges can be addressed best at the local or sub-national level. For example, more than 60 percent of the SDG targets will be best delivered at the local level. Bearing this in mind, it isn't surprising that once engaged, local government, through ICLEI (established 1991), took a leading role in bringing their experiences to the table and helping shape better policies.

Prior to this development, most UN outcomes simply focused on the actions of national governments. It had been the general understanding that those governments should follow through on UN agreements, and had the will and ability to do so.

By 1992, though, that was a view that was starting to wear thin. It was clear that because local authorities were the closest level of government to the people, they could play a significant role in educating and promoting the kind of implementation that sustainable development demands. As we have already mentioned, Maurice Strong pushed for expanding those responsible for helping to implement Agenda 21 to the nine Major Groups, and this gave local government a real boost.

ICLEI helped local councils with guidance on how to set up Local Agenda 21s and how to develop local sustainability indicators working with their communities.

Through the 1990s ICLEI hosted workshops and conferences to help councils to share experiences and develop plans and policies. Based on this experience, the same bodies learned how to provide input at the UN level.

After the Earth Summit, representatives of European cities and towns met in 1994 and agreed to a set of sustainability principles in what was called the Aalborg Charter. This was followed by the Lisbon Action Plan (From Charter to Action, 1996) and the Hannover Call of European Municipal Leaders at the Turn of the 21st Century (2000).

By 2001, over 6,000 local authorities in 113 countries had started a dialogue with their citizens based on Chapter 28 of Agenda 21. It was one of the first times that a UN document had such a profound impact on activity at local levels.

In 2002 at WSSD (the World Summit on Sustainable Development), a new body was created to deal with sustainable development at the sub-national levels, that is, levels of government immediately below the national. This was the Network of Regional Governments for Sustainable Development (NRG4SD).

Sub-national governments, because of their intermediate position between the national and local levels, are particularly well placed for identifying the needs and capabilities of their societies for sustainable development. Sub-national governments have been effective at addressing sustainable development challenges, turning these challenges into opportunities to transition towards greener, smarter and more inclusive societies.

156 *Felix Dodds*

Regional governments are also often responsible for the elaboration and implementation of policy, legislation programmes, fiscal mechanisms and public investment plans. These are in areas the SDGs focus on such as climate action, transport, energy, agriculture, forestry, industry, spatial planning and resource management.

The NRG4SD charter framed the conversation like this:

> We believe that the implementation of sustainable development needs a strategic framework for all governments. We believe that this applies strongly in our regional spheres. Regional governments need sustainable development strategies as central frameworks for linking all their other strategies, ensuring that each is sustainable and that they are mutually supportive of each other (NRG4SD, 2002).

Since WSSD, local and sub-national governments have implemented extensive initiatives that have facilitated the success of multiple sustainable development policies such as Agenda 21, the Millennium Development Goals (MDGs), and the Johannesburg Plan of Implementation. Sub-national initiatives have also addressed climate change adaptation and mitigation strategies, nature and biodiversity conservation measures, public procurement strategies, and development cooperation projects.

In 2004, European local authorities met again in Aalborg, Denmark, and agreed to the Aalborg Commitments. These commitments consolidated ten years of local sustainability efforts into more specific commitments under nine broad themes.

The Aalborg Commitments Governance:

- We are committed to energizing our decision-making processes through increased participatory democracy.

Local management towards sustainability:

- We are committed to effective management cycles, from formulation through implementation to evaluation.

Natural common goods:

- We are committed to fully assuming our responsibility to protect, to preserve and to ensure equitable access to natural common goods.

Responsible consumption and lifestyle choices:

- We are committed to adopting and facilitating the prudent and efficient use of resources and to encouraging sustainable consumption and production.

Examples of successful MS policy development 157

Planning and design:

- We are committed to a strategic role for urban planning and design in addressing environmental, social, economic, health and cultural issues for the benefit of all.

Better mobility, less traffic:

- We recognize the interdependence of transport, health and environment, and are committed to strongly promoting sustainable mobility choices.

Local action for health:

- We are committed to protecting and promoting the health and well-being of our citizens.

Vibrant and sustainable local economy:

- We are committed to securing inclusive and supportive communities.

Social equity and justice:

- We are committed to creating and ensuring a vibrant local economy that gives access to employment without damaging the environment.

Local to global:

- We are committed to assuming our global responsibility for peace, justice, equity, sustainable development and climate protection.

After 2004, many local and sub-national councils focused more specifically on targets and action on climate change, and then on biodiversity issues, as those agendas gained global prominence.

These experiments in local democracy have faced some detractors, but criticisms made by those detractors tend to be based on the substance of particular issues under consideration and whether desired change has been achieved. Critics less often question the merits of local democracy in principle.

For example, in the US, the information being put out by organizations such as the Tea Party is often inaccurate and inflammatory.

Over the last five to ten years, critics have attempted to stop local governments in the United States from promoting sustainable development. Often, they also want the US to abandon ICLEI. At the heart of such criticism is a strong belief in local engagement coupled with a distrust for government – particularly governing bodies that are farther away from a community. Anything understood as being driven by supranational bodies such as the UN

158   *Felix Dodds*

engenders significant levels of mistrust. The challenge for the implementation of the SDGs will be to try and bridge such disagreements, perhaps by rallying around local engagement. The environment shouldn't be a left or right issue, because it affects everyone if we don't have clean water, good air to breathe and safe food. How you achieve that in a locality may differ but learning from other places is a first step and is a fundamental part of the 2030 Agenda.

Creating local jobs that help make local economies more sustainable and robust in the face of global impacts can only benefit the local community as a whole.

Since the establishment of NRG4SD in 2002, sub-national governments have been experimenting with how to make sustainable development a core aspect of their work. Perhaps one of the best examples of such experimentation is that the National Assembly for Wales passed the Well-being of Future Generations (Wales) Act in 2015. This is the main mechanism by which Wales will contribute to the achievement of the SDGs (see Box 6.2).

Box 6.2 Are regions ready? Implementing the SDGs at the sub-national level, NRG4SD Assessment Questionnaire

The National Assembly of Wales – Well-being of future Generations Act.

The Act puts into law seven well-being goals for Wales based on the principles of sustainable development. These goals reflect the economic, social, environmental and cultural dimensions of sustainable development in Wales.

This holistic strategy sets out a comprehensive plan, including indicators and follow-up mechanisms for public bodies and government long-term planning.

The Act also establishes the role of a Future Generations Commissioner for Wales and aligns accountability for achieving the goals with the public sector's overarching purpose. The 2015 Act includes a requirement for Welsh ministers to take account of any action taken by the United Nations in relation to the UN Sustainable Development in their planning for the future, and to assess the potential impact of such action on the economic, social, environmental and cultural well-being of Wales.

Another example of successful local engagement comes from the Basque Country in Spain, where they have aligned the Basque Government Programme with the 2030 Agenda (Figure 6.1).

Case study from the Basque Country

The resources of this Basque 2030 Agenda will be materialized in items of the General Budget approved by the 1Basque Country's regional Parliament with direct link to the SDGs.

The alignment of the Government Programme with the United Nations 2030 Agenda can be seen in the following scheme:

UNITED NATIONS AGENDA 2030		BASQUE GOVERNMENT PROGRAM 2017–2020						EUSKO JAURLARITZA · GOBIERNO VASCO		
OBJETIVOS DESARROLLO SOSTENIBLE (ODS)	SPHERES OF IMPORTANCE	COUNTRY OBJECTIVES		COMMITMENTS	INITIATIVES	INDICATORS	STRATEGIC PLANS		SECTORAL PLANS	LAWS
17	5	15		175	650	100	15		54	28
1. An end to poverty 2. An end to hunger/food 3. Healthy lifestyle 4. Inclusive education 5. Gender equality	PEOPLE	20% reduction in poverty Increased life expectancy Higher birth rate School dropout rate <8%. 75% of the population <25 years Basque-speaking Among the top 4 countries in terms of gender equality		65	225	33	Social Services Strategic Plan Health Plan 5th Professional Training Plan 4th University Plan 7th Equality Plan Strategic Agenda for the Basque language		18	10
6. Water and sanitation 7. Sustainable consumption and production 8. Climate change 9. Sea resources 10. Ecosystems	PLANET	20% reduction in CO2 emissions		10	35	11	4th Environmental Framework Programme		11	3
11. Economic growth and employment 12. Infrastructures and innovation 13. Energy 14. Reducing inequality 15. Cities and urban settlements	PROSPERITY	Unemployment < 10% 20,000 young people with job experience 125% of the EU's GDP 25% industrial GDP 100 strategic innovation projects Leader in terms of transparency indexes		64	278	51	Strategic Employment Plan Basque Industry 4.0 Industrialisation Plan Basque Science and Technology Plan 2017–2020 Tourism, Trade and Consumption Plan Governance and Public Innovation Plan		16	13
16. Peace and justice	PEACE	Disarming and dissolving ETA		24	80	3	Co-habitation and Human Rights Plan Public Security Plan		6	2
17. Partnerships / cooperation for development	PARTNERSHIP	New political status		12	32	2	"Euskadi – Basque Country" Internationalisation Strategy		3	

Figure 6.1 Alignment of the Basque Government Programme with the United Nations 2030 Agenda, Basque Country

160 *Felix Dodds*

These items focus on promoting equal opportunities for particularly vulnerable groups (women, children and the migrant population), reducing inequality and improving environmental management and the conservation and restoration of ecosystems; they also address investments in social protection, health, education, nature conservation, the fight against climate change and cooperation policies for development.

As an example of a first effort to finance the Agenda Euskadi–Basque Country 2030 is the Sustainable Bonds (Euskadi Sustainable Bonds-ESB) launched in May 2018. These Bonds make a visible and concrete contribution to the financing and implementation of the SDGs.

To understand Sustainable Bonds, it is worth noting that the Basque Country has had its own tax system for the last 150 years. The so-called Economic Agreement is a structure of bilateral tax and financial relations between the Basque Country and Spain. That means having an own autonomous internal revenue system through full management power, levying and collection of practically all taxes. Once collected by the autonomous internal revenue service of the region, an agreed amount (quota) is transferred to the federal government for the services it provides in the Basque Country.

In short, to carry out its public policies, the Basque Government has two financing channels: the collection of taxes and the bond issuance that, subsequently, has to be reimbursed to investors.

The "Euskadi Sustainable Bonds" promote the implementation of the Agenda Euskadi–Basque Country 2030. The resources raised through the bond issue (500 million euros this year) will be used to finance programs that address some of the social and environmental challenges identified in the Agenda.

The compliance is supported by an external review carried out by one of the three major European environmental, social and governance rating agencies: Sustainalytics.

This agency has rated the bonds as a solid, credible and transparent financial product. It has verified that the categories of eligible programs and target populations are aligned with the principles of the green and social bonds. Moreover, that the selection and evaluation of projects that can be financed, as well as the management of income, are in line with good market practices, including the integration of environmental and social criteria into the hiring policies of the Basque administration.

The 500 million euros that were raised with the Euskadi Sustainable Bond issuance will be distributed in the following way: 81 percent will go to social projects and 19 percent to green projects. All of these projects will have an impact on one, or several SDGs.

Localization of the Sustainable Development Goals

Localization of the Sustainable Development Goals has been the call sign of the post 2030 Agenda and SDG implementation. It is being supported by the Global Taskforce of Local and Regional Governments, UNDP and UN Habitat have been in partnership. Localization of the SDGs has focused on four elements:

Examples of successful MS policy development   161

1   Awareness-raising: Getting to know the SDGs at sub-national level
2   Advocacy: Including a sub-national perspective in national SDG strategies
3   Implementation: The SDGs go local
4   Monitoring: Evaluating and learning from our experience

This approach brings together the local and regional governments and enables even more positive sharing between this level of governments and the relevant UN bodies that are working at the national level in many developing countries.

Conclusion

The experience of the last twenty-five years, first with local and regional Agenda 21s, and now with the localization of the SDGs, is all about strengthening local representative democracy by increasing stakeholder engagement in helping to address what the priorities of a local or sub-national government are. After those priorities are identified in a mutually satisfactory way, the idea is that continued local engagement can help deliver on the SDG goals, whether in partnership with larger government bodies or, where relevant, making good on voluntary commitments exclusively at the local level.

The next stage in sustainable development agenda-driving is to link any sub-national and local strategy for the SDGs with the national strategies. When a government is putting together any national strategy, it should reflect the work that needs to be undertaken at all levels of government and all stakeholders and citizens in their territories.

One of the key aspects of the SDGs when they were agreed was that it was for all countries. Another key aspect was that there would of necessity be interlinkage between the 17 goals and their associated 169 targets. There are many key "nexuses" in the goals and targets but perhaps the most advanced is the conversation around the goals on energy, water, food and climate change.

The greatest impacts of climate change are obviously felt at the local level. In the past, different policy options were mostly done sectorally. That is no longer an option, because we now need to address policy options cross-sectorally as well. A friend of mine who worked in local government – Gary Lawrence (formerly Chief Planner in Seattle, Washington) – paraphrased this insight by saying that we must "embrace complexity."

What does this mean? It means that we need to have both vertical conversations between the different levels of government and also horizontal engagement with stakeholders involved in the different sectors. The development of more integrated policy will require new conversations and trade-offs between sectors.

> Multi-level governance platforms should ensure coherence between the sectoral priorities of national government departments and those of local and regional governments. Inter-municipal cooperation, including cross-border cooperation where appropriate, should be used by local governments to

162 *Felix Dodds*

jointly assess their needs, define their SDG priorities and develop programmes and plans at territorial level (Global Taskforce, 2018).

The involvement of stakeholders in the policy arena and in multi-stakeholder partnerships (see Chapter 7) has over the last twenty-five years been significant. The 2030 Agenda for Sustainable Development and within that the Sustainable Development Goals and their Targets represent a common understanding by all stakeholders including governments on what the challenges facing us are, and now we must work together to address them.

In 2018, New York City became the first city in the world to produce a voluntary report. Countries have been asked to do this, but NYC may be the beginning of a process that local and sub-national governments can emulate as they start to report on SDG implementation and the challenges they are facing.

References

Bachmann, G. (2018) The 18th SDG: Sustainable Development in a Changing World: A Changing Perspective on Sustainability. Incheon Songdo: German Council for Sustainable Development. Available online at: https://www.nachhaltigkeitsrat.de/wp-content/uploads/2017/11/Bachmann_Think_Piece_SDG_18_UN_OSD_SDTF_2016-10-27.pdf

Clark, J. and Aydin, Z. (2003) UN System and Civil Society – An Inventory and Analysis of Practices: Background Paper for the Secretary-General's Panel of Eminent Persons on United Nations Relations with Civil Society. New York: United Nations.

Earth Negotiations Bulletin (ENB) (1998) CSD-6 Highlights Wednesday, 22 April 1998. Winnipeg: International Institute for Sustainable Development. Available online at: http://enb.iisd.org/vol05/enb05103e.html

European Union (2006) European Strategy on Sustainable Development. Brussels: European Commission. Available online at: http://register.consilium.europa.eu/doc/srv?l=EN&f=ST%2010117%202006%20INIT

Germany (2018) The 2018 International Peer Review of the German Sustainable Development Strategy. Berlin: German Council for Sustainable Development. Available online at: https://www.nachhaltigkeitsrat.de/wp-content/uploads/2018/05/2018_Peer_Review_of_German_Sustainability_Strategy_BITV.pdf

Global Taskforce (2018) Roadmap for Localizing the SDGs: Implementation and Monitoring at the Subnational Level. Barcelona: Global Taskforce, UNDP and UN Habitat. Available online at: https://sustainabledevelopment.un.org/content/documents/commitments/818_11195_commitment_ROADMAP%20LOCALIZING%20SDGS.pdf

Habito, C. (1998) in Strauss, M. (1999) The Dialogue Records: The UN Commission on Sustainable Development Government / Business / Labour / NGO Dialogue Sessions. Year One: 21–22 April, 1998, 'Industry and Sustainable Development.' The Verbatim Text, with Summaries and Analysis (draft). New York: Norwegian Forum for Environment and Development.

Howell, M. (2004) A thesis submitted in fulfillment of the requirements for the degree of Doctor of Philosophy in Planning: Sustaining Dialogue A Study of the Multi-Stakeholder Dialogues at the United Nations Commission on Sustainable Development, The University of Auckland.

Examples of successful MS policy development   163

Network for Regional Government for Sustainable Development (NRG4SD) (2002). The Gauteng Declaration. Gauteng: NRG4SD. Available online at: http://www.nrg4sd.org/wp-content/uploads/2015/06/gauteng-en.pdf

Nouhan, C., Osborn, D., Cornforth, J. and Ullah, F. (2018) What Is the Role of National Multi-Stakeholder Platforms in Advancing the 2030 Agenda, and How Can They Be Best Encouraged and Supported?New York: Friends of Governance for Sustainable Development.

Sustainable Development Commission (SDC) UK (2011) Our Role – Who We Are. London: SDC. Available online at: http://www.sd-commission.org.uk/pages/about-us.html

United Nations (1992) Agenda 21 Chapter 38 Section J40. New York: UN. Available online at: http://www.un-documents.net/a21-38.htm

United Nations (1996) Report of The United Nations Conference on Human Settlements (Habitat II). Istanbul: UN. Available online at: https://www.un.org/ruleoflaw/wp-content/uploads/2015/10/istanbul-declaration.pdf

United Nations (1999) Commission on Sustainable Development, Seventh Session – Report of the Secretary General: Voluntary Initiatives and Agreements. New York: UN. Available online at: http://www.un.org/ga/search/view_doc.asp?symbol=E/CN.17/1999/20&Lang=E

United Nations (2000) Commission on Sustainable Development, Eighth Session – Report of the Secretary General: Follow-Up Work on Voluntary Initiatives and Agreements. New York: UN. Available online at: http://www.un.org/ga/search/view_doc.asp?symbol=E/CN.17/2000/17%20&Lang=E

United Nations (2009) How to Strengthen National Capacity for the Integrations of Sustainable Development Principles into Development Strategies in Countries Emerging from Conflict. Nairobi: UNDESA. Available online at: https://sustainabledevelopment.un.org/content/documents/1377EGM_NSDSReportFinal221209.pdf

United Nations (2012) The Future We Want. New York: UN. Available online at: http://enb.iisd.org/vol05/enb05103e.html

United Nations (2018) Voluntary National Reviews: Synthesis Report. New York: UN. Available online at: https://sustainabledevelopment.un.org/content/documents/210732018_VNRs_Synthesis_compilation_11118_FS_BB_Format_FINAL_cover.pdf

World Commission on Environment and Development (WCED) (1987) Report of the World Commission on Environment and Development: Our Common Future. New York: UN. Available online at: http://www.un-documents.net/wced-ocf.htm

7 Multi-stakeholder partnerships

Making them work for delivering global agreements

Jan-Gustav Strandenaes

Introduction

This book addresses the role of stakeholders in policy development and practice to develop and deliver global agreements. This chapter focusses on the role that multi-stakeholder partnerships (MSPs) might play; it is part of a trilogy of chapters with Chapters 8 and 9 being the other parts of the trilogy. Between these three chapters we will try and show where MSPs have come from, some examples of them and some guidance on how to undertake them based on the experience of the writers.

Since 2000, there have been a growing number of partnerships within and outside the United Nations. This plethora of partnerships is considered by some effective and making an impact on development, but many partnerships are evidently falling short of delivering results while incurring high transaction costs.

Multi-stakeholder partnerships have been discussed at the UN with growing intensity for the last two decades: at present the Second Committee of the UN General Assembly passes a resolution on partnerships; every year the Economic and Social Council hosts a one-day Partnership Forum (UN, 2011). MSPs have been a part of the ECOSOC's subsidiary bodies such as the Commission on Sustainable Development (1993–2013) and, most recently, attention has been focused by the UN High Level Political Forum (HLPF) – the coordinating mechanisms for the 2030 Agenda. The HLPF hosts a Partnership Exchange to share practical experience.

Following the adoption of the 2030 Agenda for Sustainable Development, there has been an emerging consensus that partnerships must be aligned with this new agenda and its identified goals. The experience of the past fifteen or more years should help in streamlining and building on already existing and successful mechanisms and processes. Is that fifteen-year experience sufficient to guarantee success?

A number of reviews, undertaken by various researchers and academics, have found that despite a rapid increase in partnerships, many are falling short of delivering on the results promised (Kupcu, 2007; Schäferhoff et al., 2009). This chapter is therefore intended to inform ECOSOC's discussion on multi-stakeholder partnerships based on some lessons learnt, so that they can become more successful in the post-2015 era.

One element that experience makes clear is that a more robust form of monitoring and review mechanism is needed to determine the success of these MSPs. Coupled with this, there have been calls for a stronger intergovernmental oversight to improve the quality and perhaps the quantity, and enable the replicating of successful MSPs.

It is well understood that MSPs are complex organizational structures, and no two seem to be completely alike. But what can be developed is a framework whose elements can inform and support the accountability of partnerships (Summary of Stocktaking Event, 2015).

The Charter for multi-stakeholder partnerships discussed in Chapter 8 can help in guiding those engaged in the development of MSPs, and in Chapter 9 we copy these ideas on designing successful MSPs which will help those planning to create one and perhaps give those that are already engaged in an MSP food for thought.

Understanding terms

One of the many problems that have emerged in the discussion on multi-stakeholder partnerships is that often they are confused or used interchangeably with other approaches such as voluntary initiatives (VIs) or public private partnerships (PPPs).

All three are relevant and, in differing situations, can be useful, but each needs to be treated separately, and each requires different approaches in reporting, capacity-building, knowledge management and key governance issues.

To start, here are basic definitions relating to the three terms (see Box 7.1).

Box 7.1 Key definitions of terms

Multi-stakeholder partnerships: for sustainable development are specific commitments and contributions, undertaken together by various partners intended to support the implementation of transformation towards sustainable development and help achieve the Sustainable Development Goals (SDGs) and other relevant sustainable development agreements. The partners can include national and sub-national governments, intergovernmental organizations (IGOs), businesses, trade unions, NGOs, academics, religious associations and indigenous peoples' organizations, among others.

Voluntary initiatives: The United Nations Conference on Sustainable Development (Rio+20) invited organizations to make individual commitments focusing on delivering concrete results for sustainable development on a voluntary basis.

Public private partnerships: are contractual arrangements between single or several public agencies (national, sub-national or local) and single or several private sector entities. Through such arrangements, the skills and assets of each sector (public and private) are shared, in delivering a service or facility for the use of the general public. Other stakeholders might be sub-contractors in a PPP.

166   *Jan-Gustav Strandenaes*

To design partnerships for the future, governments, the UN and stakeholders need to build on past successful partnerships and create a more systematic approach to Multi-Stakeholder Partnerships which are aligned to the goals and targets of the 2030 Agenda. The outcome of multilateral discussions can offer insights into problems relating to MSPs, both in terms of national, domestic issues, global priorities, national demands and global prerequisites.

The collection of experience from multilateral conferences and meetings should provide substantial insights into the complexities of how to create a set of basic principles and guidelines that can guide Multi-Stakeholder Partnerships associated with the UN, including with the existing Guidelines on Cooperation between the UN and the business sector. Such experience can be found in intergovernmental discussions at relevant forums such as the HLPF, the SAMOA Pathway, the ECOSOC Partnership Forum and other UN bodies.

Partnerships organized around the 2030 Agenda including the Sustainable Development Goals must be grounded on the SDGs' two sets of foundational elements. First, they are integrated, indivisible and universal. Second, they include environmental, social and economic dimensions. These six elements are almost always referred to – and accepted, at least in theory – but they represent serious challenges when it comes to designing and implementing MSPs.

Another current theme in sustainable development deeply affecting the development of MSPs is the growing realization of the complexity of a global sustainable development agenda. In recognition of this complexity, and in making serious efforts to integrate the six elements referred to above, the political landscape has been widening and its narrative expanding.

History of multi-stakeholder partnerships

Since the 1990s, partnerships with these various groups, including foundations, business associations and individual private sector companies, have increasingly become an integral part of many United Nations programmes' and agencies' work. These partnerships have not only complemented the efforts of the UN system to achieve its objectives, but also contributed to its renewal by introducing new methods of work. While these partnerships cannot be a substitute for government responsibilities and commitments, they continue to be instrumental in the implementation of the outcomes of the United Nations conferences and summits. This also includes the realization of the internationally agreed development goals, including the Millennium Development Goals (MSDs) and will be the case for the sustainable development goals. Successful partnerships bring each partner's core competence and experience to the table, building synergies to co-create new and impactful strategies for achieving sustainable development.

The UN Global Compact (UNGC) is the world's largest voluntary corporate sustainability initiative. It has grown to include over 9,500 corporate participants and 3,000 non-business participants based in 160 countries since its launch by former Secretary-General Kofi Annan in 2000. In line with its UN General Assembly mandate to "promote responsible business practices and UN values among the global business community and the UN System", the Global Compact encourages companies throughout the world to voluntarily align their operations and strategies with ten universally accepted principles in the areas of human rights, labor, environment and anti-corruption, and to take action in support of UN goals. UNGC's network-based governance framework reflects the initiative's multi-stakeholder and public-private character, distributing governance functions among government, business and civil society actors through several entities which engage participants and stakeholders at the global and local levels in making decisions and giving advice. (A listing of the Global Compact's Ten Principles can be found in Annex 2.)

The **General Assembly** initially addressed the issue of enhancing partnerships between the UN and all its relevant partners in 2000. Its first resolution on partnerships was simply called "Towards Global Partnerships" and it continues to address the issue on a biennial basis. Its many subsequent resolutions on the theme are simply called TGPs. The GA reviews general trends in partnerships, looking at concepts, modalities and lessons learned, and has encouraged the agencies, funds and programmes to uphold the integrity of the UN by placing greater emphasis on impact, transparency, coherence, accountability and sustainability.

The purpose of these reports and the debates they engendered was to see how partnerships could interact with the UN system: how would they perform in terms of time lines, reviews, monitoring, reporting systems, etc. How could the UN engage in MSPs and still guarantee accountability and credibility which would also safeguard the core values of the UN. That these values must not be compromised was frequently the clear message from member states.

In 2000, the Secretary-General presented the "Guidelines on Cooperation between the UN and the Business Community." It was revised twice, and now carries the name: "Guidelines on a principle-based approach to the cooperation between the UN and the business sector." This document has been in use since 2015. It sets out minimum requirements for business to follow in engaging with the UN in projects: adhere to fundamental norms and principles of the UN, be transparent and accountable. Experience, however, has shown that whereas the business sector is often trying to uphold these principles, the various UN secretariats have been rather lax, and instead used what seems pertinent to their part of the UN.

Meanwhile, **ECOSOC** began to convene **Partnership Forums**, from 2008 onwards, as part of its new mandate on Annual Ministerial Reviews. The forums include representatives from the private sector and philanthropic communities, NGOs and academia to assess how they could contribute to themes that include environmental sustainability, global public health, gender equality, education, jobs and decent work. These meetings have also served to promote partnership initiatives.

Prior to the Partnership Forum, ECOSOC had been instrumental in the creation of the **Task Force on Information and Communications Technology** (ICT Task Force), one of the first major multi-stakeholder initiatives mandated

168   *Jan-Gustav Strandenaes*

by an intergovernmental body (ECOSOC resolution 2000/29). It was the first UN body with membership representing governments (26 members), civil society organizations (4 members), the private sector (11 members) and organizations of the UN system (14 members) with equal decision-making power. Its objective was to provide leadership to the UN in helping formulate strategies to use ICTs for development and to reduce the digital divide.

As mentioned earlier, the Earth Summit in 1992 was the first conference to explicitly call for the active engagement of various "social groups" in the follow-up of Agenda 21, and to identify their roles and responsibilities. Agenda 21 identified nine stakeholder groups that could play a role in developing policy and implementing agreements (UN, 1992).

Ten years after the Earth Summit there was a substantial advance in the interaction with these stakeholders when they were allowed to formally participate in the preparatory phase of the **World Summit on Sustainable Development** (WSSD). As discussed in Chapter 6 a growing consensus had emerged among governments (and some, though not all, of the stakeholders involved) that traditional intergovernmental relations were no longer sufficient to implement sustainable development (SDIN, 2002). A primary motivation was to bring in necessary additional financial resources that it was hoped would flow from the private sector. Consequently, the WSSD incorporated suggestions for increasingly decentralized and participatory approaches that became formally known as **Type II partnerships.** Type II partnerships were meant to complement **Type I outcomes**, or agreements and commitments made by governments, and were characterized as "collaborations between national or sub-national governments, private sector actors and civil society actors, who form voluntary transnational agreements in order to meet specific sustainable development goals."[1]

The Summit negotiations concluded that Type II partnerships must meet seven key criteria:

i   They should be voluntary and based on shared responsibility.
ii They must complement, rather than substitute, intergovernmental sustainable development strategies, and must meet the agreed outcomes of the Johannesburg summit.
iii They must be international in scope and reach and consist of a range of multi-level stakeholders, preferably within a given area of work and have clear objectives.
iv They must ensure transparency and accountability.
v   They must have specific targets and timeframes for their achievement and produce tangible results.
vi The partnership must be new, and adequate funding must be available.
vii A follow-up process must be developed.

These criteria built on the **Bali Guidelines**, which were developed during the preparatory phase for the Summit (UN, 2002). (See Annex 1 for full Bali Guidelines.)

Multi-stakeholder partnerships 169

In 2003, these partnership guidelines were updated during the 11th Session of the **Commission on Sustainable Development** to, inter alia, emphasize that they should bear in mind the economic, social and environmental dimensions of sustainable development in their design and implementation; should be based on predictable and sustained resources for their implementation and should result in the transfer of technology to, and capacity-building in, developing countries. They also emphasized that the involvement of international institutions and United Nations funds, programmes and agencies in partnerships should conform to inter-governmentally agreed mandates and should not lead to the diversion to partnerships of resources otherwise allocated for their mandated programmes. The CSD decision agrees that partnerships:

- Are voluntary initiatives undertaken by governments and relevant stakeholders.
- Contribute to the implementation Agenda 21, JPoI.
- Are not intended to substitute commitments made by governments.
- Bear in mind the economic, social and environmental dimensions.
- Are predictable and sustained resources for their implementation, should include the mobilization of new resources, and where relevant, should result in the transfer of technology to, and capacity-building in, developing countries.
- Are designed and implemented in a transparent and accountable manner.
- Should be consistent with national laws and national strategies.
- Provide information and reporting and are registered with the CSD.

The outcome from the CSD was then endorsed by ECOSOC and, in December 2018, still represents the only real set of criteria and guidelines that the UN is instructed to use in relation to MSPs.

In the broadest sense, how the UN family deals with – or is trying to deal with – the partnership issue is fragmented. In 2009 the UN Office of Internal Oversight Services (OIOS) strongly proposed a unified framework for partnerships within the UN system. This was followed up a year later by a report from the Joint Inspection Unit at the UN suggesting that the Global Compact and the UN Fund for International Partnerships be merged.

The 2012 **United Nations Conference on Sustainable Development** (Rio+20) was the most inclusive UN conference to date. All stakeholders, including government, civil society and the private sector, were invited to make voluntary commitments that deliver concrete results for sustainable development. By the end of the conference, over 700 voluntary commitments were announced and compiled into an online registry managed by the Rio+20 Secretariat. Collectively, these commitments – from governments, intergovernmental organizations, business, industry, financial institutions and civil society groups, among others – represented more than $500 billion in actions towards sustainable development. These commitments have since grown to more than 1,400 with a financial commitment of around $636 million (Seth, 2013). The official process

170   *Jan-Gustav Strandenaes*

recognized these commitments by inviting the UN Secretary-General to set up an Internet-based registry, in order to make information about the commitments fully transparent and accessible to the public. In a review conducted by Stakeholder Forum and NRDC in September 2013, some initiatives had already achieved their objective, such as Microsoft fulfilling its commitment to become carbon neutral just one year after Rio+20, and the Multilateral Development Banks (MDBs) well on their way to their commitment of $175 billion to sustainable development programmes (Stakeholder Forum and NRDC, 2013). A system to monitor these individual commitments does not yet exist.

The present Secretary-General, Antonio Guterres, has taken up the mantle and proposed a system-wide approach to partnerships and is developing a more robust due diligence approach to companies.

Guterres and his staff have come up with new ideas incorporated in the proposed reform of the UN Development System (UNDS); one such idea is to extend the UN's "convening power via partnership platforms." The report advocates for embedding MSPs in the UN's core business model. He may well have picked up these ideas from the independent report on the same issue by former Director General of ILO Juan Somavia and former German Federal Minister of Environment and Executive Director of UNEP Dr. Klaus Töpfer.

The notion of global partnerships and multi-stakeholder approaches are now very much accepted to be an integral part of the multilateral cooperation, such that the theme of the **Third International Conference on Small Island Developing States** (SIDS, 2014, Apia, Samoa) was "The sustainable development of small island developing States through genuine and durable partnerships." Nearly 300 partnerships were registered in the lead-up to the Conference, addressing a range of priority areas, including sustainable economic development, climate change & disaster risk management, social development in Small Island Developing States (SIDS), health and NCDs, youth and women, sustainable energy, oceans, seas and biodiversity, water and sanitation, and food security and waste management. An important recommendation in the outcome document for the Conference was the request for a partnership framework to monitor and ensure the full implementation of pledges and commitments through partnerships for SIDS. The SIDS Action Platform was developed to support the follow-up to the Conference, including through a partnership's platform, a partnership's framework and a UN Implementation Matrix.

Whereas the first TGP from the office of Guterres stressed inclusivity as an important feature of MSPs, the later report seems less interested in this factor and rather pushes for "innovation, scalability and impact" for SDGs. UN staff has at different meetings expressed the need for precise and better coordinated rules for partnerships; however, not necessarily of a meta-governance kind. Concluding her interviews with critical NGO representatives, Beisheim writes:

> These [meta governance rules] should ideally be binding under international law and linked to a binding treaty on transnational or other business enterprises, like the one negotiated by the open-ended intergovernmental

working group that has been established by the UN Human Rights Council in 2014 (Beisheim and Ellersiek, 2017).

To enable the UN website for registering the commitments made for MSPs and Volunteer Initiatives, the UN over time developed a number of strategies to monitor the partnerships, even without an intergovernmental decision. It introduced two approaches based on the SAMOA Pathway. The first is the registering of SMART criteria – "Specific, Measurable, Achievable, Resource-based, with Time-based deliverables." It is also in the process of introducing a "traffic lights" approach to registered MSPs and VIs, in relation to the requirement that they report annually. The suggestion is that if they don't report within a year, a yellow light will be assigned against their partnership, and if they haven't reported within two years a red light will be assigned. After three years of non-reporting they would be de-listed.

The HLPF's established mandate includes a "platform for partnerships."

> The HLPF, under the auspices of ECOSOC, shall carry out regular reviews, in line with Resolution 67/290. Reviews will be voluntary, while encouraging reporting, and include developed and developing countries as well as relevant UN entities and other stakeholders, including civil society and the private sector. They shall be state-led, involving ministerial and other relevant high-level participants. They shall provide a platform for partnerships, including through the participation of major groups and other relevant stakeholders (UN, 2013).

Reviewing global partnerships

"Let a thousand flowers bloom," Nitin Desai, Secretary-General of WSSD, said in relation to MSPs, at the end of the Johannesburg Summit in 2002. A number of reviews of partnerships have been undertaken by researchers and scholars since 2002 in an attempt to answer:

- What has happened since then?
- Are they on track to deliver as they set out to do?
- What are the lessons learned from existing review mechanisms?
- How can progress be measured?
- And who has the authority to do so?

From the beginning there were questions about the scope and impact of these partnerships. Hale (2003) observed that many existing partnership initiatives from WSSD were simply re-categorized, with just a few select countries participating covering a narrow list of issue areas. The Stakeholder Forum (2006) also observed that more analysis must be done to understand which partnerships are actually delivering results, and how issues of reporting, transparency and accountability are being addressed. Such a detailed review was undertaken

172 *Jan-Gustav Strandenaes*

by the International Civil Society Centre (ICSC) in 2014 of 330 of the WSSD partnerships. The study found that:

> Thirty-eight per cent of all partnerships sampled are simply not active or do not have measurable output. Twenty-six per cent of all partnerships show activities but those are not directly related to their publicly stated goals and ambitions. An underlying problem was that many multi-stakeholder partnerships have vague and diffuse goals and lack appropriate monitoring and reporting mechanisms, making the causality between the output of the partnership and impact on the ground difficult to establish. A key finding of the ICSC study was a lack of monitoring and reporting mechanisms have generally limited the effectiveness of MSPs. Improved monitoring, evaluation and reporting are tools that will help to assess progress vis-à-vis targets and goals and will no doubt enhance the credibility of the MSPs (ICSC, 2014).

Beisheim and Liese (2014), in eight years of research on multi-stakeholder partnerships, found governance structures of MSPs are "terra incognita."

> It is often difficult to find how MSPs are monitored. Some of the monitoring systems are external, but they are not public, and also not always independent. They suggest that a transparent, accountable, efficient, participatory and qualitative governance structure is a must in order to increase the effectiveness of MSPs (Beisheim and Liese, 2014).

Two other recent key studies have served to provide more in-depth analysis of these issues and their importance for partnerships: World Vision's (2015) "Getting Intentional: Cross-sector Partnerships, Business and the Post-2015 Development Agenda" and BCG/MIT's (2015) "Joining Forces: Collaboration and Leadership for Sustainability."

While acknowledging the importance and impact of MSPs, Martens (2007) has identified a number of risks and side-effects that should be taken into account when analyzing their impact on global governance. Among those he highlights as important is the growing influence of the business sector on agenda-setting and decision-making by governments. He also cites the risks to reputation to the United Nations where they are involved in these partnerships when a partner is selected who does not respect UN norms and standards. Additionally, the proliferation of partnership initiatives, which are not coordinated, can result in isolated solutions and contribute to the institutional weakening of the UN partners involved. To the extent that partnerships are expanding at a rapid rate, the problem of coordination is expected to grow in the future. Where financing is dependent on the benevolence of individuals, unpredictable financing for the provision of public goods is also a risk inherent in the privatization of responsibility. Martens also observed that many MSPs tend to concentrate in those areas where

Multi-stakeholder partnerships   173

technical solutions can lead to quick wins such as vaccines programmes and renewable energy systems.

Challenges to the validity of a multi-stakeholder partnerships approach to deliver on UN goals and mandates is further confirmed at the operational level when one considers the many partnerships being undertaken by the various funds, programmes and agencies of the United Nations system itself. While bringing many benefits, the challenges posed by this new approach, including in terms of accountability, coherence and efficiency, should not be underestimated and should clearly require a mechanism designed to respond to these challenges and for ensuring the UN's capacity to undertake partnerships at scale. Such a mechanism would help promote integrity and transparency and help ensure the UN's mandates are preserved, provide common partnership support services across the full range of UN activities, improve UN coordination and support and backstop multi-stakeholder initiatives.

Multi-stakeholder partnerships – Success stories and lessons learned

Following are five examples of successful multi-stakeholder partnerships. They were selected based on their association with the United Nations and the fact that they have certain elements in common which speak to their success; elements that could play a role when developing criteria for future partnerships.

1 *The Global Alliance for Vaccines and Immunization (GAVI)*

Background and Objectives: Established January 2000 and has raised over $.5 billion.

Vaccine provision and development, country level immunization programmes and health systems strengthening (HSS); special focus on low-income countries.

Lead Facilitators and Funders: WHO, UNICEF, World Bank, Gates Foundation, International Federation of Pharmaceutical Manufacturer's Association, US AID (funders one-third from bilateral donors, private donations and Gates Foundation).

Governance Structure: GAVI has a secretariat and Board – one-third of Board elected on an independent basis with expertise in health.

At country level GAVI works through Interagency Coordinating Committees and Health Sector Coordinating Committees.

Outcomes and Challenges: Built on the experience of the Vaccine Initiative launched by UNICEF in 1990. Generally seen as successful in increasing the numbers vaccinated but less successful influencing vaccine pricing.

Monitoring: A Monitoring and Evaluation Framework and Strategy; ensures valid, reliable, useful performance measures are available and used to support organizational and stakeholder learning, management of strategy, improvement of programmes, mitigation of risk and reporting of performance.

174   Jan-Gustav Strandenaes

Built on the experience of the children's Vaccine Initiative launched by UNICEF in 1990, has been successful but some criticism that it can push for one approach too much.

2 The Global Polio Eradication Initiative (GPEI)

Background and Objectives: Launched by WHO in 1998 at the World Health Assembly – objective to eradicate Polio by 2000; today polio reduced by 99 percent globally.

Lead Facilitators and Funders: WHO, UNICEF, the US Centre for Disease Control, Rotary International – bilateral donors also included Russian Federation, Kuwait, UAE, Saudi Arabia and Malaysia, World Bank and African and Inter-American Development Banks.

Governance Structure: The Advisory Committee on Polio Eradication and the Global Commission for the Certification of the Eradication of Poliomyelitis and the UN Interagency Committee play vital roles with WHO regional offices, large networks of health workers, public health managers and professionals.

Outcomes and Challenges: Polio incidents have reduced by 99 percent but the commitment to global polio eradication by the World Health Assembly (WHA) is not legally binding on states, and therefore the enforcement mechanisms of GPEI are not strong.

Monitoring: GPEI operates within a broad framework of intergovernmental and interagency cooperation and participation. The Independent Monitoring Board assesses progress towards a polio-free world, convenes on a quarterly basis to independently evaluate progress towards each of the major milestones of the GPEI Strategic Plan; the IMB provides assessments of the risks posed by existing funding gaps.

3 Renewable Energy and Energy Efficiency Partnership (REEEP)

Background and Objectives: Initiated by the UK government in 2002 as a WSSD Type 2 partnership – in response to WSSD failure to agree targets for renewable energy and energy efficiency. It aimed to promote collaboration to achieve a significant increase in the use of renewable energy and energy efficiency to improve energy security and provide for reliable delivery, and deal with climate change/energy issues. Project implementation and policy advice at national level, and advocacy at global level is its main thrust.

Lead Facilitators and Funders: Traditional bilateral donors (90 projects in over 40 countries); 60 percent of REEEP's activities deal with policy and regulation, the remaining with project financing.

Governance Structure: REEEP has a governing board that is responsible to a "Meeting of Partners," which is the ultimate authority of REEEP. Projects are developed and proposed by the programme committee and final selection by the International Selection Committee.

Outcomes and Challenges: REEEP contributed to change in renewable energy. REEEP has used a multiple approach to establish national partnerships involving small-scale private sector partners, NGOs and public partners. REEEP has also financed local projects that may not have been from the outset financially viable from a market point of view. South Africa proposed targets of 5 percent of total primary energy use to come from renewable energy resources by 2010. By 2009 IAEA estimate this had reached 13.1 percent, now increased to 19 percent.

Monitoring: Has a Governing Board responsible for the conduct of the business of the organization in accordance with the Statutes, and holds office for a period of four years. It is comprised of no less than six members and meets at least once a year. Its functions are to: develop and oversee the key strategic direction of the REEEP, including targets, timeframes and funding priorities; prepare the financial rules and accounting system of the organization; consider and decide upon applications to become Partners; provide instructions to the International Secretariat (Meier and Haarstad, 2014).

4 Forest Stewardship Council (FSC)

Background and Objectives: FSC Founding Assembly in 1993, the secretariat relocated in 2003 to Bonn, Germany. Main thrust from UNCED in 1992 to establish an independent and international forest certification system. Vision: The world's forests meet the social, ecological and economic rights and needs of the present generation without compromising those of future generations through promoting environmentally appropriate, socially beneficial and economically viable management of the world's forests.

Lead Facilitators and Funders: Not-for-profit NGO with membership in over sixty countries. It is financed through a multitude of sources – individual and corporate grants, donations and projects. It has a strong collaborative relationship with various UN bodies and has over the years worked with UNEP and had projects financed through the GEF. Governments cannot be members.

Governance Structure: Board of Directors and an international secretariat with the General Assembly of members as the highest decision-making body.

Outcomes and Challenges: Formally organized as an independent non-governmental organization, works outside of national regulations with its outreach. With expertise competence and project portfolio, the FSC can function as an incubator for multi-stakeholder partnerships. The FSC administers a self-elaborated third-party certification system on wood and timber products that serves to verify whether products – 8% of global forest – are certified and 25% of all industrial round-wood production.

Monitoring: FSC has developed twelve system indicators under four main categories – economic, social, environmental and general. The FSC Monitoring and Evaluation Program has also developed a Code of Good Practice for Assessing the Impacts of Social and Environmental Standards, and works with ten credibility principles integrated in the FSC monitoring work: sustainability,

176   Jan-Gustav Strandenaes

improvement, relevance, rigor, engagement, impartiality, transparency, accessibility, truthfulness, efficiency.

5 The UN's Global Compact's CEO Water Mandate

Background and Objectives: Launched by the UN Secretary-General, Mr. Ban-ki Moon, in July 2007, the UN Global Compact's CEO Water Mandate is called "a unique public-private initiative designed to assist companies in the development, implementation and disclosure of water sustainability policies and practices" (United Nations Global Compact, 2012).

The Water Mandate is developed under the UN Global Compact's three environment principles derived from the Rio Declaration on Environment and Development. They are: business should support a precautionary approach, should promote greater environmental responsibility and should encourage the diffusion of environmentally friendly technologies.

Based on analysis of the global water situation, there is a clear realization that water and sanitation management are vital in both developing and developed economies. Its structure covers six key areas and is designed to assist companies in developing a comprehensive approach to water management. The six areas are: Direct Operations; Supply Chain and Watershed Management; Collective Action; Public Policy; Community Engagement; and Transparency (from the CEO Water Mandate by Global Compact).

Lead Facilitators, Funders and Financing: Utilizing frameworks such as the UN Global Compact, companies can participate in collective efforts to address water sustainability. Several organizational units will also be involved. Among these are: UNICEF's Water, Environment and Sanitation Program; IFRC Water and Sanitation Program; the World Economic Forum Water Initiative and collaborations with other relevant UN bodies and intergovernmental organizations – e.g., the World Health Organization, the Organisation for Economic Co-operation and Development, and the World Bank Group, the Stockholm International Water Institute, UNEP Collaborating Centre on Water and Environment, UNESCO's Institute for Water Education.

Participation in the CEO Water Mandate is restricted to existing business members of the UN Global Compact. Core CEO Water Mandate Secretariat functions are financed by Mandate-endorsing companies via their general annual contributions to the UN Global Compact.

Governance Structure: The CEO Water Mandate is run by a secretariat and the core CEO Water Mandate Secretariat functions are underwritten by Mandate-endorsing companies via their general annual contributions to the UN Global Compact.

The Mandate Secretariat is run as a partnership between the UN Global Compact Office and the Pacific Institute.

Outcomes and Challenges: One of the largest water-using companies, Pepsico, has stated they are pursuing water-saving policies after having come in contact with the water initiative. By several accounts, other companies have done the same, and this may be attributed to the outreach and advocacy policy of the Water Mandate.

The Water Mandate has set rigorous standards for reporting on companies' activities in water-related areas, and the reporting policy follows those of the GRI. The polices of the Mandate further state that reporting must include a description of actions and investments undertaken in relation to the CEO Water Mandate in its annual Communications on Progress for the UN Global Compact. Reference must be made to relevant performance indicators such as the water indicators found in the Global Reporting Initiative (GRI) Guidelines.

Finally, the companies must be transparent in dealings and conversations with governments and other public authorities on water issues.

Monitoring: The Water Mandate reports through a system called Corporate Water Disclosure, which is the act of reporting information to stakeholders (investors, non-governmental organizations, consumers, communities, suppliers and employees) related to the current state of a company's water management, the implications for the business and others, and the company's strategic responses. Disclosure is a critical component of a company's water management efforts and of water-related sustainability more generally.

The review of these partnerships reveals that all five had solid organizational structures and were given clear objectives, a defined timeline, well-organized and strong facilitators, and secured funding. Having a clear, well-defined and easily understood objective was crucial: people could easily relate to it, and feel ownership because its thematic approach was clear and logical; funders could see and understand what they contributed money to; staff could easily grasp what their mandates and programmes were, and could also developed ownership; and with a clear and well-defined purpose and objective, monitoring and evaluation became possible, was not cumbersome to execute, and with a reasonable timeline, evaluation and monitoring could lead to adjustments – when and if needed.

Though GAVI has been slightly criticized for being top-down, and also seen as having influenced health policy in certain countries, the Alliance scores relatively high on good governance structures, meeting targets, as accessible to public and also for having a structure with built-in flexibility so project profiles could be assessed over time, and direction altered if conditions on the ground changed. The same can be said for GPEI, REEEP, FSC and the CEO Water Mandate. Another strong feature in the governance structure is a fairly well-developed monitoring system with good feedback mechanisms. A functional monitoring system also allows for solid resource management, which in turn is necessary for present and future funding.

Multi-stakeholder partnerships – Success stories and lessons learned

Not all MSPs are trying to do the same thing. Marianne Beisheim (SWP) came up with a useful classification of three different types of MSPs:

178 *Jan-Gustav Strandenaes*

1 MSPs for sharing knowledge – these exchange information between various stakeholders and disseminate knowledge to help achieve goals and targets (e.g., GWP – the Global Water Partnership).
2 MSPs for providing services to deliver the goals and targets (e.g., GAVI – the Vaccine Alliance).
3 MSPs for setting standards – these established standards and norms in areas where there are currently no (or no adequate) regulatory mechanisms to advance the delivery of the goals and targets (e.g., AWS – the Alliance for Water Stewardship).

This approach helps with capacity-building, with knowledge management, and with quantifying the contribution that MSPs are actually making to help deliver the SDGs and their targets. This has been an effective approach in furthering the MSP narrative.

Possible options and elements for developing a robust, enduring and dynamic framework and platform for the review of multi-stakeholder partnerships

Looking ahead, there is emerging consensus that means of implementation will be incorporated into each sustainable development goal and that multi-stakeholder partnerships could therefore be linked with each SDG. Many member states and other stakeholders have asked for a rigorous and participatory review and monitoring framework to hold governments, businesses and international organizations accountable for results.

These reviews would also have the following benefits:

- Providing a platform for UN member states and the wider international community to take stock of the role, trends, strategies, innovations and financing of voluntary multi- stakeholder partnerships and their contribution to advancing international development.
- Promoting greater understanding of diverse partnership models and approaches and their key success factors for purposes of replication.
- Monitoring and gauging the performance and impact of multi-partnership initiatives.
- Increasing the transparency and accountability of partnership commitments in support of the Post-2015 Development Agenda.
- Identifying and making recommendations on ways and means to enhance the coherence and effectiveness of multi-stakeholder partnerships.
- Increasing insight into the business and financial models behind scalable development solutions delivered through partnership modalities.

Due Diligence, the UN, the private sector and MSPs – New opportunities

At present there is no system-wide due-diligence mechanism or arrangement regulating the relationships between the UN system and private sector companies with which the UN might want to associate that could be applied, for instance, in relationship with MSPs. With a growing interest from UN agencies, programmes and entities to engage with the private sector, the importance of developing a due-diligence mechanism has taken on new importance. As we submit this book the UN Secretary-General is expecting a report on this issue from an internal UN review team headed by the heads of UNICEF and ILO.

Several UN units have, for the time being, utilized the UN Global Compact's values and criteria as that mechanism. One such agency is the UN Economic Commission for Europe (UNECE), one of five regional UN Economic Commissions.

In its collaborations with the private sector through the PPP constructs, UNECE states that companies must be a member of the Global Compact or in the process of joining it. UNEP has adopted the same approach. This approach is and should be a temporary one as it unfortunately is no guarantee for a proper due-diligence process at the UN. Global Compact may at the moment have de-listed over 6,000 companies for not reporting or adhering to its standards, but it doesn't have the staff to do an effective check on the voluntary reports being submitted. Hence this process is seriously flawed.

This is why the development of two new initiatives on benchmarking could be of critical importance to develop an improved oversight system for monitoring MSPs working on sustainable development.

The Corporate Benchmarking on Human Rights (CBHR) is a unique collaboration led by investors and civil society organizations dedicated to creating the first open and public benchmark on corporate human rights performances. Mark Wilson, the CEO of the insurance corporation AVIVA, said:

> Competition is a beautiful thing when it is used to do good. For the first time we have a public measure of companies' human rights performance which will focus attention in the boardroom on their performance versus other companies and allow investors to ask the right questions. More transparency and a desire to improve in the rankings will spark a race to the top in corporate human rights (CHRB, 2017).

Many UNGC members did not do well in the independent review of their human rights policy and actions. Below are a few examples from the 2017 report measuring companies' fulfilment of Human Rights qualities. 100 per cent is, of course, the optimum score. Any number below 100 indicates some lack of respect for Human Rights or a flaw in the operational performance of the company:

- Pepsi: 22 percent
- Starbucks: 25 percent
- Woolworth: 25 percent
- Shell: 37 percent
- Coca-Cola: 40 percent
- GAP: 44 percent

180 *Jan-Gustav Strandenaes*

Another initiative is the World Benchmarking Alliance (WBA), which is a similar coalition consisting of a wide variety of stakeholders. These range from civil society and business networks, to financial institutions and multi-lateral organizations. The WBA is in the process of producing its first report on benchmarking companies on the SDGs. The UNGC is also a member of this coalition.

If the UNGC is to become the due-diligence mechanism for the UN and its relationship with companies, then the benchmarking reports from the two new benchmarking alliances presented above will play a critical role. Presenting an outside view and analysis of companies' performance, it would be possible to use these benchmark reports to assess whether or not the voluntary reports submitted by member companies to the UNGC are accurate. This in turn may provide UNGC with opportunities to challenge the voluntary reports should the content of these differ from those of the benchmarking organizations.

The UN Joint Inspection Unit published its report on the United Nations system in September 2018: "Private sector partnerships arrangements in the context of the 2030 Agenda for Sustainable Development." The report suggests a role for an outside rating system of companies which the UN could utilize.

> Organizations also note there are obvious benefits stemming from external due diligence assessments, and that the United Nations system should continue to engage private sector companies that specialize in rating the sustainability of prospective United Nations partner companies based on their environmental, corporate and social performance (including on human rights) (UN, 2018).

The following Table 7.1 is a summary of criteria for reviewing multi-stakeholder partnerships (Beisheim and Liese, 2014).

Administrating responsibility through meta-governance and Goal Facilitators

We have asserted several times in this book that a well-organized system, with access and participation possibilities for all, and with functioning institutions and basic advances for justice, and respect for the rule of law, is the best possible hope for being able to develop a world with a sustainable future. The multilateral system with its many successful global institutions is an administrative guarantor for this to happen. And it's true that to keep such an administrative system relevant it must also be subject to rethinking and open to innovative ways of ensuring accountability.

Today, however – after seventy years of cooperative global efforts – that system is now being challenged by leaders who are dealing with human rights and justice as if they were commodities to be sold on a competitive market.

We think that stakeholder democracy can counter such irresponsible tendencies, and MSPs are essential elements of such a democratic system. We also realize that we face opposition to the idea of a stakeholder democracy with

Multi-stakeholder partnerships 181

Table 7.1 Criteria for reviewing multi-stakeholder partnerships

Elements for reviewing partnerships initiatives
Is the initiative in line with internationally agreed goals and targets, including the SDGs and others linked to conference follow-up?
Is the initiative new or an extension of an existing commitment?
Does the initiative have specific aims and objectives with clear and measurable outputs and deliverables and a defined timeline with benchmarks?
Is the initiative a multi-stakeholder initiative with a list of members?
Is there a clear governance structure and a management plan in place?
Are there adequate resources (including financing, staff and technical expertise, and in-kind contributions) for the initiative to deliver its target?
Is there an effective monitoring process in place?
Does the initiative have potential for transformative or high impact?
Does the initiative reflect the substantive and geographic diversity of the commitments made?
Do partners adhere to the 10 principles of the UN Global Compact?
Is there a transparent reporting process in place?

multi-stakeholder implementation and participation. The cry for innovative and out-of-the-box thinking is all the same voiced by political leaders and decision makers all over the world. Still, as Marianne Beisheim wonders:

> To what extent do policymakers and other relevant actors integrate these insights into multi-stakeholder partnerships – especially as regards the relevant conditions for success – when calling for and fostering new partnerships for the SDGs? (Beisheim and Ellersiek, 2017)

"The existence of a governance environment, which co-determines what works well and what not, and what is a preferred style of policy preparation, of policy instruments and of involvement of stakeholders, is sometimes ignored" (Meuleman et al., 2016).

Beisheim has given such ideas much thought, and has devised the following chart (Figure 7.1) of the governance structure at the UN on the 2030 Agenda:

Can this system be subjected to innovative thinking? Instead of changing or reforming, perhaps revisiting a process that has worked within the system, and may be reused?

One possible strategy which could promote a coordinated approach to partnerships around each SDG through "Goal Facilitators." This could lead to the creation of a meta-partnership to deliver each SDG and their targets. A meta-partnership would be made up of stakeholders, including governments and intergovernmental bodies who are engaged in working together to deliver a particular target at any level. Each meta-partnership should have a governance structure that represents all stakeholders engaged in the partnership.

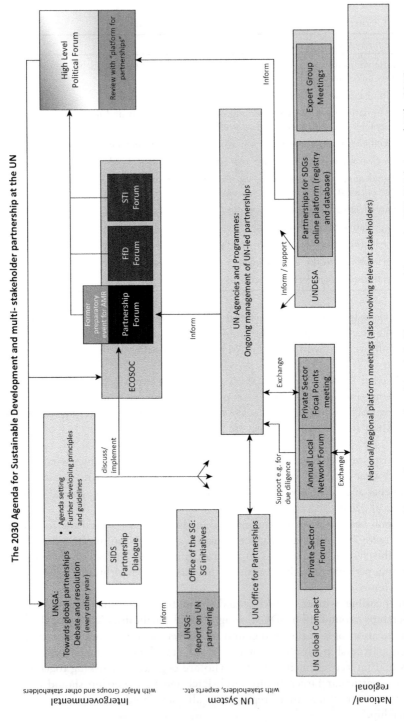

Figure 7.1 The 2030 Agenda for Sustainable Development and multi-stakeholder partnerships at the UN (Beisheim and Nils, 2016)

Multi-stakeholder partnerships 183

This type of approach would enable a "one-stop shop" for information on implementation, capacity-building, technology-sharing and would ensure transparency and a knowledge-based supported through an assigned UN agency or programme.

The Goal Facilitators system with lead UN agencies may be one way of involving the entire UN family. For targets of the Means of Implementation, those that are relevant would be seen as cross-cutting and should be taken on board by all partnerships.

Most SDGs are thematically identified, and it would not pose a great difficulty in finding a corresponding unit within the UN family to be assigned as a Goal Facilitator. For those SDGs that are known as "homeless" a secretariat with competence and defined responsibility could easily be established. Easily, that is, if the nations of the world are serious about the 2030 Agenda and its implementation. The following example – relating to the health goal (SDG 3) – may serve to illustrate the strategy we're suggesting: WHO could take the responsibility for the meta-partnerships for the health goal. This would then include a partnership to deliver each target. Monitoring, reviews and general reporting would be coordinated by WHO and presented at HLPF.

Bringing together MSPs that work on the same Goal will enable far greater capacity-building, knowledge management and quantification, none of which has been adequately achieved, to date. Perhaps there is a role for the UN Partnership Office in helping to put together and support this new administrative ecosystem we are suggesting. The Partnership Office could also help to ensure the interlinkages of the SDGs. This particular element – plus combined universality and the three dimensions of sustainable development – are the key differences between the MDGs and SDGs. It would create champion partnerships which could be quantified in their contribution to delivering the SDGs.

One way to address the interlinkages and the issue of universality is to utilize what has been termed as "nexus thinking." Often referred to as an element of the new narrative describing this century's political landscape, it allows for a wider space to implement groupings of the Goals that are closer related than others. "The food-water-energy-climate nexus" is an example of such interlinkages. Some nexus projects are already informally happening. The Blue Economy Conference (2018) in Kenya is one example. The Nexus Conferences (2014 and 2018) at Chapel Hill, University of North Carolina, is another. Perhaps the most significant is the biannual Dresden Nexus Conferences in Germany looking at Sustainable Management of Environmental Resources. The nexus narrative is clearly growing, but it needs a more defined and succinct roadmap. One issue mentioned at each of these nexus conferences is their ability to address gaps. The UN Office of Partnerships might be a good place for a "nexus responsibility" to be consciously developed and administrated, and presented to future MSPs for implementation.

184 *Jan-Gustav Strandenaes*

The UN Secretary-General, the General Assembly, ECOSOC, HLPF and partnerships

Beginning in earnest with then UN Secretary-General Kofi Anan, partnerships became an item on the agendas of the UN. Anan showed that the SG's agenda-setting power could influence politics, and through his initiative, the UN adopted the idea of the Global Compact as a partnership. Ban Ki-moon, his successor as Secretary-General, launched various transformational multi-stakeholder initiatives, such as Every Woman Every Child (EWEC), the Zero Hunger Challenge, Global Pulse and Sustainable Energy for All (SE4All). (An elaboration of these examples can be found in Annex 3.) These multi-stakeholder transformative initiatives were seen as innovative partnership mechanisms that included stakeholders from all relevant sectors and utilized the core competences of each to catalyze wide-scale changes in behavior, achieving greater impact because the benefits accrue broadly. They aimed to create a lasting impact on crucial systemic issues and create broader economic impact in terms of sustained, inclusive and equitable economic growth and job creation, which member states have defined as a vital role for partnership. One of the key criticisms is that they had no member state oversight.

The present Secretary-General, Antonia Guterres, has picked up the baton of partnerships. In 2017 he delivered a report titled "Secretary-General's Report on Re-positioning the UN Development System to Deliver on the 2030 Agenda." As part of the repositioning, the SG recognized the role that MSPs might play. The report expressed that the Development System:

> can only be realized with a strong commitment to partnerships at all levels between governments, private sector, civil society and others ... With this recognition, we must harness the convening power of the United Nations through platforms where stakeholders can meaningfully engage, build trust, exchange know-how and technologies, strengthen relationships and bring synergy and coherence to achieve results.
>
> We will also need to embed multi-stakeholder partnerships into the core business model of the UN development system, pooling system-wide expertise across the partnership spectrum (UNGA, 2017).

As the MSP issue is firmly placed on the international, regional and national agendas, it seems obvious that the General Assembly will continue to play a role in the evolving issue of MSPs. From an insignificant beginning with partnerships referred to merely as an issue for development aid in the late 1980s, the UN GA will now have a broad oversight over partnerships that are linked to the United Nations through the agenda item "Towards Global Partnerships." The importance of MSPs has permeated the UN system, and with the 2030 Agenda, the Economic and Social Council, ECOSOC has been given a growing and important role with the issue of partnerships and the UN. ECOSOC is also the body that coordinates the activities of the United Nations system and, as

Multi-stakeholder partnerships 185

such, it is uniquely situated to provide oversight of partnership initiatives or commitments in which the UN system is involved. ECOSOC could therefore set the broad parameters for partnerships that apply to the whole of the UN system and could initiate the idea of Goal Facilitators within the UN system.

Established by paragraph 84 in the Rio outcome document of 2012, and given its mandate in UNGA resolution 67/290, the HLPF has become the primary venue to discuss partnerships and its ramifications for the 2030 Agenda. As mentioned previously in this chapter, HLPF:

> Shall follow up and review progress in the implementation of all the outcomes of the major United Nations conferences and summits in the economic, social and environmental fields, as well as their respective means of implementation, improve cooperation and coordination within the United Nations system on sustainable development programmes and policies, promote the sharing of best practices and experiences relating to the implementation of sustainable development and, on a voluntary basis, facilitate sharing of experiences, including successes, challenges and lessons learned, and promote system-wide coherence and coordination of sustainable development policies (UN, 2013).

The paragraph further states that regional processes as well as deliberations in ECOSOC and the Development Cooperation Forum shall also be integrated in this work. But it does not stop there. HLPF shall also conduct thematic reviews of the various SDGs. These thematic reviews shall be carried out annually at HLPF under the auspices of ECOSOC and should provide the occasion for individual countries to voluntarily present their own national reviews of progress, today institutionalized as so-called VNRs (Voluntary National Reviews). Ideally these VNRs could provide opportunities to discuss lessons learned in each country's implementation of the 2030 Agenda and to review both short-term outputs and long-term outcomes related to attaining the goals.

The resolution (67/290) also mandated HLPF the task to provide a platform for partnerships, including the participation of Major Groups and other relevant stakeholders (paragraph 8). Member states could consider reviewing multi-stakeholder partnerships of a global nature in the same thematic areas that given year. The HLPF should also benefit from any outcomes from ECOSOC's review of partnership principles and guidelines. Consideration could also be given for ECOSOC to commission a study of a "lessons learnt" review of partnerships which could be shared with HLPF and the General Assembly.

MSP Charter – not a panacea, but a way forward

There are no globally agreed guidelines for MSPs, their composition, values, responsibilities or accountability issues. Twenty-five years have elapsed since Agenda 21 called for multi-stakeholder partnerships to play an active and crucial role in transforming this world into a sustainable one, a demand repeated

186   *Jan-Gustav Strandenaes*

in the 2030 Agenda. This lack of any new guidelines for MSPs since the UNGA endorsed the CSD 2003 principles, the so-called Bali Guidelines, has caused a growing frustration among many people actively involved and engaged in MSPs today. As this chapter has shown, there is now wide experience and knowledge on what has worked and what has not concerning MSPs.

Instead of letting the feeling of frustration dominate, a coalition of stakeholders led by the MSP Institute and the Tellus Institute took the collected experience and knowledge and decided to create a new narrative for the MSP discourse. Their analysis of the political landscape in the second decade of the twenty-first century illustrated a growing paradox: on one side the landscape offered more possibilities for humanity than ever before in the annals of history; on the other side there was a clearly identified lurking danger to explore and utilize these possibilities. This political danger was threatening to undermine the multilateral system and its positive functions based on the system of mutual respect for agreed and accepted norms and values.

Bearing this in mind, but eager to work with and in support of the multilateral system, these stakeholders decided to create an MSP Charter (see Chapter 8) – as a serious contribution to the MSP discourse. It identifies its objective to be: to "enable a focused discussion on such a shared vision, and synthesize key principles in a brief document. The Charter can be used to promote principles and best practice." Informed by an International Advisory Board of present and former government representatives and non-state stakeholders, the MSP Charter will hopefully help fertilize the MSP narrative, challenge the UN and its member states and in the meantime inspire new partnerships to at least start using the Charter as a guiding tool (MSP Charter, 2018). Another idea that has been suggested is to see if the Charter can inspire the development of a certification scheme as well.

Where do we go from here?

Partnerships, or more specifically MSPs, are now part of the delivery mechanism for global policy agreements. As we have argued in the theory of change stakeholders are now both helping governments make better informed policy decisions and through MSPs they are helping them deliver those policy decisions.

In this chapter, we have tried to describe the evolution of partnerships – and it would be very fair to say that it has not been a straightforward evolution.

The major difficulty isn't in the theory; it has been in creating a recognized mutually supportive and accountable process to be able to help those partnerships deliver their full potential. Chapters 8 and 9 try to give some of the best ideas on how to do that backed up by the experience of the last fifteen years.

We now have enough experience and knowledge to make MSPs so much better and more impactful. We should be able to report each year at the HLPF on how many people have gained access to water or how many have moved out of extreme poverty ($1.25 a day).

Multi-stakeholder partnerships 187

There is general agreement that we can only build a sustainable future by working together in close cooperation.

In order to move to a fully effective, outward-reaching system of partnerships that not only provides services but empowers broad groups of people, a model is required that emphasizes cooperation and trust. Such a model might be compared to the traditional Nordic model of economic and social negotiations that successfully brings together key stakeholders to work on issues as co-equals.

There are some exciting developments just starting where countries such as Germany are setting up national multi-stakeholder partnership platforms to help share and build capacity to deliver. This new development needs more countries piloting it as we move forward and share those lessons at the HLPF.

As mentioned at the beginning of this chapter there are also new versions of partnerships emerging, where we identified the difference between MSPs and PPPs. We are now also seeing public–private partnerships and NGOs and other stakeholders forming legal relationships with industry and government to deliver on sustainable development. These new approaches need to be guided by principles for SDG partnerships. However, as yet, governments have not agreed to any new principles. We hope this will change and change soon.

We can't come back in 2030 and say "if only we had been more robust with our guidance and help on partnerships."

Note

1 "Type II's partnerships/initiatives are complementary to the globally agreed 'Type I' outcomes: they are not intended to substitute commitments by governments in the 'Type I' documents, rather they should contribute to translating those political commitments into action. Given the broad range of issues currently being negotiated, it should not prove difficult to link a 'Type II' initiative to the negotiated outcome" (UN, 2002).

Annex 1 Bali Guidelines on partnerships

Objective of partnerships

Partnerships for sustainable development are specific commitments by various partners intended to contribute to and reinforce the implementation of the outcomes of the intergovernmental negotiations of the WSSD (Programme of Action and Political Declaration) and to help achieve the further implementation of Agenda 21 and the Millennium Development Goals.

Voluntary nature/respect for fundamental principles and values

Partnerships are of a voluntary, "self-organizing" nature; they are based on mutual respect and shared responsibility of the partners involved, taking into

188 *Jan-Gustav Strandenaes*

account the Rio Declaration Principles and the values expressed in the Millennium Declaration.

Link with globally agreed outcomes

Partnerships are to complement the intergovernmentally agreed outcomes of WSSD: they are not intended to substitute commitments made by governments. Rather they should serve as mechanisms for the delivery of the globally agreed commitments by mobilizing the capacity for producing action on the ground. Partnerships should be anchored in the intergovernmentally agreed outcomes of WSSD (Programme of Action and Political Declaration) and help achieve the further implementation of Agenda 21 and the Millennium Development Goals.

Integrated approach to sustainable development

Partnerships should integrate the economic, social and environmental dimensions of sustainable development in their design and implementation. They should be consistent, where applicable, with sustainable development strategies and poverty reduction strategies of the countries, regions and communities where their implementation takes place.

Multi-stakeholder approach

Partnerships should have a multi-stakeholder approach and preferably involve a range of significant actors in a given area of work. They can be arranged among any combination of partners, including governments, regional groups, local authorities, non-governmental actors, international institutions and private sector partners. All partners should be involved in the development of a partnership from an early stage, so that it is genuinely participatory in approach. Yet as partnerships evolve, there should be an opportunity for additional partners to join on an equal basis.

Transparency and accountability

Partnerships should be developed and implemented in an open and transparent manner and in good faith, so that ownership of the partnership process and its outcomes is shared among all partners, and all partners are equally accountable. They should specify arrangements to monitor and review their performance against the objectives and targets they set and report in regular intervals ("self-reporting"). These reports should be made accessible to the public.

Tangible results

Each partnership should define its intended outcome and benefits. Partnerships should have clear objectives and set specific measurable targets and timeframes for their achievement. All partners should explicitly commit to their role in achieving the aims and objectives of the partnerships.

Funding arrangements

Available and /or expected sources of funding should be identified. At least the initial funding should be assured at the time of the Summit, if the partnership is to be recognized there.

New/value-added partnerships

Ideally, partnerships for sustainable development should be "new," i.e., developed within the framework of the WSSD process. In case of ongoing partnerships, there has to be a significant added value to these partnerships in the context of the WSSD (e.g., more partners taken on board, replicating an initiative or extending it to another geographical region, increasing financial resources, etc.).

Local involvement and international impact

While the active involvement of local communities in the design and implementation of partnerships is strongly encouraged (bottom-up approach), partnerships should be international in their impact, which means their impact should extend beyond the national level (global, regional and/or sub-regional).

Follow-up process

Partnerships should keep the Commission on Sustainable Development informed about their activities and progress in achieving their targets. The CSD should serve as a focal point for discussion of partnerships that promote sustainable development, including sharing lessons learnt, progress made and best practices.

Opportunities to develop partnerships for sustainable development will continue after the WSSD. Submissions of partnerships after the Summit will be considered in the follow-up process.

Annex 2 Global Compact Principles

Human rights

Principle 1: Businesses should support and respect the protection of internationally proclaimed human rights; and
Principle 2: make sure that they are not complicit in human rights abuses.

190   *Jan-Gustav Strandenaes*

Labor

Principle 3: Businesses should uphold the freedom of association and the effective recognition of the right to collective bargaining;
Principle 4: the elimination of all forms of forced and compulsory labor;
Principle 5: the effective abolition of child labor; and
Principle 6: the elimination of discrimination in respect of employment and occupation.

Environment

Principle 7: Businesses should support a precautionary approach to environmental challenges; Principle 8: undertake initiatives to promote greater environmental responsibility; and
   Principle 9: encourage the development and diffusion of environmentally friendly technologies.

Anti-Corruption

Principle 10: Businesses should work against corruption in all its forms, including extortion and bribery.

Annex 3: Leadership initiatives of the Secretary-General – Partnership commitment platforms (Ki-moon, 2012)

Every Woman Every Child

Every Woman Every Child is a global movement launched by the Secretary-General to save and improve the lives of 16 million women and children within five years. To date, more than 400 partners from a range of stakeholder groups, including over 70 governments, have made specific commitments to advance women's and children's health under this initiative. Each commitment maker is required to report annually on progress related to the implementation of their commitment.
   All commitments advancing goals outlines in the *Global Strategy for Women's and Children's Health* are encouraged, in particular those which are long-term (e.g., over several years), are sustainable (e.g., public private partnerships with sustainable business models) and innovative (e.g., innovative policies, new low-cost technologies, innovative partnerships, innovative business models). Most importantly, commitments must have measurable impact.

Sustainable Energy for All (SE4All)

In September 2011, the Secretary-General launched the Sustainable Energy for All initiative and shared his vision for how governments, business and civil society, working in partnership, can make sustainable energy for all a reality by

2030. Today, thousands of partners from all regions and sectors have committed to work towards realizing the initiative's transformative agenda and objectives. A robust accountability framework is being established to foster transparency and enable the tracking of the many voluntary commitments to the initiative.

Global Pulse

Global Pulse was established to tackle an emerging and highly forward-looking issue area: the use of real-time data for decision-making. Big data is produced by the public, is held closely by private sector and may be used by governments to better serve the public. Yet data sharing between these entities is problematic for reasons related to personal privacy, business risk and national sovereignty. The topical nature of "big data" made Global Pulse an early and visible leader in this new policy space, which has attracted multi-stakeholder partners from inside and outside the UN system.

The Zero Hunger Challenge

The Zero Hunger Challenge has opened the door to the certainty that hunger can be eliminated in our lifetime, if all stakeholders work together. It has brought a renewed focus to nutrition, food waste, agriculture, women's empowerment and sustainability – and to the necessary interconnectivity of all these areas. Not only has the will to end hunger increased, but there is now the knowledge that it cannot be accomplished without the integration of all other elements of the Challenge – nor without engagement from all sectors.

The Climate Summit

The Secretary-General hosted the Climate Summit in September 2014 to engage leaders and advance climate action and ambition. The Summit served as a public platform for leaders at the highest level – all UN member states, as well as finance, business, civil society and local leaders from public and private sectors – to catalyze ambitious action on the ground to reduce emissions and strengthen climate resilience and mobilize political will for an ambitious global agreement by 2015 that limits the world to a less than 2-degree Celsius rise in global temperature.

The Climate Summit focused on concrete action and solutions for accelerating progress in areas that can significantly contribute to reducing emissions and strengthening resilience – such as agriculture, cities, energy, financing, forests, pollutants, resilience and transportation. New commitments, new ideas and new financing for significant actions to address the challenge of climate change dominated the announcements made by more than 100 heads of state and government and leaders from the private sector and civil society at the Climate Summit.

192 Jan-Gustav Strandenaes

References

BCG/MIT (2015) Joining Forces: Collaboration and Leadership for Sustainability. Available online at: http://sloanreview.mit.edu/projects/joining-forces/?utm_source= UNGC&utm_medium=referral&utm_campaign=susrpt14

Beisheim, M. and Liese, A. (eds.) (2014) *Transnational Partnerships: Effectively Providing for Sustainable Development?*Palgrave Macmillan.

Beisheim, M. and Nils, S. (2016) Multi-Stakeholder Partnerships for Implementing the 2030 Agenda: Improving Accountability and Transparency. Independent Analytical Paper for the 2016 ECOSOC Partnership Forum. New York: UN. Available online at: https://www.un.org/ecosoc/sites/www.un.org.ecosoc/files/files/en/2016doc/partnership -forum-beisheim-simon.pdf

Beisheim, M. and Ellersiek, A. (2017) A Partnership for the 2030 Agenda for Sustainable Development – Transformative, Inclusive and Accountable? SWP Research Paper. German Institute for International and Security Affairs.

Corporate Human Rights Benchmark (CHRB) (2017) Press Release. Available online at: https://www.corporatebenchmark.org/2017-results-press-release

Hale, T. (2003) Managing the Disaggregation of Development: How Johannesburg "Type II" Partnerships Can Be More Effective. Woodrow Wilson School, Princeton University. Available online at: https://www.princeton.edu/~mauzeral/wws402f_s03/ JP.Thomas.Hale.pdf

International Civil Society Centre (ICSC) (2014) Multi-Stakeholder Partnerships Building Blocks for Success. Berlin: ICSC. Available online at: http://icscentre.org/area/m ulti-stakeholder-partnerships

Ki-moon, B. (2012). New York: UN. Available online at: http://sustainabledevelopment. un.org/partnerships.html

Kupcu, F. M. (2007) Paper 5: Ideas for Launching and Evaluating New Partnerships/ Initiatives and Reinforcing Ongoing Ones. London: Stakeholder Forum.

Martens, J. (2007) Multi-Stakeholder Partnerships – Future Models of Multilateralism? Dialogue on Globalization, Occasional Papers, No. 29/January 2007. Berlin: Friedrich Ebert Stiftung.

Meier, U. and Haarstad, J. (2014) Review of Support to the Renewable Energy and Energy Efficiency Partnership, REEEP Review. Norad Collected Reviews 8/2014. Norad.

Meuleman, L., Niestroy, I. and Strandenaes, J.-G., (2016) From PPP to ABC: A New Partnership Approach for the SDGs. IISD.

MSP Charter (2018) A Project of MSP Institute and Tellus Institute. Available online at: http://msp-charter.org/

Seth, N. (2013) Foreword in Fulfilling the Rio+20 Promises: Reviewing Progress since the UN Conference on Sustainable Development. New York: UN.

Schäferhoff, M., Campe, S. and Kaan, C. (2009) Transnational Public –Private Partnerships in International Relations: Making Sense of Concepts, Research Frameworks, and Results. *International Studies Review* 11: 451–474.

SIDS (2014) Partnerships. New York: UN. Available online at: http://www.sids2014. org/partnerships

Stakeholder Forum (2006) Strengthening the Johannesburg Implementation Track. London: Stakeholder Forum.

Stakeholder Forum and NRDC (2013) Fulfilling the Rio+20 Promises: Reviewing Progress since the UN Conference on Sustainable Development. London: Stakeholder

Forum. Available online at: http://www.nrdc.org/international/rio_20/files/rio-20-rep ort.pdf

Summary of Stocktaking Event (2015) Summary of Stocktaking Meeting of Inter-governmental Negotiations on the Post-2015 Development Agenda. New York: UN. Available online at: https://sustainabledevelopment.un.org/content/docum ents/5913Summary%20of%20IGN%20Stock%20Taking%20Mtg%2019_21%20Jan %202015.pdf

Sustainable Development Issues Network (SDIN) (2002) Taking Issue: Questioning Partnerships. New York: SDIN. Available online at: http://www.sdissues.net/sdin/ docs/takingissue-no1.pdf

United Nations (1992) Agenda 21, Chapter 23, Sections 1 and 2. New York: UN. Available online at: http://sustainabledevelopment.un.org/content/documents/Agenda21.pdf

United Nations (2002) Prepcom IV Annexed Further Guidance for Partnerships/Initia-tives – An Explanatory Note by Vice-Chairs Jan Kára and Diane Quarless, as an Addendum to the Chair's Explanatory Note. New York: UN. Available online at: http:// www.johannesburgsummit.org/html/documents/prepcom3docs/summary_partnerships_a nnex_050402

United Nations (2011) General Assembly Resolution 66/223, Towards Global Partner-ship. New York: UN. Available online at: http://www.un.org/en/ga/search/view_doc. asp?symbol=%20A/RES/66/223

United Nations (2013) General Assembly Resolution 67/290, Format and Organizational Aspects of the High-Level Political Forum on Sustainable Development. New York: UN. Available online at: https://sustainabledevelopment.un.org/index.php?page= view&type=111&nr=1888&menu=35

United Nations (2018) The UN Joint Inspection JIU/REP/2017/8. The United Nations System – Private Sector Partnerships Arrangements in the Context of the 2030 Agenda for Sustainable Development. Available online at: https://www.unjiu.org/sites/www. unjiu.org/files/jiu_rep_2017_8_english_1.pdf

United Nations General Assembly (UNGA) (2017) Repositioning the United Nations Development System to Deliver on the 2030 Agenda: Our Promise for Dignity, Pros-perity and Peace on a Healthy Planet. Available online at: http://undocs.org/A/72/684

United Nations Global Compact (2012) The CEO Water Mandate. New York: UN. Available online at: https://ceowatermandate.org/

World Vision (2015) Getting Intentional: Cross-Sector Partnerships, Business and the Post-2015 Development Agenda. New York: World Vision. Available online at: http:// www.wvi.org/united-nations-and-global-   engagement/publication/getting-intentiona l-cross-sector-partnerships

8 Principles for multi-stakeholder processes

Minu Hemmati

Introduction

The experience with multi-stakeholder partnerships (MSPs) over the last fifteen years has been mixed. At the center of this has been that there is a lack of shared understanding of what partnerships are, how they should work and what they should accomplish.

Unfortunately, there is a lack of shared understanding of what partnerships are – i.e., the current reality – and what they should be. There is hardly a shared vision of what we should aspire to when creating and operating in partnerships and what core principles should be included. Some guidance has been provided by UN agreements and there are some guidebooks and tools for practitioners, but there is hardly a growing community of practice and practitioners, and no common voice of such a community sharing their experiences, building a shared body of knowledge, and articulating their quality standards.

This was the background to the MSP Charter project, undertaken by the MSP Institute – Multi-Stakeholder Processes for Sustainable Development eV – and the Tellus Institute in 2017–2019.[1]

This chapter provides a summary of existing guidance for MSPs with a focus on principles; some of the key literature is being presented along with the MSP Charter developed 2017–2019. The MSP Charter includes references to practical aspects of putting its principles into practice. In addition, the chapter offers implementation guidance by providing summaries of key handbooks and tool guides as well as links to relevant organizations, institutes and networks.

Background

The objective of the MSP Charter project was to enable a focused discussion on a shared vision, and synthesize key principles in a simple, brief document. By articulating a positive vision and valued principles of MSPs, the Charter is aiming to promote high-quality standards, thus contributing to increasing the quality of MSP practice and maximizing their contributions to realizing the SDGs. The Charter can be used to promote principles and best practice.

The MSP Charter is based on existing agreements, research and practical experience synthesized in various handbooks and how-to guides (see Table 8.4). It is also based on dialogue with and detailed feedback from members of a global multi-stakeholder advisory group of experts and practitioners, and a two-day multi-stakeholder workshop held on the margins of the High-Level Political Forum (UN HLPF) in July 2017 in New York ("Making MSPs Work for the SDGs"). In addition, a wide consultation process among stakeholders was conducted, using an open Internet-based call for comments.

The following understanding of MSPs and stakeholders is underpinning this work:

Multi-stakeholder partnerships for sustainable development are defined as a means through which partners from different societal sectors can jointly support the transformation towards sustainable development and help achieve the 2030 Sustainable Development Agenda and the Sustainable Development Goals (SDGs). In MSPs, partners engage in a co-creation process, combining resources and sharing risks so that the ownership of the partnership and its outcomes are shared among all partners.

Using such a multi-stakeholder approach also means that:

- MSPs are inclusive in nature, involving all relevant actors in their area of work.
- MSPs can be arranged among any combination of partners, including governments, regional groups, local authorities, non-governmental actors, international institutions, private sector partners and other relevant stakeholders.
- MSPs use a participatory approach where all partners are involved from an early stage, helping to shape and develop the partnership.
- MSPs remain open for including additional partners as the partnership may evolve over time.

There are numerous MSPs fitting this definition, from local to global levels, working on all kinds of sustainable development issues: Examples of multi-stakeholder partnerships for sustainable development principally range from small collaborative projects of individual organizations and institutions that address local challenges to international partnerships tackling global issues. Goals and activities can center on capacity-building and knowledge exchange, market development, technological innovation or standard-setting. Many of the international initiatives operate local or national centers that implement a global standard, and network amongst each other to share lessons learned and support each other's work.

Stakeholders are defined as those who have an interest in a particular decision, either as individuals or representatives of a group or organization/institution. This includes people who influence a decision, or can influence it, as well as those affected by it (Hemmati, 2002).

196 Minu Hemmati

The principles discussed in this chapter are meant for **multi-stakeholder processes**. There is some confusion about different terms – multi-stakeholder processes, partnerships, dialogue, participation, and so on. "Multi-stakeholder processes" seems the broadest term and includes various levels of engagement that can be described along a continuum of more or less intense, interactive, collaborative and long-term forms of communicating and working together across boundaries of sectors, levels and silos (see Table 8.1).

Principles of multi-stakeholder processes

Principles of multi-stakeholder processes have been articulated in the context of sustainable development agreements and their implementation, in particular since the early 2000s. The main sources that also served as the basis for the MSP Charter are summarized below.

Table 8.1 Levels of engagement (author)

	Hearing	One-off dialogue event	Regular dialogue	Multi-stakeholder steering body	Multi-stakeholder partnership
Type of interaction	One-way conversation	Two- or multi-way conversation	Two- or multi-way conversation	Two- or multi-way conversation/ collaboration	Two- or multi-way collaboration
Description	Convener receiving input: research, planning, policy	Convenor engaging in exchange: research, planning, policy	Convenor engaging in exchange over longer period: regular policy review, planning review	Joint responsibility, steering adjustments, steering results	Joint decision-making, implementation planning, activities, monitoring & evaluation (M&E)
Outputs	Input received on one side; potentially increased understanding	Input received on both sides; potentially new thinking emerges	Input received on both sides; potentially new thinking emerges; stakeholder influence increases	MoU or other institutional arrangement; shared results	MoU or similar arrangement; action plans; shared project outputs; M&E arrangements

→ from event → to process →
→ from listening → through exchange → guidance → to collaboration →

Table 8.2 Key principles and strategies of multi-stakeholder processes (Hemmati, 2002)

Principles	*Strategies*
Accountability	Employing agreed, transparent, democratic mechanisms of engagement, position-finding, decision-making, implementation, monitoring, evaluation; making these mechanisms transparent to non-participating stakeholders and the general public
Effectiveness	Providing a tool for addressing urgent sustainability issues; promoting better decisions by means of wider input; generating recommendations that have broad support; creating commitment through participants identifying with the outcome and thus increasing the likelihood of successful implementation
Equity	Levelling the playing-field between all relevant stakeholder groups by creating dialogue (and consensus-building) based on equally valued contributions from all; providing support for meaningful participation; applying principles of gender, regional, ethnic and other balance; providing equitable access to information
Flexibility	Covering a wide spectrum of structures and levels of engagement, depending on issues, participants, linkage into decision-making, time-frame, and so on; remaining flexible over time while agreed issues and agenda provide for foreseeable engagement
Good governance	Further developing the role of stakeholder participation and collaboration in (inter)governmental systems as supplementary and complementary vis-à-vis the roles and responsibilities of governments, based on clear norms and standards; providing space for stakeholders to act independently where appropriate
Inclusiveness	Providing for all views to be represented, thus increasing the legitimacy and credibility of a participatory process
Learning	Requiring participants to learn from each other; taking a learning approach throughout the process and its design
Legitimacy	Requiring democratic, transparent, accountable, equitable processes in their design; requiring participants to adhere to those principles
Ownership	People-centered processes of meaningful participation, allowing ownership for decisions and thus increasing the chances of successful implementation
Participation and engagement	Bringing together the principal actors; supporting and challenging all stakeholders to be actively engaged
Partnership/cooperative management	Developing partnerships and strengthening the networks between stakeholders; addressing conflictual issues; integrating diverse views; creating mutual benefits (win–win rather than win–lose situations); developing shared power and responsibilities; creating feedback loops between local, national or international levels and into decision-making

Table 8.2 (Con.)

Principles	Strategies
Societal gains	Creating trust through honouring each participant as contributing a necessary component of the bigger picture; helping participants to overcome stereotypical perceptions and prejudice
Strengthening of (inter)governmental institutions	Developing advanced mechanisms of transparent, equitable and legitimate stakeholder participation strengthens institutions in terms of democratic governance and increased ability to address global challenges
Transparency	Bringing all relevant stakeholders together in one forum and within an agreed process; publicizing activities in an understandable manner to non-participating stakeholders and the general public
Voices, not votes	Making voices of various stakeholders effectively heard, without disempowering democratically elected bodies

Table 8.3 Seven principles of effective MSPs (Brouwer et al., 2015)

Principle	Related perspectives, models, theoretical ideas
1: Embrace systemic change	1. Assessing the complexity of a situation 2. Soft systems methodology 3. Adaptive management 4. Four quadrants of change
2: Transform institutions	1. Supporting and obstructing institutions 2. Systems thinking 3. Framework for institutional analysis 4. Linking institutional change
3: Work with power	1. Types of power 2. Rank 3. Expressions of power 4. Faces of power 5. Empowerment
4: Deal with conflict	1. Causes of conflict 2. Continuum of conflict 3. Interest based negotiation
5: Communicate effectively	1. Dialogue 2. Non-violent communication 3. Powerful questions and active listening 4. Cultural issues and communication
6: Promote collaborative leadership	1. Six aspects of leadership 2. Belbin Team Roles 3. Balancing results and relationships
7: Foster participatory learning	1. Experiential learning cycle 2. Learning styles 3. Single, double, triple loop learning

Principles for multi-stakeholder processes · 199

In the book *Multi-Stakeholder Processes for Governance and Sustainability – Beyond Deadlock and Conflict* (Hemmati, 2002), the following key principles and strategies of multi-stakeholder processes are being suggested (see Table 8.2):

The MSP Guide (Brouwer et al., 2015) offers seven principles that make MSPs (more) effective. These principles are based on experience and on discussions with academics and practitioners. Each principle has a theoretical underpinning and descriptions of practical application. For each principle, there are three or four perspectives – these are conceptual models and theoretical ideas that help to explain the principle and illustrate the practical implications (see Table 8.3).

Partnerships2030, the MSP-related programme run at the German agency for international cooperation (GIZ), has identified success factors of MSPs and offers them as principled guidance for multi-stakeholder partnerships (see Table 8.4):

Table 8.4 Success factors of partnerships (author)

Success factors	Components
Cooperation management	Involving relevant partners Respectful communication Establishing a common "language"
Steering & resources	Neutral project secretariat Inclusive and transparent decision-making and steering structures Sustainable resource mobilization
Project management	Implementation and results orientation Clear roles Transparent communications strategy
Monitoring, evaluation and learning	Process and results monitoring Evaluation and reporting Learning processes and capacity development
Context	Global context Meta-governance
Common strategy & future planning	Jointly developing clear objectives Common leadership and responsibility High-level support

UN resolutions on multi-stakeholder partnerships

The most comprehensive UN decision on partnerships to date is contained in paragraphs 21–24 of the ECOSOC decision at its 61st session in 2003.

Other relevant UN decisions and resolutions are listed in the bibliography at the end of this chapter, including as the UN General Assembly regular so-called "global partnerships resolutions" that focus on the UN Global Compact with business.

200 Minu Hemmati

The guiding principles contained in these decisions can be summarized as follows:

- **Voluntary nature:** actors and stakeholders come together in partnerships at their free will, and with everyone benefitting in ways they desire and need
- **Transparency:** public announcements; registration; regular reporting
- **Credibility:** putting announced activities into practice and reaching stated objectives
- **Accountability:** exchanging relevant information with governments and other stakeholders; regular reporting
- **Participation:** open and participatory in nature
- **Multi-stakeholder**, i.e., including three or more stakeholders in the partnership
- Reflecting **sectoral and geographical balance** (as appropriate, depending on the partnership)
- Integrating the **three pillars of sustainable development**: ecological, economic and social
- Resulting in **technology transfer and capacity-building** in developing countries (as appropriate, depending on the partnership)
- Making a **genuine, concrete, additional contribution** to agreed sustainable development goals
- Adhering to **agreed plans and priorities at national level**
- Conforming to **intergovernmental agreed mandates**
- Being based on **predictable and sustained financial resources** while not drawing funds away from other agreed mandates
- Aiming at **transforming** our world towards sustainable development

This is what the international community has articulated that it wants to see in terms of multi-stakeholder partnerships for sustainable development. In other words: multi-stakeholder partnerships like that reflect these principles are deemed to help realize sustainable development.

The MSP Charter: Principles of multi-stakeholder partnerships for sustainable development

The common challenge of sustainable development requires the joint commitment of all stakeholders. Multi-stakeholder partnerships are a way of joining forces, to build on the strengths of each partner, and to complement all partners' capacities and capabilities for the benefit of all.

Partnerships strive for true transformation towards realizing the 2030 Agenda for Sustainable Development, which includes the Sustainable Development Goals (SDGs), in a joint effort to leave no one behind. Partnerships should do their utmost to adhere to the following principles for multi-stakeholder partnerships (MSPs) for sustainable development:

Define clear objectives: Supporting global goals, national and regional plans

MSPs should have jointly defined specific objectives, contributing to globally agreed goals and outcomes, grounded in their local interpretation and relevance of these goals, and consistent with relevant initial conditions, strategies and policies of the countries, regions and communities where their implementation takes place.

MSPs should complement other governmental, intergovernmental and stakeholder activities and initiatives towards the implementation of Agenda 2030 and the SDGs. They serve to mobilize and combine the capacities of different stakeholders and citizens for achieving the transformative agenda on the ground. Their ambition may extend beyond national goals and regulations.

Each MSP should specify its implementation methodologies and dedicated resources, and set specific, measurable, achievable, reasonable and time-bound targets for their achievement (SMART approach). MSPs should also clearly define when they are to conclude after reaching their objectives, and have an exit strategy. All partners should explicitly commit to their well-defined role in achieving the aims and objectives of the respective MSP.

All this should be captured in a written partnership agreement, endorsed by the leadership of each partner organization, and made publicly available.

Uphold fundamental principles and values

MSPs for sustainable development are based on mutual respect, trust and benefit, equity, and shared responsibility of the partners involved, taking into account the Rio Declaration Principles, the Universal Declaration of Human Rights, and the values expressed in Agenda 2030, respecting indigenous and local knowledge, as well as national regulations. Potential partners need to meet minimum standards, and due-diligence procedures should be in place. Business partners should consider joining the UN Global Compact. Stakeholders[2] should comply with the Istanbul Principles, and consider joining the Civic Charter.

Apply integrated and systemic approach

MSPs for sustainable development should strive to integrate the economic, social and environmental dimensions of sustainable development in their design and implementation. They should take a systemic approach, build a shared understanding of the whole system context and take this into account when devising their work program. This includes looking at all factors, their interlinkages, relevant institutions, rules and assumptions and aiming to transform all elements that need change and development in order to achieve sustainable development.

202   Minu Hemmati

Adopt multi-stakeholder approach

MSPs can be arranged among any combination of partners, including international institutions, governments, regional groups, business, civil society, academia and other stakeholders.

MSPs should in their initial stage undertake a stakeholder mapping and analysis. MSPs are inclusive in nature. All those that are affected by their work and all those that (can) influence the issues at hand need to be identified and engaged. Following the 2030 Agenda's "leaving no one behind" principle, MSPs should also identify and engage marginalized groups that may be affected by their work. This may include investing in building partners' capacities such as training of specific groups.

All partners should be involved in the development of the MSP from an early stage, so that it is genuinely participatory. Yet as partnerships evolve, there should also be opportunities for additional partners to join on an equal basis if appropriate.

Levels and kinds of engagement of partners can vary – from core partners implementing activities together, through engaging in a subset of activities to participating forums of consultation.

Ensure that form follows function

MSPs are the strategy of choice when individual organizations cannot tackle an issue on their own, hence they are often set up to address intractable, complex, wicked, systems-wide challenges/opportunities.

MSP designs and set-ups will be unique, and will always depend on their specific objectives and conditions under which they operate. MSPs need to invest significantly in their governance structures and their core organizations and secretariats.

Promote good governance

MSPs should have robust governance structures in place, including inclusive, transparent and accountable processes of preparing and making decisions, policies on actual and potential conflicts of interests, and mechanisms for resolving disputes.

MSPs for sustainable development should address potential power differences, diverse interests and potential conflict among partners in a constructive manner so as to ensure equity, inclusiveness and fairness in all decisions and activities concerning the partnership, and harnessing lessons learned.

Promote transparency and accountability

MSPs for sustainable development should be developed and implemented in an open and transparent manner and in good faith. All partners are equally accountable for what they do. They are accountable to each other. Moreover, MSPs are accountable to the public.

An accountability map and strategy should be developed identifying the elements of accountability relevant to the specific MSP. Both internal and external stakeholders should be engaged in this, using clear communication strategies. Subsequently, MSPs should specify arrangements to monitor and review their performance against the objectives, targets and milestones they set. Reports should be made regularly and should be made accessible to the public, including financial information. Available and/or expected sources of funding and/or investment should be clearly identified.

MSPs for sustainable development should keep relevant public institutions informed about their activities and progress in achieving their targets. Depending on the levels and topics of their work, this may include United Nations' bodies, governments at national, sub-national and/or local levels.

MSPs should actively take part in relevant review processes, sharing lessons learned about factors of success and failure, and strategies for scaling up and out.

Organizations and individuals can serve as promoters and brokers of MSPs by reaching out to potential partners, building relationships with stakeholders, and bringing them together to explore collaboration. Those who convene MSPs should adhere to the same principles to be considered legitimate conveners, champions and/or partners in MSPs.

Build effective communication and leadership

Effective communication is a key success factor for MSPs. High-quality facilitation and joint reflection within the partnership is required.

In successful MSPs, both formal and informal leadership roles are identified, valued and leveraged to enable the cross-sector approach.

Foster learning

Participatory, collective learning is at the heart of MSPs. In the process of learning, different partners' perspectives become clear, and mutual understanding can grow so that diversity can indeed foster creativity and innovation, overcoming obstacles along the way to implementing objectives. MSPs should organize and foster learning loops, and secure and publish the lessons learned.

Implementation guidance: Resources and tools for designing, implementing and facilitating MSPs

Principles are one thing – putting them into practice is quite another. The MSP Charter includes some practical aspects of putting its principles into practice. More comprehensively, various handbooks, how-to guides, tools and collections of examples are available providing guidance for implementation, from planning and brokering through implementing the various MSP phases to

204 *Minu Hemmati*

(joint) monitoring, evaluation and learning. Below is a selection of the best and most popular of such materials, most of which can be found on the Internet, and many free of charge.

The website of the MSP Institute also provides these and further sources, and is being regularly updated.[3]

Hemmati, M. (with contributions from F. Dodds, J. Enayati and J. McHarry) 2002. Multi-stakeholder Processes for Governance and Sustainability: Beyond Deadlock and Conflict. London: Earthscan

This book provides guidance for MSP designers, brokers, facilitators and coaches, as well as policy processes and institutions dealing with multi-stakeholder participation and partnerships, grounding recommendations in analyses of values, experience and science.

Chapter 7, "Designing MSPs: A Detailed Guide," provides general considerations and detailed guidance for key elements that are largely also mirroring typical phases of MSPs (see flow diagram on p. 211), namely:

- **Context:** process design; linkages to decision-making; issue identification; stakeholder identification; facilitation back-up; funding
- **Framing:** group composition; goals; agenda
- **Inputs:** stakeholder preparations; agreed rules and procedures; power gaps; capacity-building
- **Dialogue/meetings:** communication channels; facilitation/chairing; rapporteuring; decision-making (*); closure
- **Outputs:** documentation; action plan implementation (*); ongoing MS processes; impact official decision-making (*); and
- guidance for aspects that are relevant **throughout the process**: meta-communication; relating to non-participating stakeholders; relating to the general public (* optional)

Chapter 8, "The Short-cut," gives a brief summary of "**Principles of Stakeholder Participation and Partnership**" where key principles are listed along some brief notes about strategies that can help put these principles into practice. The chapter also provides a practical "**Checklist for MSP Designers.**" It is a list of key points that need to be addressed when designing multi-stakeholder processes. Not all processes need to include all of these components but they are suggested for consideration in order to gain clarity and not overlook necessary activities.

Brouwer, H. and J. Woodhill (with M. Hemmati, K. Verhoosel and S. van Vugt) 2015. The MSP Guide: How to Design and Facilitate Multi-Stakeholder Partnerships. CDI: Wageningen/Practical Action

This seminal guide offers a practical framework for designing and facilitating collaborative processes that work across the boundaries of business, government, civil society and science, supporting those who are involved with MSPs as stakeholders, leaders, facilitators or funders. The guide discusses **conceptual foundations and practical tools**, including a clear four-phase process model, a set of seven core principles, key ideas for facilitation, references to sixty participatory tools for analysis, planning and decision-making, and many practical examples from around the world. It draws on science, experience, expertise as well as training materials used at the Centre of Development Innovation (CDI), at Wageningen University & Research Centre. CDI also maintains a **web portal on MSPs**[4] offering information, materials, links and other useful resources as well as a platform for exchange among practitioners.

Brouwer, H. and J. Brouwers 2017. **The MSP Tool Guide: Sixty Tools to Facilitate Multi-Stakeholder Partnerships.** *CDI: Wageningen*

This compilation of sixty tools is a companion to *The MSP Guide*, the Wageningen University & Research CDI resource on how to design and facilitate effective multi-stakeholder partnerships. *The MSP Guide* is also available in French.

Partnerships2030 – Promoting multi-stakeholder partnerships for sustainable development

The German Federal Ministry for Economic Cooperation and Development (BMZ) commissioned Partnerships2030, a platform for promoting multi-stakeholder partnerships and supporting the implementation of the 2030 Agenda. Partnerships2030 strengthens existing multi-stakeholder partnerships, launches new initiatives and provides information on all partnership matters.

Studies and manuals in the Platform's MSP Library include guidance for first steps, working with stakeholders and their networks, developing partnering agreements, institutionalizing partnerships, conducting impact assessments, and more.[5]

EcoAgriculture Partners

EcoAgriculture Partners is a catalyst, pursuing a multi-pronged approach to make an impact at the landscape, national, regional and international level and working to mainstream integrated landscape management around the world. EcoAgriculture Partners also works on creating partnerships for action and advocacy, and it serves as the secretariat for the "Landscapes for People Food and Nature Initiative," a multi-stakeholder initiative with partners from governments, intergovernmental organizations, civil society organizations and business initiatives.[6]

Tools, manuals and guidance literature

Tools, manuals and guidance literature for sustainable landscape management include:

206 *Minu Hemmati*

De Graaf, M. et al. 2017. *Assessing Landscape Governance: A Participatory Approach*. Trobenbos International & EcoAgriculture Partners

Heiner, K. et al. 2017: *Public-Private-Civic Partnerships for Sustainable Landscapes: A Practical Guide for Conveners*. IDH, the Sustainable Trade Initiative & EcoAgriculture Partners

Kusters, K. et al. 2016. "Guidelines: Participatory Planning, Monitoring and Evaluation of Multi-Stakeholder Platforms in Integrated Landscape Initiatives." Working Paper

The Partnering Initiative (TPI) builds country-level platforms to catalyze partnerships; undertakes action research; develops individual and organizational partnering capacity; and directly supports partnerships around the world. The website offers **information and tools** for professional development, support services, and resources.[7]

Tennyson R. 2011. *The Partnering Toolbook: An Essential Guide to Cross-Sector Partnering*. The Partnering Initiative (IBLF)

The Partnerships Resource Centre (PrC) is a (virtual) network of professionals, academics and practitioners around the world that share and collect information on selecting appropriate partnerships and increasing their efficiency, impact and effectiveness.

The Partnerships Resource Centre (PrC) is a specialist research centre at Rotterdam School of Management, Erasmus University. It connects scientifically sound research and practitioner experience of cross-sector partnerships to aid sustainable and inclusive development.[8]

Partnership Brokers Association is an international professional body for those managing and developing collaboration processes; providing **tools, publications, networking events**, etc.[9]

Partnerships in Practice (PiP) provides **advisory, research and training services** to strengthen partnership approaches for sustainable development.[10]

MSI Integrity: The Institute for Multi-Stakeholder Initiative Integrity is a nonprofit organization dedicated to understanding the human rights impact and value of voluntary multi-stakeholder initiatives (MSIs) that address business and human rights. MSI Integrity researches key questions surrounding the effectiveness of MSIs, facilitates learning and capacity building in the field, and develops **tools to evaluate initiatives from a human rights perspective**, focusing in particular interest on how MSIs include, empower, and impact affected communities.[11]

MSI Integrity & International Human Rights Clinic at Harvard Law School, 2017. *MSI Evaluation Tool*, v.1.0.

The Collective Leadership Institute is an internationally operating nonprofit organization with focus on educational programs in the area of Leadership and Stakeholder Dialogues.[12]**Guidance literature** includes:

Kuenkel, P. et al. 2016. *Working with Stakeholder Dialogues: Key Concepts and Competencies for Achieving Common Goals* – a practical guide for change agents from public sector, private sector and civil society.

Kuenkel, P. et al. 2011. *Stakeholder Dialogues – Manual*. A GIZ publication.

Principles for multi-stakeholder processes 207

CIVICUS: The global alliance of civil society organizations and activists is dedicated to strengthening citizen action and civil society throughout the world.[13] It also provides guidance and toolkits for all areas of civil society organizations' work, including dialogue and partnerships, for example:

Hemmati, M. and F. Rogers. 2015. *Towards New Social Contracts: Using Dialogue Processes to Promote Social Change.* Johannesburg: CIVICUS – World Alliance for Citizen Participation (in English, Français, Espanol, Arabic)

CIVICUS & International Civil Society Centre. 2014. *Partnership Principles. For Cooperation between Local, National and International Civil Society Organisations.* CIVICUS & ICSC

Promoting Effective Partnering (PEP): The PEP Facility, supported by the Dutch Ministry of Foreign Affairs as co-chair of the Global Partnership for Effective Cooperation, is committed to building the quality and effectiveness of partnering efforts worldwide.

PEP seeks to facilitate better access to proven partnering knowledge and expertise, and to identify gaps where such knowledge and expertise does not yet exist.

The website provides reports, case studies, tools, trainings, blogs, and more meant to support all those who work in and with partnerships. PEP has also identified "17 factors for 17 goals" to guide effective partnering to deliver the SDGs.[14]

The **Institute of Development Studies (IDS) Participatory Methods** website provides resources to generate ideas and action for inclusive development and social change. It explains participatory methods – from program design to citizen engagement – their use, problems and potentials.[15]

The **Consensus Building Institute (CBI)** is a nonprofit organization founded by leading practitioners and theory builders in the fields of negotiation and dispute resolution. They engage in research and teaching, and offer tools for analysis, design and facilitation.[16]

The **Community Development Resource Association (CDRA)** is a non-governmental African organization advancing learning about development processes and intervention. The site offers resources, information on programs and courses, etc.[17]

The **International Association of Facilitators** was created by a group of professionals in order to have an avenue for exchange, professional development, trend analysis and peer networking. It has over 1,200 members in more than sixty countries. There is a specific methods database at that can be searched by purpose and group size, and offers brief descriptions, how-to's and materials on over 560 **methods of working with small and large groups.** Many of them are useful for different phases and challenges in MSPs, helping to build trust, enhance creativity and problem solving, increase ownership and improve implementation of agreements.[18]

The **National Coalition for Dialogue and Deliberation (NCDD)** "is a network of innovators who bring people together across divides to discuss, decide and act together on today's toughest challenges." It is a gathering place, a resource center, a news source and a facilitative leader for this community of practice. The website offers resources, access to networks of dialogue practitioners, information about events, and news.[19]

208 Minu Hemmati

Notes

1 See www.msp-charter.org
2 Among the stakeholders formally recognized in the UN are the so-called "Major Groups" that were defined in Agenda 21, the main outcome document of the Rio Earth Summit in 1992. They include the following: Women, Children and Youth, Indigenous Peoples, Non-Governmental Organizations, Local Authorities, Workers and Trade Unions, Business and Industry, Scientific and Technological Community, and Farmers.
3 www.msp-institute.org
4 www.mspguide.org
5 www.partnerschaften2030.de
6 https://ecoagriculture.org
7 https://thepartneringinitiative.org
8 https://www.rsm.nl/prc/
9 www.partnershipbrokers.org
10 http://partnershipsinpractice.co.uk
11 http://www.msi-integrity.org
12 http://www.collectiveleadership.de
13 https://www.civicus.org
14 http://www.effectivepartnering.org
15 http://www.participatorymethods.org
16 www.cbuilding.org
17 http://www.cdra.org.za
18 www.iaf-world.org.
19 www.ncdd.org

Bibliography

1 UN decisions relating to MSPs

2002 (January) UNGA Resolution (56/76) Towards Global Partnership
2002 (July) Bali Guiding Principles
2003 (June) UN Commission Decision on Partnerships for Sustainable Development including Criteria and Guidelines
2004 (February) UNGA Resolution (58/129) Towards Global Partnerships
2005 (December) UNGA Resolution (60/215) Towards Global Partnerships
2007 (December) UNGA Resolution (62/211) Towards Global Partnerships
2010 (March) UNGA Resolution (64/223) Towards Global Partnerships
2012 (March) UNGA Resolution (66/223) Towards Global Partnerships
2014 (February) UNGA Resolution (68/234) Towards Global Partnerships: A Principle-Based Approach to Enhanced Cooperation between the United Nations and All Relevant Partners
2015 (December) UNGA Resolution 70/224 Towards Global Partnerships: A Principle-Based Approach to Enhanced Cooperation between the United Nations and All Relevant Partners

2 UN background papers

Atkisson, A. 2015. MSPs in the Post-2015 Development Era: Sharing Knowledge and Expertise to Support the Achievement of the SDGs. Paper prepared for UN DSD. New York.

Beisheim, M. and N. Simon. 2016. Multistakeholder Partnerships for Implementing the 2030 Agenda: Improving Accountability. Analytical paper for the 2016 ECSOC Partnership Forum.

ECOSOC Committee of Experts on Public Administration. 2018. Challenges for Institutions in the Transformation towards Sustainable and Resilient Societies. Contribution by the Committee of Experts on Public Administration to the 2018 Thematic Review of the High-Level Political Forum on Sustainable Development. Seventeenth Session, 23–27 April 2018.

Expert Group Meeting. 2016. Multi-Stakeholder Partnerships on Implementing the 2030 Agenda, 2016: Improving Accountability and Transparency. Organized by UNDESA, February 2016.

Hoxtell, W. 2016. MSPs and the 2030 Agenda: Challenges and Oversight Options – Challenges and Options for Oversight at the United Nations. UNDESA Expert Group meeting "Strengthening the role of Member States in the review of multi-stakeholder partnerships for implementing the 2030 Agenda." December 2016.

3 UN Agencies and Programmes

Executive Board of the UN Development Programme and of the UN Population Fund. 2008. The UNDP Accountability System: Accountability Framework and Oversight Policy. UN Doc DP/2008/16/Rev.1. New York: United Nations.

FAO Committee on Food Security – High Level Panel of Experts on Food Security and Nutrition (HLPE). 2018. Multi-Stakeholder Partnerships to Finance and Improve Food Security and Nutrition in the Framework of the 2030 Agenda. HLPE Report #13, June 2018.

Joint Inspection Unit. 2006. Oversight Lacunae in the United Nations System. UN Doc. JIU/REP/2006/2. Geneva: United Nations.

UN Economic Commission for Europe. 2018. Draft Guiding Principles on People-First Public-Private Partnerships (PPPs) for the United Nations Sustainable Development Goals. Part II – The 8 Guiding Principles for People-First PPPs.

4 Key literature on MSPs

Andonova, L. B. and M. A. Levy. 2003. Franchising Global Governance. Making Sense of the Johannesburg Type II Partnerships. In O. S. Stokke and O. B. Thommessen (eds.) *Yearbook of International Co-Operation on Environment and Development 2003/2004*. London: Earthscan.

Beisheim, M. and N. Simon. 2015. Meta Governance of Partnerships for Sustainable Development: Perspectives on How the UN Could Improve Partnerships' Governance Services in Areas of Limited Statehood. Berlin: SWP.

Beisheim, M. and N. Simon. 2016. Multi-Stakeholder Partnerships for Implementing the 2030 Agenda: Improving Accountability and Transparency. Independent analytical paper commissioned by UNDESA.

210   *Minu Hemmati*

Beisheim, M. and A. Ellersiek. 2017. Partnerships for the 2030 Agenda for Sustainable Development: Transformative, Inclusive and Accountable? SWP Research Paper 2017/ RP 14, December 2017.

Brouwer, H. and J. Woodhill, with M. Hemmati, K. Verhoosel and S. van Vugt. 2015. *The MSP Guide: How to Design and Facilitate Multi-Stakeholder Partnerships.* Centre for Development Innovation, Wageningen University.

Brouwer, H. and J. Brouwers. 2017. *The MSP Tool Guide: Sixty Tools to Facilitate Multi-Stakeholder Partnerships.* Wageningen: CDI.

Global Development Incubator. 2015. More Than the Sum of Its Parts: Making Multi-Stakeholder Initiatives Work. USAID.

Heiner, K., L. Buck, L. Gross, A. Hart and N. Stam. 2017. Public-Private-Civic Partnerships for Sustainable Landscapes: A Practical Guide for Conveners EcoAgriculture Partners and IDH-Sustainable Trade Initiative. Washington, DC:EcoAgriculture Partners.

Hemmati, M. 2002. *Multi-Stakeholder Processes for Governance and Sustainability: Beyond Deadlock and Conflict.* London: Earthscan.

Hemmati, M. 2015. Engagement and Communication for Implementation and Review. Contribution to UN EGM "Social Development and the Agenda 2030." New York, October 2015.

Hemmati, M. and R. Whitfield. 2003. The Future Role of Partnerships in the Follow-Up to Johannesburg. Suggestions for Effective Mechanisms at the National, Regional and International Level. London: Stakeholder Forum.

Hemmati, M. and F. Rogers. 2015. Multi-Stakeholder Engagement and Communications for Sustainability. Beyond Sweet-Talk and Blanket Criticism – Towards Successful Implementation. London: CatalySD.

Hemmati, M. and F. Dodds. 2016. *High-Quality Multi-Stakeholder Partnerships for Implementing the SDGs.* New Frontiers Publishing.

Hemmati, M. and F. Dodds. 2017. Multi-Stakeholder Partnerships for Sustainable Development. Three-part blog series.

International Civil Society Centre. 2014. MSPs: Building Blocks for Success (by Pattberg & Widerberg). Berlin: ICSC.

Isaacs, W. 1999. *Dialogue and the Art of Thinking Together.* New York: Doubleday.

Kahane, A. 2001. How to Change the World: Lessons for Entrepreneurs from Activists. *Reflections*, Vol. 2, No. 3, pp. 16–29.

Lederach, J. P. 2003. *The Little Book of Conflict Transformation.* New York: Good-Books, Skyhorse Publishing.

Martens, J. 2007. Multistakeholder Partnerships – Future Models of Multilateralism? Berlin: Friedrich Ebert Stiftung.

OECD. 2015. Development Co-Operation Report 2015: Making Partnerships Effective Coalitions for Action. Paris: OECD Publishing.

Parks, W. et al. 2005. *Who Measures Change? An Introduction to Participatory Monitoring and Evaluation of Communication for Social Change.* South Orange, NJ: Communication for Social Change Consortium.

Pinnington, R. 2014. Local First in Practice. Unlocking the Power to Get Things Done. London: Peace Direct.

Rein, M. et al. 2005. Working Together. A Critical Analysis of Cross-Sector Partnerships in Southern Africa. Cambridge, UK: The University of Cambridge Programme for Industry.

Tennyson, R. 2011. *The Partnering Toolbook. An Essential Guide to Cross-Sector Partnering.* The Partnering Initiative (IBLF).

UNDESA. 2007. Participatory Dialogue: Towards a Stable, Safe and Just Society for All. Report commissioned by UN DESA Department for Social Policy and Development (by Minu Hemmati). New York: United Nations.

World Vision. 2014. Getting Intentional: Cross-Sector Partnerships, Business and the Post-2015 Development Agenda. Milton Keynes, UK.

World Vision. 2014. Reaching the Unreached: Cross-Sector Partnerships, Business and the Post-2015 Development Agenda. Milton Keynes, UK.

World Vision. 2015. Advancing the Debate: Cross-Sector Partnerships, Business and the Post-2015 Development Agenda. Milton Keynes, UK.

World Vision and The Partnering Initiative. 2016. Agenda 2030 Implementation: Delivering on the Promise. Uxbridge and Oxford, UK.

9 Designing successful multi-stakeholder partnerships

Susanne Salz, Bernd Lakemeier, Laura Schmitz, and Jana Borkenhagen

The chapter's authors wish to thank Lili Mundle, Nina Ouan and Johanna Moster as well as all participants of a workshop series held in Germany in 2018 for their valuable contributions.

Introduction

Multi-stakeholder partnerships are a complex undertaking. This chapter gives practical tips for setting up and running MSPs. The advice is based on the experiences of several MSPs as distilled in a series of workshops held in Germany in 2018 at the initiative of the MSP project Partnerships2030 based at the Gesellschaft für Internationale Zusammenarbeit (GIZ).

1 First steps in Multi-Stakeholder Partnerships

How can a new partnership best be started and what are the points to be considered? This section outlines the first steps in MSPs (see Figure 9.1) and provides practical tips.

a) Point of departure

The idea of starting a new partnership or cooperation is often a result of an encompassing (sectoral) social problem or a current crisis, or the desire and need for change. The exact reasons vary. The initiative to start a partnership might come from any stakeholder. MSPs are suitable in a wide range of contexts and for a broad range of issues. They can be local, national or global in scope.

Practical tips

- Early definition of the goal and related clarification of the question "Is a multi-stakeholder partnership the right method to achieve this goal?".
- Ensure added value of a new partnership. This can be done by answering the key questions "Is there a partnership that works?" and "Does it make sense to start another partnership?".

Designing successful MSPs 213

Figure 9.1 First steps in an MSP (authors)

b) Initiating a partnership

Organizations, companies and/or individuals can initiate a new partnership. The motivation and the conviction to tackle the problem and the associated challenges are important. The individual stakeholder is not alone but shares the willingness to tackle a challenge together with others from different sectors.

Practical tips

- Mobilize network.
- "Stakeholder mapping": Which other stakeholders are there in the field? Which other partnerships exist already?
- Definition of the vision: What is the goal of a potential partnership?
- "Copy-paste principle": learn from other partnerships and their way of working together, adopt existing mechanisms if necessary, to avoid reinventing the wheel.

c) Finding partners

After identifying the challenge, potential partners are identified. This can be done via bilateral talks, an open exchange of interested parties or the mobilization of existing networks. Building trust on all sides of the involved parties is particularly important, so potential partners can imagine future cooperation in which compromises will be made, decisions are taken, and a leap of faith is often necessary. In addition, cultural realities and differences of the potential partners and the desired target group should be taken into account.

Practical tips

- Ensure funding and resources while avoiding short-term financing and financing from a sole principal financier.
- Early stage analysis of potential new partners and their review (due diligence), ongoing stakeholder analysis in the further process.
- A partnership can be started with just a few partners in order to start the process sooner. Other partners can join in future.
- Develop, strengthen and constantly ensure trust and credibility.
- Strive for transparency.
- If necessary, identify and delegate tasks to an intermediary, e.g., in the form of a secretariat to ensure neutrality and fairness.

214 *Salz, Lakemeier, Schmitz, and Borkenhagen*

- Clearly define and communicate the roles and needs of the respective actors.
- Individual actors define their "red line" (maximum compromise or concessions possible) and communicate these as transparently as possible to partners.

d) Partnership starts to operate

After stakeholders have been identified as potential partners, the content and organizational work can start. Setting a joint objective is the immediate focus. The actors should ideally already agree on working modes that accompany and determine the cooperation. Answering the key questions "How does the collaboration work?" and "How are decisions made?" helps to determine the first structures on which the content work can build.

Practical tips

- It takes patience and time:
  - Take your time (as little as possible, but as long as necessary),
  - Consider long decision-making processes when planning a partnership,
  - Set communication rules (especially for internal votes),
  - Be prepared for possible frustration, and
  - Engage in expectation management of the participating actors.

- Develop decision-making and communication structure and, if necessary, note it in a "Code of Conduct."
- Define milestones and intermediate goals.
- Keep stakeholders "in line," e.g., by:
  - Internal communication of small, interim victories and progress, while avoiding premature external communication of unsecured results,
  - Offers of peer-learning formats,
  - Implementation of joint projects with scalability, and
  - Knowledge sharing and knowledge management inside the partnership and with external partners.

- Generally, keep internal and external communication separate.
- Regular and self-critical reflection (also during the process and the other first steps).
- Keep area of action and work as small and specific as possible.
- Clearly define responsibilities and ownership.
- In-person exchange and meetings (formal as well as informal) for the purpose of exchange, trust-building and mediation between the partners.
- Identify high-level key figures as a "door opener" to promote the partnership and its attractiveness.

Designing successful MSPs 215

e) Challenges across phases and steps

Along the individual steps, the interested parties often encounter major and minor challenges. Some examples of these are:

- Resources: Where do financial resources, time and personnel come from to start a partnership?
- Stakeholder management: Which potential partners are identified and approached?
- Organization: How is the cooperation structured and organized? Does it need a neutral organization unit (e.g., a secretariat)?
- Equal participation: Are all actors equal in cooperation? What are decision-making processes?
- Building trust: How can actors develop mutual trust?
- How can misunderstandings and prejudices be removed/tackled?
- Expertise: Which of the respective actors has the necessary technical expertise? Who has knowledge in the field, in the target group and the potential (partner) countries?

In a nutshell, relevant key points about initiating a partnership are illustrated in short in Table 9.1.

2 Institutionalization of MSPs

Once a new MSP has been launched and starts to operate, questions about the institutionalization arise. In that context, the legal form, the governance structure and funding are important elements that influence each other (see Figure 9.2).

An initial issue to consider is when and why to institutionalize an MSP. The institutionalization of an MSP is not an end in itself, but a step in the partnership process. Institutionalization becomes useful or necessary, such as to have the possibility to jointly fundraise and spend funds.

Table 9.1 Overview: Starting a partnership (authors)

Why start a partnership?	*To address a (cross-sectoral) societal challenge.*
What does a partnership need?	Motivation, willingness to work together and to compromise.
Who participates in a partnership?	Ideally actors from civil society, academia, private sector and state.
How do you work in a partnership?	Ways of cooperation vary and need to be customized to the context and the partners.
How long does the first phase last?	On average 2.5 to 3 years.

216 *Salz, Lakemeier, Schmitz, and Borkenhagen*

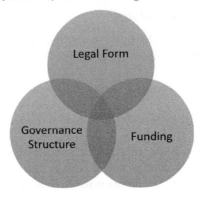

Figure 9.2 Three elements of the institutionalization of MSPs (authors)

a) Legal form

One key factor for choosing the potential legal form of an MSP is to identify the country in which the legal entity will be registered. Within most countries, there will be several options of legal forms available for MSPs. Multi-stakeholder partnerships have a charitable purpose, which influences the choice of the legal form.

As soon as the actors have agreed on certain structures, elaborated the form of cooperation and decided on a long-term goal of the MSP, it is helpful to seek legal advice in order to discuss the specific legal options available and to clarify the next steps.

b) Governance structure

The governance structure is another element of the institutionalization of an MSP. The purpose of a governance structure is to define joint decision-making and joint implementation. As MSPs deal with a wide range of sustainable development themes, partnerships and their objectives are also multifaceted. Therefore, there is no "one-size-fits-all" governance structure that can be applied to all MSPs. However, during the workshop and in the evaluation of various studies, it was apparent that certain structures and bodies are widespread, as explained in the following (Partnerships2030, 2017). The governance structure should be kept as simple as possible to avoid unnecessary effort. Especially at the beginning, as well as in smaller MSPs, simplified versions of the bodies could be a good option.

General assembly: The general assembly (also known as member forum or membership platform) usually unites all members and participants of the MSP. The general assembly provides space for exchange between the stakeholders, and through face-to-face meetings (usually 1–2 annually) or digital communication often forms the foundation of the MSP.

Other features include:

- Election of the steering committee,
- Mandating the steering committee, and
- Adoption and signing of (public) obligations (such as memorandum of understanding or terms of reference defining tasks and duties of members).

Steering committee: The steering committee (also known as board, board of directors or steering group) is commonly the decision-maker of the MSP. The executive power is often shared equally amongst actors from the different stakeholder groups – government, business, civil society and academia – to anchor the principle of equality in the governance structure. The members of the steering committee are typically elected by the general assembly. The steering committee is responsible for the strategic orientation of the partnership.

Other features include:

- Setting the decision mechanism (consensus, majority vote, right of veto, etc.).
- Making decisions.
- Defining the strategy of the partnership.
- Administration of the budget.
- Commissioning of the secretariat's work.
- Reporting to the general assembly on decisions.
- In some cases: mandating the working groups on the content of the work.

Secretariat: The secretariat is a neutral actor in an MSP. In smaller MSPs, one or more partners sometimes fulfill this function, while larger MSPs often create a new body or organizational unit.

The secretariat is officially commissioned by the steering committee and usually performs the following functions:

- Process facilitation.
- Completion of administrative and logistical tasks.
- Preparation of general assembly and steering committee meetings.
- Assistance to the steering committee in decision-making.
- Processing of the reports of the steering committee and the general assembly.

Working groups: Some MSPs integrate working groups as bodies in their governance structure. They develop content and prepare working proposals. Individual members often voluntarily team up based on interests. Through the use of working groups, the secretariat is relieved of the content-related work, which ensures neutrality.

Working groups typically perform the following functions:

- Development of content based on a mandate by the steering committee,
- Content and preparation for the steering committee, and
- Reporting the results to the general assembly and the steering committee.

c) Funding

The question of funding is often pressing for both new and established partnerships. The gathering of stakeholders into a partnership is often initially accomplished through short-term (1–3 years), mostly external (donor) funding, unless start-up capital already exists. In terms of sustainability, it is advisable to ensure long-term funding of the partnership and avoid full funding from a single financier. However, in practice long-term funding and avoidance of a single financier often turns out to be difficult. It has proved helpful to consider tax implications of the legal form at an early stage.

3 Impact and impact assessment of and in MSPs

In MSPs diverse partners jointly tackle sustainable development challenges. In doing so, questions of impact and impact assessment arise: What does impact mean and how to assess it?

a) Understanding impact of MSPs

In comparison to the impact achieved via classical means like projects, the impact of multi-stakeholder partnerships has an additional component. Just like with classic projects, MSPs have an impact on the sector and target group. In addition, however, they also have an impact on the stakeholders within the MSP (as illustrated in Figure 9.3). This impact on stakeholders within an MSP is referred to as social impact.

It is helpful for MSP secretariats and backbone organizations to understand and consider their own impact separately from that of the MSP as a whole, as shown in Figure 9.4.

Basics based on OECD/DAC criteria: Impacts can be planned or unplanned, positive or negative, intended or unintended. They appear in the short, medium or long term and are related to the activities of the MSP directly or indirectly.

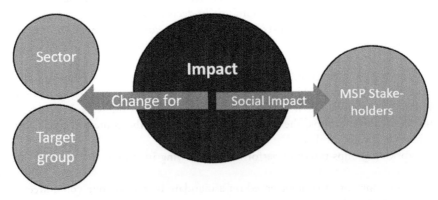

Figure 9.3 Impact of MSPs (authors)

Designing successful MSPs 219

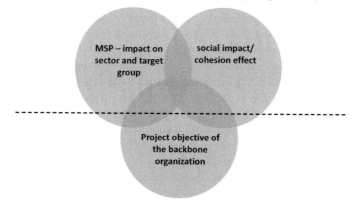

Figure 9.4 Impact and MSP – three perspectives (authors)

The so-called impact chain supports the consideration of impact of an MSP by breaking down the different impact levels (see Figure 9.5).

The five core criteria for effectiveness of the OECD Development Assistance Committee (DAC) can be adjusted to the evidence of impact of MSPs (OECD, 1991):

- Relevance: Is the MSP's objective relevant? Is an MSP the appropriate instrument to achieve the objective? Does the MSP create benefits compared to other approaches?
- Efficiency: Are the resources contributed by partners, such as time, money, staff, in proportion to the results achieved or the benefits of the MSP?
- Effectiveness: Are there countable and measurable results of the MSP at the output level? Are there qualitative changes at the outcome level due to the generated results?
- Sustainability: Is the MSP likely to provide lasting benefits? How sustainable and self-supporting are the institutionalized structures of the MSP?
- Impact: Does the MSP achieve transformative change?

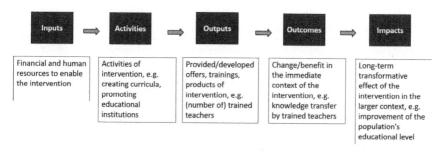

Figure 9.5 MSP impact chain (authors)

220   *Salz, Lakemeier, Schmitz, and Borkenhagen*

Impact of MSP – social impact: The fundamental ways of thinking and acting of stakeholders involved in MSPs can change through their interaction in an MSP. New patterns of interaction emerge from new internal dynamics based on cooperation, trust and joint action. These remain even beyond the cooperation within the MSP, leading to transformative changes of behavioral patterns of the stakeholders. MSP participants report on their experiences in their wider networks and thus contribute to dissolving stereotypes. In addition, there is often an increased willingness of the stakeholders to cooperate again in other projects, to exchange information informally periodically or to act more inclusively and sustainably.

MSPs thus have effects that go beyond the change processes initiated by the MSP. These impacts are referred to as the social impact of MSPs.

Impact of MSP – impact on sector and target group: In order to understand the impact of an MSP on the sector and the target group, the following questions should be considered:

- Outcomes: What is achieved for whom? When does the outcome occur?
- Mechanisms: What kind of factors and processes have made these outcomes possible? How are the mechanisms that produce change interrelated?
- Additionality: What is the contribution of the MSP to the observed impact (keyword contribution)? Has the MSP put forth the impact (keyword attribution)? Would the impact have been achieved even without the MSP? Has the MSP achieved more than what individual actors would have achieved working on their own?

Practical tips

How can MSPs navigate impact?

Sketching the overall objective: What kind of outcome can be promised and realized? For whom and where should the effects take place?

The overall objective and impact of an MSP should be aligned with the type of MSP, its size and context. The different types of MSPs might help to pursue different kinds of impacts (see Table 9.2).

Defining the overall objective: What do we want to achieve? What are our goals?

Table 9.2 Types of MSPs and kinds of impacts (authors)

Standardization partnership	Focus on setting standards and norms. The impact aims at transforming an entire sector.
Service partnership	Concrete implementation and realization of activities at the local or regional level, where the impact is to be delivered.
Knowledge partnership	Knowledge sharing aims to alter the actions of MSP stakeholders based on the information received.

Designing successful MSPs 221

The overall objective (or "theory of change") of the MSP should be discussed with all stakeholders from the beginning so that they develop a common understanding. It is important to bear in mind that there are different dimensions of objectives:

- The common goal of the MSP (what do we want to achieve together?),
- The long-term developmental objective (what do we as an MSP want to contribute to?), and
- The varying objectives of each MSP stakeholder.

In general, it is recommended to execute a problem analysis as a baseline and to articulate clear, measurable goals and review mechanisms.

Since multi-stakeholder partnerships usually involve an intense initiating phase, their implementation and impact will only show later. Therefore, MSPs require longer time horizons than classical project work.

Involvement of stakeholders: Who is involved?

The dialogue should be strategic: relevant and influential stakeholders can drive the process forward as a core group. However, too many stakeholders in the core group can slow down the process, as it is primarily about building trust within the group.

In order to gain further relevant stakeholders for the MSP, establishing business cases and demonstrating the benefit of involvement for different groups is helpful.

During the ongoing process, new stakeholders might join or drop out. Therefore, it is important to keep the impact model updated, especially when new stakeholders join.

Working together as equals: How do we want to cooperate?

Inclusive and participatory decision-making and implementation is essential when it comes to the sustainable impact of an MSP as it determines legitimacy and scope of the partnership. Stakeholder groups should therefore be able to engage in an equal way.

Institutionalized governance structures, as already explained, prepare the ground of the partnership and provide an agreement about the way in which stakeholders will work together. Among other things, it is important to ensure that governance structures ensure stakeholders work together as equals, so comments and suggestions are included from everyone.

Working in MSPs is at its core about the interaction of the engaged stakeholders. Building trust between the stakeholders is an integral factor for achieving impact. As for this, building a common identity and establishing a sense of "we" can be helpful for the joint activities.

Continuous monitoring and evaluation: How do we achieve success? How do we ensure learning?

An important success factor for the impact potential of MSPs is sound process management. Joint learning, continuous development and improvements are the basis for the efficiency and effectiveness of an MSP. It is helpful to monitor short-term outcomes in order to ensure continuous learning, to make adjustments and to manage expectations. Measuring medium-term outcomes is important to evaluate changes that occur.

b) Impact assessment

Impact assessment is relevant and essential in many ways – it provides accountability towards donors, target groups and active stakeholders of the MSP. Impact assessment is not simply about control, but rather about monitoring and evaluation (M&E) in order to document successes and ensure learning (see Figure 9.6).

The goals of impact assessment are:
Comprehension: How can the process be managed?
Control: Are the tasks implemented by the responsible stakeholders?
Learning: How do processes work between stakeholders and how does the MSP operate?
Legitimacy: What kinds of activities lead to which kinds of results and who contributes?

Practical tips

- *Who assesses?* MSPs are responsible for their M&E process. External support and advice on M&E as well as training for the steering committee, the secretariat and/or other bodies can be helpful. In case of standards and certification, it is useful to involve independent third parties.
- *Why assess?* Impact assessment requires capacities (time, money, effort). It should be emphasized that M&E legitimizes and improves the impact of all MSP stakeholders. This requires the evaluation of the impact on the target group as well as monitoring the MSP and the relationships between the stakeholders themselves.
- *What to assess?* Possible contents and aims of an evaluation are the monitoring of progress, examination of the relevance and achievement of objectives, assessment of impacts and examination of causal hypotheses.

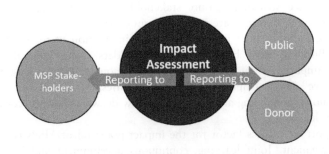

Figure 9.6 Impact assessment of MSPs (authors)

Designing successful MSPs 223

- *When to assess?* Assessment should take place in several stages: ex ante to improve the planning of an intervention (baseline setting); continuously to improve the processes; and ex post to assess the actual impact. It should be kept in mind that it is difficult to assess the long-term impact of MSPs.
- *How to assess?* Impact assessment can be both quantitative and qualitative, whereby triangulation of data is recommended. Standardization is not the golden way. The aim is to find solutions that work within the respective system.
- *How to proceed?* It should be noted that monitoring and evaluation belong together. Questions about the M&E system should be considered in good time in order to establish it as early as possible while staying flexible during the ongoing process.

Questions MSPs should ask themselves

- Why do we need an M&E system?
- What kind of information does each individual partner need?
- What do we need to know/find out?
- What resources/capacities/conditions do we have?
- What data do we need for this?
- When do we need which data?
- How do we guarantee the quality of data?
- Who needs to be involved?
- Who carries out the M&E process?
- How do we deal with the results internally?
- How do we share the data with others?
- How does the MSP contribute to change? Does the MSP achieve its objectives?
- What do we do if things do not turn out as planned?

Exemplary illustration of the M&E process

The MSP for sustainable tuna handline fisheries serves as a case study to illustrate a possible M&E process of an MSP. The World Wide Fund for Nature (WWF) acts as the backbone organization for this MSP.

The MSP's objective is:

> The establishment of multi-stakeholder partnership dialogue structures in order to promote fairer tuna supply chains and sustainable management of yellowfin tuna stocks as well as improvement of the socio-economic situation of small-scale handline fishers, aiming to secure their livelihoods in the long-term, in the Philippines (see Table 9.3).

Table 9.3 The M&E process of the MSP for sustainable tuna fisheries in the Philippines MSP case study (WWF, 2019)

Step 1 – Project idea, topic & rough goal	The MSP is the result of a predecessor project. Idea, topic and goal developed in a dialogical exchange.
Step 2 – Common objectives	The vision and the overall objective as well as the project and sub-objectives were developed. Objectives for the content and the process were defined. The process objectives deal with the development of dialogue structures and institutionalisation.
Step 3 – Deciding on the format	Is an MSP the right instrument to achieve the objectives? Which reasons do the different stakeholder have for their engagement?
Step 4 – Objective and sub-objectives with indicators	In a workshop, advised by the Collective Leadership Institute (CLI), a core group (also known as a container of change) agreed on the definition of the overall objective and formulation of six sub-objectives linked to indicators.
Step 5 – Ongoing M&E	*In the project application,* training sessions with external experts on the monitoring process were included. *In the planning phase,* personnel resources have been considered and dedicated to M&E activities. A person, responsible for the monitoring process of the MSP, was appointed. *Every three months,* the backbone organization produces an internal report on current events and discussions. The aim is to reflect on the process and effectiveness of project activities, to fine-tune and adapt the MSP dialogue process and other project activities as necessary. Partners and other relevant stakeholders are updated on a regular basis via e-mail communication and during regular meetings. *A comprehensive report informs the donor annually*; review is the indicators and tracks the progress. *Once a year,* external experts conduct an assessment applying the MSC Standard (Marine Stewardship Council), a benchmark tool to measure progress towards sustainable fisheries management, in order to assess the status quo of the project fishery. *Other activities,* support the livelihoods impact assessment and measure progress towards increasing sustainability in the fishing sector. To name but a few, those activities include: surveys on households and their income situation (i.e., indebtedness), number of harmful and/or sustainable subsidies from authorities to the tuna fisheries on site, measurement of the fishing capacity of handline fishing and analysis of profit margins along the supply chain. *Consultancy and support,* from external experts on technical matters.

Designing successful MSPs 225

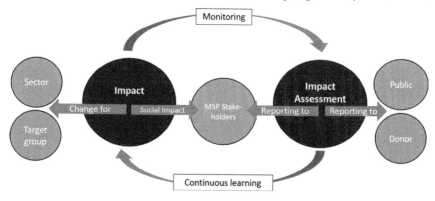

Figure 9.7 Impact and impact assessment of MSPs (authors)

Figure 9.7 summarizes how impact and impact assessment relate to MSPs. MSPs affect the sector and the target group on the one hand and the MSP stakeholders on the other (referred to as social impact). Assessing the impact of an MSP is relevant for the MSP stakeholders, for the public and the donors. The impact of an MSP is captured via impact assessment and ensures continuous learning.

References

OECD (1991), The DAC Principles for the Evaluation of Development Assistance, adapted to DAC Criteria for Evaluating Development Assistance. Available online at: http://www.oecd.org/dac/evaluation/daccriteriaforevaluatingdevelopmentassistance.htm

Partnerships2030 (2017), Multi-Stakeholder Partnerships in the Context of Agenda 2030: A practice-Based Analysis of Potential Benefits, Challenges and Success Factors. Available online at: https://www.partnerschaften2030.de/wp-content/uploads/2017/10/Viadrina_EN_WEB.pdf

WWF (2019), Partnership Program towards Sustainable Tuna. Available online at: https://wwf.org.ph/what-we-do/food/pptst/

10 The challenges ahead

I and the other authors hope you enjoyed the book and found it challenging as well as useful.

We tried to cover a number of themes, all of which could be (and in some cases are) separate books in their own right.

Stakeholder democracy fits within the paradigm of democracy in general. This book argues that stakeholders strengthen representative democracy, while recognizing that the definition of democracy has itself changed over time.

The continuum used in this book is one that moves from representative democracy towards participatory democracy, and the theory of change we have tried to flesh out is that involving stakeholders in the decision-making process makes better informed policy, which in turn means that stakeholders are more likely to want to be involved in the delivery of that policy by themselves or in partnerships with others.

This book attempts to bridge the space between multi-stakeholder policy engagement and multi-stakeholder partnerships. It is always difficult to combine those two things, but I think we managed it. If you are only interested in understanding how to engage in multi-stakeholder partnerships, there are ideas here on how to do that while improving the work that you already do. If you are interested in how stakeholders have helped develop policy, we have tried to share some examples that you might build from.

The number of different ways to engage more people in democratic discourse is increasing, which is good news. Unfortunately, we have also seen how the same channels can be used by outside forces to undermine democratic institutions.

> We also have to be honest that many people have lost their trust in conventional politics and the vision of the future these are presenting: as in long-term thinking and sustainable development. There is uncertainty as to what this is all about, even among experts. In addition, we see in many countries a growing disconnect between politics and the expectations of the people (Bachmann, 2018).

The challenges ahead 227

The steps towards a more "global citizen" approach and a more engaged population in countries, cities and communities will require a more informed population than we have at present.

When science is challenged or undermined by negative corporate or political interests, then we must tread carefully. In recent years, we have witnessed the positive and negative impacts of the Internet on news consumption to the point where it is unclear to many which news is factual and which is not.

There will be huge challenges over the coming decade as new technologies impact our lives to an unprecedented degree. The new industrial revolution will build on the digital and information revolution of the past decades, and we will see tipping points on a number of technological and ecological areas.

In this decade, there will be ever-increased automation and, in some areas, robots employed to do more and more of what we used to do. Driverless cars, taxis, lorries (or trucks, in the American vernacular) and trains all coming sooner than we expect. 3D printing is doing amazing things, including printing human organs – how will that impact manufacturing?

Just over twenty years ago, Dolly became the world's most famous sheep because she was a clone. As I write this, China has just cloned a monkey. Will we see the first human cloned in the next ten years? If so, what does that mean?

We are now in an era of the Internet of things, and we order more and more online. What will be the long-term impact on our local shopping centers? Will we have wearable Internet or even have the Internet embedded into our bodies? Where will nanotechnology and quantum computing take us? You get the idea.

Are we ready for these disruptive technologies? Who will be left out of this new revolution? Are our democratic institutions strong enough to withstand these rapid changes?

Changes can be incorporated into society, and change is often good, but these changes on so many fronts will require stable governments that have long-term strategies – not short-term electoral promises – to ensure we all benefit.

Stakeholder engagement in the policy arena offers a way of helping governments address these new challenges. It offers a way of stabilizing democratic institutions and helping to chart a shared vision for the path forward.

Engaging stakeholders singularly or in groups for help with delivering on policy agreements inevitably means that we will be building more robust communities.

In other words, this approach offers a way to try and ensure that this new industrial revolution is for everyone, not just for the few. This next generation need not be a generation of crisis or fear – it could be a generation of hope and solidarity.

We have the chance to decide to work together. This book shows a path whereby engaging stakeholders increases the likelihood of creating and preserving sustainable communities in which there is less inequality. We want to be able to absorb change quickly, and see ourselves working together as part of a global community. Without a vision of this kind, the future looks darker and more dangerous than it might otherwise be.

References

Bachmann, G. (2018) The HLPF We Need to Support the 2030 Agenda. Incheon Songdo: German Council for Sustainable Development. Available online at: https://www.na chhaltigkeitsrat.de/wp-content/uploads/2018/11/20181029_Bachmann_UN_SDTF_ 2018.pdf

Index

Page numbers in **bold** refer to figures, page numbers in *italic* refer to tables.

2030 Agenda for Sustainable Development 92–93, 126, 153, 154, 162, 164, 200

Aalborg Charter 155
Aalborg Commitments Governance 156–157
absolute monarchies 37
Abzug, Bella 50, 59
accountability 3, 12, 87, 103, 104, 129–130, 132, *198*, 200, 202–203
accreditation 12
advocacy democracy 37
African Development Bank Framework for Enhanced Engagement with Civil Society Organizations 113–114
Agenda 21 1, 11, 15, 50, 52–54, 57–58, 60, 78, 94, 126, 148, 152, 154–155, 156, 161, 168, 185–186; implementation assessment 147; Local Authorities Initiatives 64; Major Groups implementation review 60–61
Agenda Euskadi–Basque Country 2030 158, **159**, 160
Agenda for Sustainable Development 2–3, 8
Agenda of Science for Environment and Development into the Twenty-first Century 50
Agné, H. 127–128, **128**
agriculture 142–144, *144*
Alinsky, S. 115
alternative facts 94
American Dream, the 22
"A New Global Partnership: Eradicate Poverty and Transform Economies Through Sustainable Development" 90
Annan, Kofi 70, 166, 184

ANPED 63
anticipatory democracy 37
anti-globalization 108–109
Arab Spring 101
Aristotle 24–25, *24*, 100, 107
Armstrong, Neil 45
Assembly of the People 26
assessment 140; MSP impact 222–223, **222**, *224–225*, 225, **225**
associational life 102–103
association, freedom of 116
Athenian democracy 24–25, *24*, **25**
automation 227
Awiti, Alex 102

Bachmann, G. 226
Bäckstrand, K. 127, 129
Bahá'í 35–36
Bali Guidelines 168, 186, 187–189
Bartram, J. 100
Basque 2030 Agenda 158, **159**, 160
Basque Country 158, **159**, 160
Beer, Henrik 45–46
Beisheim, Marianne 170–171, 172, 177–178, 181
Bendis, B. M. 22
Benson, Emily 55–56, 80–81
Bergen 51–52
Berlin Wall, fall of 101
Beyond 2015 89
big data 23
Blue Economy Conference 183
Bonn Dialogues 62
Bonn Freshwater Conference 69
Bradley, Arthur 103
Brazil 74, 82
Bretton Woods Agreement 42

230   *Index*

Bretton Woods monetary system 42
Brexit 23, 38
Brouwer, H. 199, 204–205
Brouwer, J. 205
Brugmann, Jeb 51
Brundtland Bulletin 51–52
Brundtland, Gro Harlem 10, 47–48
Buchanan, James McGill 114
Bureau for the Commission on Sustainable Development 136
business and industry 2
"Business Charter for Sustainable Development" (ICC) 50
Business Council for Sustainable Development 50
Bussche, Baron Axel von dem 46

Caballero, Paula 84
Calhoun, C. 106–107
Cambridge Analytica 23
Cameron, David 90
Campaign for a United Nations Parliamentary Assembly (CUNPA) 38–39
capacity-building 140
Caracas 51
Cardoso, Fernando Henrique 70
Cardoso Report 70–73
casino capitalism 110
Catholic Church 32
cellular democracy 37
Center for Technology, Policy, and Industrial Development, Massachusetts Institute of Technology (MIT) 145
centralization 104
Centre for Our Common Future 47, 48–49, 51–52, 83
challenges 9
champions 135–136
change, theory of 1
China 39
chlorofluorocarbons 43
Chomsky, Noam 108–109
Churchill, Winston 93–94
citizens panels 38
Civic Forum 101
CIVICUS 73
civil society 12–13, 99–121, 132; account-ability 103; as associational life 102–103; Cardoso Report and 70–73; and CFS 76; definition 100–102, 111–112, 112–114, 119–120; and devo-lution of power 110; global 106; as the good society 104–106; and NGOs

112–113, 120; principles 115–118; as a public sphere 106–108; role 111, 119; social movements 108, 108–110; stakeholder approach 112–114, 120; threats to 114–119; tripartite approach 119–120; and trust in government 110–111; twenty-first century 111–114
Civil Society Support Mechanism 80
Civil Society Task Force 80
climate change, local impacts 161
Climate Summit 191
Clinton, Bill 146
closed societies 104
coalitions 3
collaborative democracy 13
Collective Leadership 206–207
colonialism 37
Commission of the Economic and Social Council 53
Commission on Global Security, Justice and Governance 39
Commission on Human Settlements 135
Commission on Sustainable Development 53–54, 54–55, 134, 164, 169; agriculture dialogues 142–144, *144*; "Days of Major Groups" 58; Decision 7/6 141; dialogue days 137; end of MSDs 68–70; intersessional process 146–147; MSD major group interventions 138, *139*; MSDs 136–147, *139*, *143*, *144*, *146*; multi-stakeholder dialogues *139*; NGO Steering Committee 56–57, 61, 63, 136, 138, 147; policy impacts 147; role 136; sustainable energy and transport dialogues 145–147, *146*; tourism dialogues 141–142, *143*; voluntary initiatives 139–141, 144–145; WSSD and 66–68
commitment 140
Committee on Non-Governmental Organizations 54
Committee on World Food Security 76–78; CFS Bureau and Advisory Group 77
communication 13, 140, 203; right to 117
communism 32; fall of 101
community 100
Community Development Resource Association 207
competition 179
complexity 166
Conference on Environment and Development. *see* Earth Summit, Rio, 1992

Index 231

confirmation bias 119
conflict 13
consensus 9, 13
Consensus Building Institute 207
consensus decision-making 35–36
constituencies 13
constitutional monarchies 37
consult 13
context, multi-stakeholder dialogues 139
Convention on the Elimination of All
    Forms of Discrimination
    against/nlWomen (CEDAW)
    73–74
Conway, Kellyanne 94
cooperation, right to 117
cooperative pluralism 102
Corporate Benchmarking on Human
    Rights 179
Corporate Human Rights Benchmarking
    105–106
corporate social responsibility 104–105
corporatization 23
cosmopolitan democracy 106
Crane, Edward H. 114
critical theory 107
Cromwell, Oliver 28
culture, homogenization 42
Czechoslovakia 32, 101

Dahrendorf, Ralf Gustav 120
"Days of Major Groups" 58
debate 13
decisions and decision-making 1, 9, 13, 15,
    35–36, 128, 129, 130–132, 132
Declaration of the Rights of Man and of
    the Citizen 31
deliberative democracy 37
democracy 38; advancement 23; Age of
    Enlightenment 28–30; challenges facing
    23; Churchill's appreciation for 93–94;
    collaborative 13; corporatization 23;
    cosmopolitan 106; Declaration of the
    Rights of Man and of the Citizen 31;
    definition 23; direct 14; English 27–28;
    as evolving system 2; government types
    36–37; Greek 24–25, 24, 25; history
    22–39; indirect 14; Jeffersonian 22;
    liquid 15, 38; local 157; Madisonian 22;
    participatory 2, 17, 22, 33–36, 94, 100,
    120–121, 226; Quaker model 34–36;
    renewal 23; representative 2, 14,
    18, 22, 23–24, 34, 94, 100, 120, 226;
    Roman Republic 26–27, 27; Switzerland
    31; twentieth century 31–33; types of

23–24, 37–38; undermining 226; world
    parliament 38–39
Democracy Without Boarders 39
democratic deficit 14, 71
democratic governments, types of 36–37
democratic institutions, global level 125
democratization, third wave of 9
de Montfort, Simon 27
Desai, Nitin 62–63, 171
de Tocqueville, Alexis 102
development 108
Development Cooperation Forum 185
development events 108
dialogue 14
dictatorships 31–32
direct democracy 14
discussion 14
disenfranchised groups 129
disruptive technologies 227
Dodds, Felix 62, 90, 105
Donostia Declaration 82–83
Dubcek, A. 33
due-diligence 106, 178–180
duty to protect, states 118

Earlham College 35
Earth Negotiations Bulletin 139
Earth Summit 2002, Regional
    PrepComms 145
Earth Summit, Rio, 1992 1, 2, 10, 11, 15,
    43–44, 94, 125, 148, 154–155, 168;
    agreements 52–54; preparatory process
    51–52; stakeholder follow-up 54–58;
    UK stakeholder follow-up 57–58
EcoAgriculture Partners 205
economic crisis, 2008 110, 114
Edwards, Michael 99, 100, 106, 119
Emerald City Comic Convention 22
emergence 2
empowerment 3
engagement: NGO 44–46; priorities 93;
    with stakeholders 2–3; stakeholders 7,
    8, 12, 44–46, 67–68, 70, 70–81, 86, 93,
    129, 132, 134–135, 227
Engels, F. 32
English Civil Wars (1642–1651) 27–28
English democracy 27–28
Enlightenment, the 28–30, 100
environmental agreements 43–44
environmental, social and governance 105
Environment Liaison Center
    International 63
environment, the, and globalization 43–44
European Commission 58

232   *Index*

European Union 59–60, 113, 154
Euskadi Sustainable 160
Every Woman Every Child 190
expression, freedom of 117

fake news 23, 103, 111
Farman, Joe 43
fascism 31
financial leakages 142
First International Conference on
    Chemicals Management (ICCM1) 75
Flacks, R. 34
Food and Agricultural Organization 76
Forest Stewardship Council 175–176, 177
Founex Report on Development and
    Environment 45
France 29–30, 31, 151
franchise 14, 32
Frankfurt School of Sociology 107
freedom 14
Freedom House 23–24
French Revolution 30, 30–31
Friends of Governance for Sustainable
    Development 152–153
Friends of the Earth 45
Fukuyama, Frances 9
Fulfilling the Rio+20 Promises (Stake-
    holder Forum) 87
funders, national platforms 93
funding 131–132, 160, 218; MSPs 171, 218
future challenges 226–227

"The Future We Want" 91; 87–8 87

Gambari, I. 39
General Agreement on Trade and Tariffs
    (GATT) 44
general assemblies 216
Gereluk, Winston 51
German agency for international
    cooperation 199
German Council for Sustainable
    Development 150
German Federal Ministry for Economic
    Cooperation and Development 205
Germany 66, 149, 150, 187
Gingrich, Newt 110
Giuliani, Rudy 94
Global Agreement on Trade and Tariffs
    (GATT) 42
global agreements 8
Global Alliance for Vaccines and Immu-
    nization 173–174, 177, 178
global citizen approach 227

Global Climate Action Summit,
    California, 2018 79
Global Compact Principles 189–190
Global Forum 49
globalization 15, 108–109; cultural 42;
    definition 41; emergence 41; and the
    environment 43–44; expansion 42
global level approaches 9
Global Policy Forum 72–73
Global Polio Eradication Initiative
    174, 177
global public policy (GPP) networks 15
Global Pulse 191
Global Reporting Initiative 93, 105
Global Reporting Initiative (GRI)
    Guidelines 177
global trade, emergence 41
Global Water Partnership 178
Glorious Revolution, the 28
Goal Facilitators 181, 183, 185
GONGOs (Government-Organized
    NGOs) 112
good society, the 104–106
Gorbachev, M. 32–33
Gore, Al 58
governance 15, 44; accountability 12, 130;
    global 125–126, 127, 128; legitimacy
    127; MSPs 172, 173–177, 180–181, **182**,
    183, 202, 216–217, 221
government: role 11; trust in 110–111;
    types of democratic 36–37
Greek democracy 24–25, *24*, *25*
guided democracy 37
guilds 26–27
Guterres, Antonio 170, 184

Habermas, Jurgen 107
Habitat II Agenda 59
Habitat II Conference 58–59, 134–136,
    137; Second Committee 59–60
Habito, Cielito 138
Hales, David 62
Hale, T. 171
Hamburg, Arjan 59–60
Hamilton, A. 30
Hannover Call of European Municipal
    Leaders 155
Harding, N. 32
Haudenosaunee Confederacy Grand
    Council 35
Havel, Václav 101
Hayden, T. 34, 36
hearing 15
Hegel, Friedrich 100, 101

Index 233

Held, David 106
Hemmati, M. 199, 204
Henry III, King 27
High-Level Meeting (HLM) on AIDS 80
High-Level Panel of Eminent People on
the Post-2015 Development Agenda
90–91
High-Level Panel of Eminent Persons 89
High-Level Panel of Experts on Food
Security and Nutrition (76–77
High-Level Panel on Global
Sustainability 90
High Level Political Forum 17, 79, 164,
171, 185, 187, 195
Hill, Tony 55–56
history 11
Hobbes, John 100
Hohnen, Paul 3
Horkheimer, Max 107
Howell, Megan 63–64, 68,
143–144, 147
human rights 104, 105, 179–180
Hungary 32
Huntington, Samuel 9

ideology 15
impact assessment, MSPs 222–223, **222**,
224–225, *225*, **225**
impact chain, MSPs **219**
impact, MSPs 218–223, **218**, **219**, 220, **222**,
224, *225*, **225**; assessment 222–223, **222**,
224–225, *225*, **225**; impact chain **219**;
OECD/DAC criteria 218–219; on sector
and target group 220; social impact
220; types of *220*
impetus, multi-stakeholder dialogues 139
implementation gap 126
implementation guidance, MSPs 203–207
implementation of decisions 15
Indigenous Peoples 2
indirect democracy 14
industry: MSDs 61; and SDGs 93
industry leaders 49–50
inequality 114
information, access to 131–132
Institute for Multi-Stakeholder Initiative
Integrity 206
Institute of Development Studies, Participatory Methods website 207
interactive democracy 37–38
intergovernmental negotiations sessions
92–93
intergovernmental organizations 12,
127, 129

Inter-governmental Panel on Climate
Change 11
interlinkages 10
International Advisory Board 186
international arena 134–136
International Association of
Facilitators 207
International Bonn Water Conference 62
International Chamber of Commerce 13,
49–50
International Civil Society Centre 172
International Council for Local
Environmental Initiatives 51,
65–66, 155
International Council for Scientific
Union 50
International Facilitation Committee
49, 59
International Fund for Agricultural
Development 76
international law 15
International Union for Conservation of
Nature 44–45, 47
Internet of things 227
Internet, the 36, 48, 102–103, 110, 227
investor rights 108–109
Iraq War 107
Iroquois nation 35

James II, King 28
Jeffersonian democracy 2, 22
Jefferson, T. 30
Johannesburg Plan of Implementation 82,
153, 156
John XXIII, Pope 32
justice 22, 25, 26, 104

Kakakhel, Shafqat 136
Kaldor, Mary 106
Kamau, Macharia 91, 92
Keanes, John 107
Kelber, Mim 50
Kennedy, J. F. 33
Kennedy, Robert 1
Keynes, John Maynard 42
Ki-moon, Ban 184
King, Martin Luther, Jr. 121
Korosi, Csaba 91
Korten, David 108

Lawrence, Gary 65, 161
leadership 203
League for Industrial Democracy 33–34
League of Nations 42

234 *Index*

learning 203
Lebanon 151
legal form, MSPs 216
legitimacy 127, 127–128, 128–129, 132
Lerner, Steve 49
Levellers, the 28
liberal environmentalism 126–127
liberty 15
Liese, A. 172
Lindner, Chip 2, 47, 48–49, 52
liquid democracy 15, 38
Lisbon Action Plan 155
literature review 124–133; accountability
  129–130; decision-making 130–132;
  implementation guidance 203–207;
  legitimacy 127–128, 128–129; liberal
  environmentalism 126–127;
  multi-stakeholder partnerships 126–127,
  132–133; representation 129; stakeholder democracy 125–126,
  132–133
Litsios, Socrates 57–58
lobbying 59
Local Agenda 21 64–66, 126
local authorities, role 154–155
local democracy 157
Local Governments for Sustainability 13
localization, Sustainable Development
  Goals 160–161, 161
local level, multi-stakeholder dialogues
  154–160, 159
Locke, John 100
London School of Economics Centre for
  Civil Society 111–112
long-term planning 8–9
Lula da Silva, Luiz Inácio 82

McCarthy, Joseph 32
Madisonian democracy 2, 22
Madison, J. 30
Major Groups 11, 15–16, 17, 53, 56, 59,
  60, 125, 208n2; Agenda 21
  implementation 60–61; agriculture
  dialogues 144, 144; CSD interventions
  138, 139; CSD involvement 69; MSDs
  137; priorities 63; Rio+20 89; role
  74–75, 82; sustainable energy and
  transport dialogues 146, 146, 147;
  tourism dialogues 142, 143; WSSD
  preparatory
  meetings 63
Martens, J. 172–173
Martin, Nigel 101
Marx, Karl 32, 101

Massachusetts Institute of Technology
  (MIT), Center for Technology, Policy,
  and Industrial Development 145
Mayr, Juan 142
meta-communication 16
meta-governance 170–171, 180–181,
  182, 183
Middle Ages 27
Millennium Development Goals 79, 88,
  156, 166
Mill, J. S. 29
Ministerial Round Table Dialogues 74
Moldan, Bedrich 145, 147
monitoring 140
Montreal International Forum 101
Montreal Protocol 43
Moore, Franklin 62
Morganthau, Henry 42
MSI Integrity 206
multi-lateral cooperation 8–9
Multilateral Development Banks 170
Multilateral Environmental Agreements
  52–54
multilateralism 8–9, 12, 124, 127
multi-level governance platforms 161–162
multi-sector approach 10
multi-stakeholder approach, policy development 10
multi-stakeholder democracy 7–8
multi-stakeholder dialogues 59–62,
  136–147, 139, 143, 144, 146; agriculture
  142–144, 144; assessment 140; Cardoso
  Report and 70–73; commitment 140;
  context 139; dialogue days 137; Habitat
  II Conference 135; impetus 139; industry 61; lessons 62–64, 69; Major Groups
  137; monitoring 140; opposition 69;
  outside the UN 62; participation 140;
  policy impacts 147; process 136–137,
  144; purpose 139; replication 140;
  respect 140; sustainable energy and
  transport dialogues 145–147, 146;
  tourism 62, 141–142, 143; trust 140;
  verification 140; water 61; WSSD
  62–64, 66–68
multi-stakeholderism 3
multi-stakeholder partnerships 16, 95, 126,
  164–191, 226; accountability 200, 202–
  203; challenges facing 215; Charter 133,
  165, 185–186, 194, 194–195, 200–203;
  communication 203; definition 165, 195;
  design 166, 212–225; due-diligence 178–
  180; first steps 212–215, 213, 215; form
  202; funding 171, 218; future

Index 235

developments 186–187; Global Compact Principles 189–190; goals 221; governance 172, 173–177, 180–181, **182**, 183, 202, 216–217, 221; guidelines 166, 167, 168, 185–186, 187–190, 194–207; history 166–171; impact 218–223, **218**, *219*, *220*, **222**, *224*, *225*, **225**; impact assessment 222–223, **222**, *224–225*, *225*, **225**; impact chain **219**; implementation guidance 203–207; initiation 213; institutionalization 215–218, **216**; lack of shared vision 194; leadership 203; legal form 216; lessons 173–181, **182**, 183–186; levels of engagement 196, *196*; literature review 126–127, 132–133; mobilization 213–214; monitoring and review mechanism 165, 173–177, 178, *181*; North–South inequalities 129; objectives 201, 212, 214; opening 214; partners 213–214; plethora of 164; point of departure 212; principles 194–207, *197–198*, *198*; proliferation 171; reviews 171–173; sector and target group impact 220; social impact 220; success factors 199, *199*; sustainability 218; terminology 165–166; theory of change 221; transparency 202–203; Type II partnerships 168, 187n1; types 177–178; Un mandates 173; UN resolutions on 199–200; UN Secretary-General leadership initiatives 190–191; UN system 184–185; validity 173; values 201
multi-stakeholder policy development 134–162, 226; capacity-building 140; communication 140; global level 136–147, *139*, *143*, *144*, *146*; international arena 134–136; local level 154–160, *159*; Multi-Stakeholder Dialogues 135; national level 147–154, *149*, *153*; stakeholder engagement 134–135
multi-stakeholder processes 9; background 194–195; definition 196; implementation guidance 203–207; levels of engagement 196, *196*; MSP Charter 200–203; principles 194–207, *197–198*, *198*
Murphy, M. 23
mutualism 102
MY World survey 89–90

National Assembly for Wales 158
National Coalition for Dialogue and Deliberation 207

National Councils for Sustainable Development (NCSD) 94, 148–154, *149*, *153*
National Economic and Social Councils 148
National Rifle Association 114
national strategy 161
Nayar, Anita 59
negative tendencies 9
neo-liberal policies 42
Network 92 48
network democracy 38
Network of Regional Governments for Sustainable Development 1, 155–156, 158
New Left 73
new social partnerships 16
New York 89, 162
Nexus Conferences 183
nexus responsibility 183
nexus thinking 183
non-governmental organizations 2, 13, 16, 18; and civil society 112–113, 120; coalitions 49; engagement 44–46; funding 112; Government-Organized 112; informal 78; local 112; membership-based 112; operational cooperation 56; and SDGs 93; second generation 55–56; UN accredited 44
non-state actors 13, 16–17
non-state stakeholders 12
norms 60
North–South inequalities 129
Nouhan, Charles 152–153, 154
Nyon 49

Obama, Barack 118
objectives 201
OECD 12
Old Left 73
on behalf of 17
one-party states 37
open societies 104
Open Working Group 10
operational cooperation 56
optimism 9
other stakeholders 17
"Our Common Future" (Brundtland) 48
ownership 127, 130
Oxenford, Matthew 110
Oxfam 105
ozone layer 43, 50

Paine, T. 30
Paris Agreement on Climate 11, 94

236 Index

Paris Commune 29–30
parliamentary republics 36; with a ceremonial/non-executive president 36–37
participation 17, 131, 140
participation gap 126
participatory democracy 2, 17, 22, 33–36, 94, 100, 120–121, 226
Partnering Initiative, The 206
Partnership Brokers Association 206
Partnership Forums 167
Partnerships2030 199, 205
partnerships, commitment to 8
Partnerships in Practice (PiP) 206
Partnerships Resource Centre 206
peaceful assembly, freedom of 117–118
PepsiCo Inc 105–106
Permanent Forum on Indigenous Peoples 2
Pew Research Center 23
Plato 26, 37
policy development, multi-stakeholder 10, 134–162; international arena 134–136; Multi-Stakeholder Dialogues 135; stakeholder engagement 134–135; stakeholder involvement 11
policy-making: complexity 130–131; global 128
political landscape 8
political participation 131
pollution, transboundary 43
Popper, Karl 104, 119
populism 23
Porritt, Jonathon 57, 152
Port Huron Statement 33–34, 73
Post-2015 Development Agenda 89
"Post Johannesburg: The Future of the CSD" (Stakeholder Forum) 67–68
power 17; devolution of 110
Prague Spring 32, 33
Pratchett, T. 36–37, 39
presidential republics 36
privatization 171
process 17–18
Promoting Effective Partnering 207
proportional representation 110–111
protectionism 124
psychographics 23
public choice theory 114–115
public private partnerships 18, 165, 176–177, 179
public space 110
public sphere 106–108
Putney Debates 27–28

Quaker Decision-Making model 34–36

radical democracy 38
Razali, Ismail 60
Reagan, Ronald 42
"Realizing the Future We Want" (UN) 88
referenda 31
Reinicke, W. 15
relevant stakeholders 3
Renewable Energy and Energy Efficiency Partnership 174–175, 177
replication 140
representation 129, 132
representative democracy 2, 14, 18, 22, 23–24, 34, 94, 100, 120, 226
representativity 18
"Resilient People, Resilient Planet: A future worth choosing" 90
resources 118
respect 140
responsibilities 1, 11
responsibility, privatization of 171
rights 1, 11
right-wing networks 103
Rio+5 56, 137, 146
Rio+20 74, 84–85, 152–153, 169–170; High-Level Panel Reports 90–91; MY World survey 89–90; national consultations 89; outcome document 91; preparatory sessions 85–93; stakeholder Dialogue days 86–88; stakeholder engagement 86; Sustainable Development Dialogues 88–89; thematic consultations 89
Rio+20 Stakeholder Forum 82–84
Roman Republic 26–27, 27
Romero, Christy Goldsmith 110
Rousseau, J. J. 28–29
Royer, Lucien 51
rumor cascades 111

SAMOA Pathway 171
Save the Children Fund 88
Schmidheiny, Stephan 50
Schwab, Klaus 114
SDG Compass, the 93
SDGfunders.org 93
Second World War 32, 42
semi-presidential republics 36
separation of powers 30
short-termism 9
ShughartII, F. W. 114–115
siloed expertise 10
singular-focused approach 10

Index 237

Sirlef, Ellen Johnson 90
Small Island Developing States, Third International Conference on 170
SMART criteria 171, 201
Snyder, Timothy 11
social capital 100, 102
social contract, the 28–30, 100
social division 101
social media 89–90, 103, 104, 110, 111
social movements 108, 108–110
Socrates 24
Somavia, Juan 170
sovereignty, of the people 14
Soviet Union 32–33
Special Inspector General for the Troubled Assets Relief Program 110
stakeholder concept 2
Stakeholder Empowerment Project report (2009) 55–56
Stakeholder Empowerment Project, Stakeholder Forum 80–81
Stakeholder Forum 1, 57, 59, 62, 65, 66–67, 148, 152, 171; Donostia Declaration 82–83; *Fulfilling the Rio +20 Promises* 87; Stakeholder Empowerment Project 80–81; Stakeholder Standard 81
stakeholder forums 18
stakeholder groups 2–3
stakeholder mapping 119
stakeholders: and Agenda 21 52–54; definition 7, 18, 195; Earth Summit follow-up 54–58; Earth Summit preparatory process 51–52; emergence 46–47; engagement 7, 8, 12, 44–46, 67–68, 70, 70–81, 86, 93, 129, 132, 134–135, 227; engagement with 2–3; equity 70; follow-up process 53; importance 71; non-state 12; other 17; relevant 3; Rio+20 and 82–84; role 74–75, 82–83; UN accredited 54
Stakeholder Standard, Stakeholder Forum 81
Starbucks 105–106
state interference, freedom from unwarranted 116–117
statement 18
steering committees 217
Stockholm Conference 45–46
Strategic Approach to International Chemicals Management (SAICM) 75–76
Strong, Maurice 2, 45–46, 48, 48–49, 49–50, 50, 51, 52, 155

Students for a Democratic Society 33–34
sub-national governments 155–159, 159, 160
Superman 22
sustainability, definition 7
Sustainable Bonds 160
sustainable development 10, 52, 108, 124, 126–127
Sustainable Development Commission 152
Sustainable Development Councils 53
Sustainable Development Dialogues 86–87, 88–89
Sustainable Development Goals 8, 10, 70, 79, 84–85, 90–91, 91–92, 93, 94, 106, 121, 126, 151, 154, 155, 160–161, 161–162, 166, 183
Sustainable Development Goals Open Working Group 91–92
Sustainable Development Information Network 63
sustainable energy and transport dialogues 145–147, *146*
Sustainable Energy for All 190
Sweden 66
Switzerland 31

Tandon, Rajesh 101
targets 126
Task Force on Information and Communications Technology 167–168
Taylor, David 141
Tebbit, Norman 42
Thatcher, Margaret 42
"The Future We Want" 91; 87–8 87
theory of change 221
Third International Conference on Small Island Developing States 170
Third World Network 63
timelines 126
Töpfer, Klaus 170
tourism 62, 141–142, *143*
"Towards Global Partnerships" (UN) 167, 184–185
trade unions 50–51, 138
transparency 3, 18, 104, 105, 202–203
Tribal Assembly 26
tribal societies 104
Trump, Donald 94, 110, 119
trust 110–111, 140, 220, 226
truth 22, 35–36, 94, 110
twentieth century democracy 31–33
Twitter 103, 111
Type II partnerships 168, 187n1
Type I outcomes 168, 187n1

238 *Index*

Ukrainian Revolution, 2014 101
UNAIDS 80
UN Commission on Sustainable Development 1, 60, 152
UN Conference on Human Settlement. *see* Habitat II Conference
understand 18
UN Development System 170
UN Division on Sustainable Development 61
UNDPI NGO Conference 84–85
UN Economic Commission for Europe 51–52
UN Framework Convention on Climate Change 146
UN Global Compact 93, 166–167, 179–180, 184, 199
UN Guiding Principles for Reporting Framework 113
UN Guiding Principles on Business and Human Rights 104–105
United Cities and Local Governments 13
United Kingdom 1, 152; Bill of Rights (1689) 28; Brexit vote 23, 38; Earth Summit follow-up 57–58; English democracy 27–28; local authorities 66
United Nations 15, 42, 47; 19th General Assembly Special Session 60; accreditation 12; accredited stakeholders 54; Charter 16, 44; Earth Summit follow-up 54–56; Earth Summit preparatory process 51–52; Economic and Social Council 12, 44, 54, 55, 77, 164, 167–168, 184–185; ECOSOC Resolution 1996/31 55; General Assembly 59–60, 136, 145, 167, 184; General Assembly hearings 79–81; Guidelines on Cooperation 166, 167; level of focus 155; MSP history 166–171; MSP mandates 173; MSPs 184–185, 190–191; Office of Internal Oversight Services 169; operational cooperation 56; Resolution 38/161 47; Resolution 47/191 54–55; Resolution 67/290 185; Resolution 1296 44–45; resolutions on MSPs 199–200; Second Committee of the UN General Assembly 164; Secretary-General 184, 190–191; Specialized Agencies 16; stakeholder engagement 70–81; Technical Support Team 90
United Nations Conference on Environment and Development 48, 49

United Nations Conference on Sustainable Development 169–170
United Nations Conference on the Human Environment 45–46
United Nations Convention on Biological Diversity 43
United Nations Convention to Combat Desertification 43
United Nations Department of Public Information 84–85
United Nations Environment and Development 57–58
United Nations Environment and Development UK Committee 57–58
United Nations Environment Programme (UNEP/UN Environment) 43, 46, 74–75
United Nations Framework Convention on Climate Change (UNFCCC) 43, 78–79
United Nations Parliamentary Network 39
United Nations World Commission on Environment and Development 147–148
United States of America: Constitution 30; democracy 30; Electoral College 30; federal government 30; House Committee on Un-American Activities 32; local governments 157–158; Presidential Election, 2016 23, 38; Students for a Democratic Society 33–34; the Tea Party 157; Trump presidency 119; trust in government 110–111
UN Joint Inspection Unit 180
UN Non-Governmental Liaison Service 55–56
UN Partnership Office 183
UN's Global Compact's CEO Water Mandate 176–177
UN Special Rapporteur on the Rights of Indigenous People 2
UN system 9, 12, 13, 16
Upton, Simon 62, 141–142
USAID 62

values 18, 201
Vancouver 48–49
vanguard 19
verification 140
Vienna Convention for the Protection of the Ozone Layer 43
Vienna International Conference 50
voices, stakeholder 2
voluntary action 102
voluntary initiatives 19, 87–88, 139–141, 144–145, 165, 171

Index 239

Voluntary National Reviews 185
Vosoughi, S. 111
voting, proportional representation 110–111

Waller-Hunter, Joke 136, 138
Wall Street Journal 108
Washington Post 94
water 61, 62, 69, 176–177, 178
Well-being of Future Generations (Wales) Act 158
Wen, Jichang 101
White, Dexter 42
Wilson, Mark 179
women 59
Women's Environment and Development Organization 50, 59
Woodhill, J. 204–205
working groups 217
World Bank 12, 76, 112–113
World Bank Global Public Policy Program 15
World Benchmarking Alliance 106, 180
World Business Council for Sustainable Development 13, 93
World Charter for Nature 47

World Congress of Local Governments for a Sustainable Future 51
World Congress of the International Confederation of Free Trade Unions 51
World Economic Forum 109, 114
World Food Programme 76
World Metrological Organization 43
World Movement for Democracy 115
world parliament 38–39
World Social Forums 109–110
World Society for Animal Protection 90
World Summit on Sustainable Development 3, 62, 62–64, 65, 66–68, 126, 147, 148, 149, 155, 168, 171–172
World Trade Organization 15, 44, 108
World Urban Forum 51
World Vision 172
World Women's Congress for a Healthy Planet 50

Young, Oran 60
Yudhoyono, Susilo Bambang 90

Zero Hunger Challenge 191
zombie partnerships 130

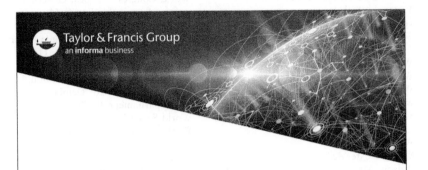